G000058853

WHAT TWEEPLE ARE SAYING

'This book is Robert Caldini's "Influence" on steroids!'

~ SHELAGH JONES - @SpiritusShelagh
Founder/CEO Spiritus Spiritual Marketing Directory
www.spiritus.co

'Lynn Serafinn has written THE guide to using Twitter...Tweep-e-licious is far and away the **clearest, most practical, usable, and ethical guide** for how to build your own 'tribe' on Twitter. It's definitely **motivating me** to finally get serious about using Twitter. **A must-read!'**

~ RICH GALLAGHER - @GallagherPOC
Author of the #1 customer service bestseller
What to Say to a Porcupine and The Customer Service Survival Kit
www.pointofcontactgroup.com

'Lynn Serafinn is the Twitter Queen! ...She launched my book, Blast Off, to #1 using many of the methods in her new book, Tweep-e-licious. If you want to add **power to your social media punch,** this is the book to read, hands down!"

~ ALLISON MASLAN - @AllisonMaslan
Author of #1 Entrepreneurship bestseller, Blast Off! www.myblastoff.com

'My company Sound Orange had been on Twitter for nearly two years, but we were stuck at around 700 unresponsive followers for the longest time. We had no real idea of what to Tweet or how to connect with the audience we wanted to reach. Then, I started working with Lynn, who began applying the same strategies she discusses in her book Tweep-e-licious!. Lynn immediately showed me how much potential content our site already contained, and within a few weeks I wrote over 600 highly relevant Tweets with ease. I automated this content using Lynn's suggestions, and focused on building relationships on Twitter. After three months, we had **over 4000** *highly engaged followers* and *our monthly* **web subscriptions increased by 200%**. *All in all,* **Lynn's Twitter strategies work!**'

~ANADI TAYLOR- @MediaForTheSoul

Founder, Sounds Orange and iMediaLibrary

www.soundsorange.com; www.imedialibrary.com

'*If you are serious about Twitter for Business,* **Tweep-e-licious is bursting at the seams** *with great tips which are* **both practical and ethical**. *This book will show you how* **you can create a powerful network for business success!**'

~ ALISON PERRY - @Purpledognet

Director The Purple Dog Network - www.thepurpledog.net

'*...a* **masterful job** *of conveying how to effectively use Twitter to promote your organization. Whether you're an experienced tweep or a novice, you'll pick up a number of* **ideas you can apply immediately**. *Hat's off to Lynn!*'

~KENT HUFFMAN - @KentHuffman @8Mandates

Author of *8 Mandates for Social Media Marketing Success*- www.8Mandates.com

'*Lynn Serafinn's Tweep-e-licious is* **the definitive guide for businesses who wish to increase their influence** *and use Twitter effectively in their marketing.*'

~ CHARLY LEETHAM - @charlyjl

Founder/CEO of Ask Charly Leetham,

Online Business Implementation Experts - www.askcharlyleetham.com

'*Tweep-e-licious! brings you a wealth of tried-and-tested tools to help you* **get the very best out of Twitter** *with* **minimal expense and effort**. *It's the* **perfect read** *for anyone who wishes to fully* **engage in the Twitterverse in a way that feels really GOOD for you and your followers.**'

~ CALLIE CARLING - @MoonPoppy

'Playfull Genie Muse' - www.createavity.com

'*This special book from Lynn Serafinn shows us* **how to do amazing by doing good—one Tweet at a time!**'

~LISSA BOLES - @TheSoulMapper

www.TheSoulMap.com

@!

RT! **RT!** **RT!** **RT!** **RT!** **RT!**

Tweep-e-licious!

158 Twitter Tips & Strategies
for Writers, Social Entrepreneurs & Changemakers
Who Want to Market Their Business Ethically

(that's exactly 140 characters!)

Lynn Serafinn

Author of *The 7 Graces of Marketing*

international #1 bestseller in marketing & business ethics

Published in Great Britain by Humanity 1 Press

Copyright © Lynn Serafinn, 2012
1st printing, December 2012

Edited by Vrinda Pendred
Cover design by Renee Duran
Author's photograph by Andy Adams, Bedfordshire, UK

All rights reserved. No part of this publication may be reproduced, stored in a retrieval system, or transmitted in any form or by any means, electronic, mechanical, photocopy, recording or otherwise, without prior written permission of the copyright owner. Nor can it be circulated in any form of binding or cover other than that in which it is published and without similar condition including this condition being imposed on a subsequent purchaser.

Humanity 1 Press
Unit 36, 88-90 Hatton Garden,
London, EC1N 8PN
England

Any queries relating to this publication or author may be sent to
info@humanity1press.com

This book is also available in electronic format.
Please visit
www.the7gracesofmarketing.com/tweep-e-licious
for details.

ISBN: 978-0-9568578-4-2

*Dedicated to all the wonderful people in the emerging
7 Graces Community, who inspired me to write this.*

Thank YOU for buying this book!

To show my appreciation, I have some gifts for you:

1) A free 90-minute *Tweep-e-licious!* audio class AND
2) A downloadable PDF with all the resources discussed in the book,
with clickable links so you can find them quickly and easily.

To claim your gifts, go to:

http://the7gracesofmarketing.com/tweep-resources.
*When prompted, enter coupon code: **TWITTERLOVE***

CONTENTS

INTRODUCTION:
THE LITTLE TWEET THAT ROARED

Back in the summer of 2009, I met an author on Twitter named @TonyEldridge. Tony, who ran a blog called *Marketing Tips for Authors*, asked me to write an article sharing some of the marketing strategies I had used to propel my first self-published book *The Garden of the Soul* to become a top-20 spirituality bestseller on Amazon. To be perfectly honest, when Tony first asked me to do this, I felt more than a bit miffed. *Hmmph!* I thought. *Here I've spent two years pouring my heart and soul into a book and all people want to know is how I marketed it? They don't care about my book; they just want to sell their OWN books. Some bloody nerve!* While I didn't voice these thoughts to Tony at the time (I did tell him later, and we both had a good laugh), I continued to grumble and complain to myself for two days, wondering what I could possibly gain from writing such an article. But my annoyance would soon prove ironic, for Tony's offer was about to open the door to something spectacular that would change my life forever.

I stopped playing prima donna and decided that writing for Tony's blog would be a good idea. Being resentful and miserly about sharing my marketing tips had only left me feeling cynical and disconnected; making the choice to be open and generous just 'felt' better. Besides, I'd be mentioning my book in the article even if I wasn't talking directly about it. It could be good publicity. So I got over my hissy fit, dusted myself off and wrote an article on the importance of marketing your book long before it is published. I called the article 'Pre-Natal Care for Your Book'. [1]

When Tony published my article on his blog in October 2009, he sent out this Tweet to his followers:

'Pre-Natal Care for Your Book' by @LynnSerafinn
http://bit.ly/RJvaKI

Within two days, I received a Tweet from one of Tony's followers named @AllisonMaslan. Allison had never heard of me before, but when she saw Tony's Tweet she clicked the link and read the article I had written. Allison contacted me to ask if we could talk on Skype. When we spoke a day or so later, Allison told me she was getting ready to release her new book *Blast Off* through Morgan James Publishers. She said she was impressed with what I had written in my article and that she would like to hire me to create a book launch campaign for her book. Although I had been working behind the scenes as a marketing coach and consultant, this would be my first full-blown book launch apart from my own. Having learned from my mistakes, I wasn't going to be satisfied bringing Allison only into the top 20; I told her I wanted her book to go all the way to the top. Set with this intention, when Allison and I launched *Blast Off* in January 2010, the book did indeed hit the #1 spot in the entrepreneurship category on Amazon.

Both our professional lives were transformed significantly as a result of the success of that campaign. Allison's #1 status helped propel her into a thriving career as a television show host and high-profile mentor for entrepreneurs. I suddenly found myself with a long queue of author clients hoping I could help them achieve similar success. Within half a year, I built a whole new business with a team of seven people working with me to create dozens of bestseller launches, the vast majority of them reaching #1. But I began to notice my approach to marketing was significantly different from other approaches I had seen, and there were many things about mainstream marketing I viewed as unethical or harmful. This led me to write my book *The 7 Graces of Marketing: how to heal humanity and the planet by changing the way we sell*, which quickly became an international #1 bestseller in business ethics, marketing, and business communication when it was released in December 2011.[2]

While writing *Tweep-e-licious!* in autumn 2012, *The 7 Graces of Marketing* was selected as a finalist in the Brit Writer Awards and offered a foreign language translation deal in Indonesia. I am also on the threshold of establishing the 7 Graces Project, a social enterprise the aim of which will be to provide an educational alternative, business incubator and mentorship scheme for a new generation of ethical, community-focussed entrepreneurs.

I often tell people that 'Twitter changed my life'. Truly, it has. But this change doesn't end with me: because I work exclusively with social changemakers, when the impact of their work spreads as a result of the marketing projects we create together, they in turn help transform the lives of many, many other people all around the planet.

And that is the story of the astounding butterfly effect of a *single* Tweet.

Perhaps you already have your own Twitter butterfly effect story to tell. If not, my hope is that you will by the time you read and apply the strategies in this book.

WHY I WROTE THIS BOOK

Over the past few years, I've read hundreds of complaints from people on both Facebook and Twitter about how they don't 'get' Twitter. Just about every new client who comes to me admits they don't know how to use Twitter, and their lack of knowledge shows in the poor results they are reaping from it. It occurred to me that there was a need for a Twitter 'how to' guide, written by someone who knew how to make the most of the phenomenon. But I long resisted writing such a guide because I knew that almost as soon as I published it, it would probably become obsolete due to constant change in the technology of social media.

I first took a chance by putting together a short (now discontinued) Kindle eBook called *Social Media on Autopilot* in January 2012, hoping this would help give people a few useful technical tips about social media automation using a variety of third-party applications. Sure enough, while *Social Media on Autopilot* sold a lot of copies and received nice reviews when it first came out, within a month, Twaitter (one of the five software platforms I discussed in that book) completely changed when it introduced its new platform called Gremln. Within another month, Ping had been sold out to Seesmic and bore almost no resemblance to the product I had reviewed in the book. Then, both TweetDeck and HootSuite also changed some of their features, rendering just about all of my technical information obsolete. Finally, Tweet Adder[6] became the defendant in a major court case with Twitter (something I'll talk about shortly). This experience drove a formidable nail in the coffin of the idea of putting any effort into writing another book on social media in the future.

But then, quite impulsively I decided to write this book, *Tweep-e-licious!*, about two months ago. The idea came to me after I had hosted an online meeting with members of our 7 Graces community. During the meeting, I asked the group, 'If this project could give you one thing, what would it be?' Many people came forward to share what they most wanted, and nearly everyone said roughly the same thing: 'I want to be in a community of other ethical business owners who share my values so I don't feel like I'm a weirdo,' and 'I want help with *getting the word out* about my business so I can make a living.'

Addressing *both* of these desires is the intent of this book. It is not merely a book of quick 'how to' tips on using Twitter that are likely to become obsolete in a few months. Rather, it is a comprehensive book of '7 Graces' *marketing strategies* to help you create a compelling, effective and ethical online marketing platform that focuses on people, values, and clarity of purpose. Thus, while some of the technical information I shall be sharing with you will probably change over time, my hope is that the strategies and ethos within this book will help writers, social entrepreneurs and changemakers develop their brands online for many years to come.

WHY TWITTER?

I believe Twitter is a vital component in the social media 'machine'. Those who choose to ignore it or don't make an effort to develop it just because they don't 'get' it are seriously missing out on a major asset for their business. If you doubt there could be any power in 140-character micro-blogging, consider this: according to *Alexa's* 'Top Sites', Twitter currently[3] has a global rank of 8th of all websites on the Internet:

1. Google - google.com

2. Facebook - facebook.com

3. YouTube - youtube.com

4. Yahoo! - yahoo.com

5. Baidu.com - baidu.com (Chinese search engine)

6. Wikipedia - wikipedia.org

7. Windows Live - live.com

8. Twitter - twitter.com

9. QQ.COM - qq.com (China's largest and most used Internet service portal)

10. Amazon US - amazon.com

SIDEBAR NOTE: *These statistics are for global rank and are typically different for a specific country. These rankings are also continually fluctuating. Even over the past few weeks as I have written this book, Google and Facebook have exchanged places several times, as have Twitter and QQ.com. And for those of you who might be wondering, LinkedIn's rank is a still quite respectable 14. The newer social network Google+ is a bit of a blur on Alexa, because it falls under 'Google' for rank. However, if you look at the Alexa site info for Google more closely, you will see that a mere 5.88% of Google's visitors go to Google+.[4]*

I find these statistics very interesting. The 'top 10' is made up of two social networks (Facebook and Twitter), the world's biggest online retailer (Amazon) and seven *search engines*. Of the seven search engines listed, two are for the emerging Chinese market and probably not used much by English speakers at all. The reason I'm referring to YouTube and Wikipedia as 'search engines' is in how they are used. These are not websites about 'themselves' but repositories of information. When you land on either YouTube or Wikipedia, the first thing you do is perform a search for information on a particular topic—a person, a song, a TV show, an historical date, a scientific fact, etc. When you look at it this way, you can see that *YouTube is the second most powerful search engine in the world* after Google (the importance of this will be explained later in this book).

These page rank statistics can help us understand perhaps THE most vital key to cracking the online marketing problem:

> *If we want to succeed online, we need to put our attention into leveraging the **relationship** between 1) search engines, 2) social media and 3) major online retailers.*

Let's first look at social media. It's probably no surprise that Facebook is the biggest social network on the Internet today, having just reached one billion registered users on 4 October 2012. But Twitter is no small fry, with currently more than half a billion active users. We can probably assume that part of Facebook's advantage lies in it being more than two years older than Twitter. Two years is a heck of lot of time in the 'techno-verse'. But I think there's more to this story.

Part of the story has to do with other technological developments made by third-party hardware and software designers. First are the mobile applications available for both Twitter and Facebook, which reportedly are now being used more frequently to access these networks than either of their web-based entry portals. On top of this, you need to take into account the fact that the vast majority of regular Twitter users today manage their Twitter accounts using third-party apps such as HootSuite, TweetDeck, Tweet Adder, Social Oomph and many others. Speaking for myself, I'd estimate the time I spend on Twitter.com compared to accessing it by other means is probably only about 10% and I'm sure I'm not an exception amongst experienced Twitter users. This means the amount of time spent on the actual Twitter *site* is a mere fraction of the time actually spent by people using Twitter *remotely*.

What this means is that Alexa's page rank for Twitter cannot possibly give us an accurate picture of the sheer magnitude of information that passes through Twitter on a daily – and hourly – basis. According to an article on Twitter's official blog on their 6th birthday in March 2012, about 340 million Tweets are sent every day (that's over *a billion* Tweets every three days).[5] As an example of how much Twitter is used, in August 2012 Twitter reported that more than 150 million Tweets about the London 2012 Olympics were sent during its 16-day window, with people Tweeting about it as frequently as 80,000 Tweets per minute.[6]

More recently, during the first 'Results Show' for *The X-Factor* UK on 7 October 2012, a massive 650,000 Tweets using the hashtag #xfactor were blasted during a 90-minute period, peaking at a rate of 29,000 Tweets per minute owing to some 'last-minute drama' between the judges.[7] And let me tell you, while that may have 'looked' like a scandal to television viewers, the folks running the @TheXFactor account on Twitter were lapping it all up. They couldn't have asked for a more powerful publicity opportunity. And the beauty of it is that their fans did all the work for them.

OK, I'm pretty sure many of you are now thinking, 'Geez, all these people Tweeting about *The X-Factor* should really get a life.' Well, yes, maybe. But if we can put aside our judgment for a minute, there is no denying that Twitter is a massive influencer in the social media spectrum and has huge potential as a marketing tool.

By now, some of you may be starting to feel more overwhelmed than ever by Twitter. You might wonder how you will ever be seen amidst this seemingly unfathomable sea of information being broadcast at lightning speed. Worse than that, you wonder how you will ever be able to make sense of it. You find it difficult to understand how this can be called 'communication' at all.

If that's where you are right now, please take a deep breath and trust me when I tell you it is my goal that, by reading this book, you will not only learn how to *use* Twitter as a strategic and *ethical* marketing tool that connects you to some of your best and closest collaborative partners and most loyal fans you will ever find, but you will also *fall in love* with Twitter without feeling you have to sell your soul to it.

WHAT DO WE MEAN BY 'ETHICAL'?

Some of you might have been attracted to this book because it mentions 'ethics' in its subtitle. Others of you might wonder what in the world 'ethics' has to do with Twitter. Before we can talk about ethics within the specific context of Twitter, let's first look at the basic concept of 'ethics' and why it is such an important topic at this particular time in history.

These days, 'ethics' is a hot topic, especially when we start talking about big business and advertising. Terms like 'corporate social responsibility' (CSR) have recently entered our business vocabulary. Generally we associate the term CSR with how well a business takes responsibility for its impact upon the environment, and how well it upholds social justice when dealing with employees and residents of the local region in which they operate. But while these are the 'mega' issues we tend to hear about in the media, the fundamental issue of 'ethics' has a far deeper and more personal purport. Carrying out our natural duty to 'do no harm' to our planet and humanity does not automatically make us 'ethical'. Ethics is not simply the absence of a negative; it is not a list of 'rules' we should follow and 'regulations' we should not break. Rather, it is a vibrant code that expresses our *values*. When we live an ethical life or run an ethical business, it means our decisions, policies and behaviour are all congruent with our values, and that these values illuminate a higher purpose and vision for the world.

What that actually 'looks like' is, admittedly, more than a bit hazy. What one person puts at the forefront of their values may not match another person's values. But I believe when we dig deeply enough and get to the core of the intent behind those values, we find a great deal of common ground. For example, I hear a lot of people say they think 'greed' is the 'evil' that drives people to be unethical. But I believe greed is just a symptom of something subtler. Beneath greed, you will always find fear—fear of loss, fear of survival, fear of rejection, or whatever. And if you dig even more deeply to look beneath the fear, you will eventually find the root cause from which the apparently 'unethical' behaviour of greediness was born: a fundamental feeling of *disconnection*. It is my view that disconnection is at the root of all so-called 'evils' in the world. When we feel disconnected from Self, people or planet, we open the door to various shades of 'unethical' behaviour. Greed is just one of the darker shades of disconnection.

It is my repeated observation that if you look beneath the surface of any 'unethical' behaviour, whether it be of an environmental, economic or societal nature, you will always find the 'Deadly Sin of

Disconnection' (as I call it in my book *The 7 Graces of Marketing*) as its point of origin. Because of this, if our view of 'ethics' is defined solely by behaviour rather than the *cause* of that behaviour, we as a society are likely never to reach consensus about what is 'ethical' and what is not. Rather, we only increase this Deadly Sin of Disconnection by putting people into categories of 'right' and 'wrong' and 'good' and 'evil'. At its most extreme, this superficial understanding of ethics can produce a polarity of thought that creates a sword of division between individuals, races and nations, and becomes the fuel of crime, terrorism and warfare.

Because of this, in this book I intend to take a core-focused perspective of ethics, where the underlying assumption is that if we are driven by a desire to create a deeper, more genuine, more respectful *connection* with others, our outward behaviour will automatically be 'ethical'. And while I will openly express my personal views on what I believe 'ethical marketing' might look like on Twitter, I do respect that you will undoubtedly have your own interpretations of what is and is not ethical, which may differ from mine.

Why Is It Important To Talk About Ethics NOW?

The idea of Corporate Social Responsibility came about in response to an urgent need of our changing times: the need to address ecological imbalance and social injustice. Similarly, while this book is at its essence a practical guide to using Twitter, my decision to incorporate ethics into this book is a response to something even more important: *the need to address how social media is changing the way we communicate.*

The rise of social media is arguably the fastest paradigm shift in communication humankind has ever experienced. In *The 7 Graces of Marketing* I shared statistics showing that our adoption of communication platforms like Facebook and Twitter has spread at lightning speed, *hundreds* of times faster than the adoption of either the telephone or television in the 20th century. Social media has slipped into our lives so quickly and so pervasively that many people find it overwhelming, confusing, or even repugnant. Others have embraced it with great enthusiasm, seeing it as an alluring, wide-open canvas for experimentation and innovation.

But within that vast, exciting world of lightning-speed change, experimentation and innovation lies a dilemma: the old paradigms for communication are being stretched and morphed into a new culture we don't fully understand yet. We're making up the rules as we go along, like a mob. When things start to get out of hand, the policy makers behind platforms like Facebook, Twitter or LinkedIn step in and announce a new set of ground rules. Then, all the end users have to shift gears and the whole mob dynamic starts again. You could say that social media is one big global communication laboratory, and that every one of us is playing a part in its creation. If we can step back from our personal feelings about social media just enough to look at it from a sociological perspective, we can perhaps begin to appreciate what a powerful and fascinating chapter in human history this is.

Our communications are no longer limited by time and space; instead they are limited to 140 characters. Our conversations are no longer with one person at a time, but with hundreds or even thousands. And because we are in the midst of a major shift in our communication paradigms, we are also in the midst of a shift in our paradigms for ethics. Our old ideas about privacy and propriety are being challenged. Many 'old school' advertisers are starting to stick out like sore thumbs when they barge into our new communication universe. We can sense that the status quo of business and marketing is changing, but we have not yet reached a *consensus* as to what is 'ethical marketing' and what is not.

Reaching that consensus is what we as a world are being called upon to do now, while we are still amidst this blitz of change. There is no point in talking about ethics AFTER things have 'settled down'. If we wait until then, the ethical standards that emerge will most likely be *the dogma* of the loudest or most powerful voice. If this happens to be a large corporate or political entity whose primary motive is to protect their financial or political interests, chances are that dogma will be only a slight variation of the old paradigm. No, we cannot wait any longer; the only sensible time to talk about ethics is when we are exactly where we are now—**confused**.

It is only within the 'mess' of our confusion that we will find our greatest resource for innovation and social change. A vibrant, new, value-driven paradigm for ethics can only be created if we begin the dialogue NOW, rather than wait for big businesses, governments or even the social media platforms themselves to make our minds up for us.

THE GREAT TWITTER ETHICS DEBATE

Right now, the topic of ethics is of particular relevance to Twitter. On 6 April 2012, Twitter announced that they had filed suit in federal court in San Francisco against what they called 'five of the most aggressive tool providers and spammers' on Twitter.[8] Although not named in their official blog, it soon became a matter of public record that the companies and individuals they were suing were 'Tweet Attacks', 'Tweet Adder', 'Tweet Buddy', James Lucerno of justinlover.info and Garland E. Harris of troption.com. Twitter's stated reasoning for going after not only some of the highest profile spammers (with allegedly hundreds of thousands of accounts set up solely for the purpose of sending out spam on Twitter) but also the software companies was to shut down 'bad actors who build tools designed to distribute spam on Twitter (and the web) by making it easier for other spammers to engage in this annoying and potentially malicious activity'.

Since the case was filed, all but one company has settled outside of court—Tweet Adder, who are still vehemently contesting the charges. In a response to Twitter's allegations on 9 July 2012, the attorneys for Skootle (Tweet Adder's company name) said, 'Tweet Adder is not "spamware". Instead, it provides businesses and individuals, including, for example, Presidential campaigns, news networks, bloggers and celebrities, with a streamlined way to manage their Twitter accounts and send automated news and updates to other Twitter users who already elected to follow their Tweets.'[9] Skootle's attorneys further argued that Twitter was unfairly prejudicing Skootle and its 'legitimate business product' by 'improper[ly] grouping' them with other defendants with 'very differing conduct and potential culpability'. They requested that Skootle be treated as a separate defendant in this case 'without confusing and prejudicial reference to other irrelevant "spammer" defendants'. The last I have heard,

Skootle's request was accepted by the court and they are now engaged in a separate lawsuit with Twitter.

I wanted to give you the most up-to-date information about this, but despite sending many letters to both Twitter and Tweet Adder, I have received no response from either company about the progress of the case, nor has there been any news about it on their blogs or forums. As of this writing, all I know is the case has yet to be resolved. There are several reasons why I am morally and ethically obligated to bring up this lawsuit at the start of this book. Firstly, as you will read later in this book, I have used the software Tweet Adder for a couple of years. I have even recommended it to clients and colleagues, and have mentioned it in many of my articles and marketing courses. I will also be mentioning it in this book, albeit taking care to be clear about Twitter's official view of this software, regardless of my own opinion. Speaking from my own experience, I have never considered Tweet Adder to be 'spamware', and I certainly have never used it to 'spam' my followers. When I look at the way Tweet Adder promotes its product on their site, it gives me no sense they are targeting anyone but legitimate Twitter users. Perhaps the feature that enables the user to 'spin' Tweets (which I've always found to be pointless) could potentially be exploited by spammers. But I feel to suggest a piece of software that is used legitimately by thousands of honest people should be banned because some dishonest people use it to send spam is kind of like saying cars should be banned because some people use them as getaway vehicles in bank robberies. In other words, I don't feel the software and the act of spamming are fundamentally related.

Amazingly, this lawsuit has been rather underplayed on the Twitter website, the only mention of it being in April, with no further details to date. I would hazard a guess that the vast majority of Twitter users have no idea it is even happening. Amongst those of us who have been following it, this lawsuit has created quite a stir; some are in firm agreement with Twitter, while others feel there are a lot of grey areas in the case. In an article on the *Above the Law* legal website, author Christopher Danzig expresses his opinion that 'Twitter will have to show something more than that the software can be used to manage Tweets from multiple accounts and automate Tweets (functionality shared by many tools that are perceived as "legitimate" by Twitter)'.[10] I am much of the same opinion. On the one hand, Twitter expressly state in their policy that using 'automated Tweets' is against official policy. However, they fail to explain what they mean by 'automated'. It cannot just refer to scheduled Tweets, as Twitter's own product TweetDeck enables the user to schedule Tweets one at a time. More than that, the widely used software HootSuite, which Twitter recently cited as a 'Twitter Certified Product',[11] allows its users to schedule as many as 200 Tweets in advance using their bulk uploader facility. The implication is that the issue for Twitter is not automation *per se*, but automation used specifically for the purposes of distributing *spam*. However, this distinction is not *explicitly* stated in their policy, which makes it difficult and confusing (and possibly scary) for end users who by all accounts behave 'ethically' but may technically be breaking the 'rules'. Without clarifying such ambiguity, it leaves both the software developers and end users in a vulnerable position, where Twitter is capable of interpreting their policy as they wish. For me, regardless of who wins the Twitter versus Skootle lawsuit, the best result would be that Twitter re-word their policy so it is finally crystal clear for all of us.

More ambiguities arise when we try to come to a clear definition of 'spam'. For example, Twitter has recently introduced the use of 'promoted' Tweets and adverts. This means that anyone who has enough money can send Tweets to everyone on Twitter, whether or not they are their followers. As a result, I frequently see adverts for McDonald's in my Twitter stream even though I do not (and would never) follow them. If spam means receiving unwanted/unrequested advertising, why is this not considered 'spam'? Some say that being subjected to adverts on Twitter and Facebook is the price we pay for it being free to use. While this may be logical, it also implies that the *only* difference between 'spam' and unwanted 'advertising' is whether or not it has been paid for.

All of this brings us to the bigger question: what is the difference between 'ethics' and 'company policy'? Are the two synonymous? *Should* they be? We think of Twitter as a private company, not a public servant; but *are* they? If they are a private company, they are free to define their Terms of Service (TOS) any way they wish. But *can* they? We found ourselves facing similar ethical dilemmas back in the

1980s with the de-monopolisation of the Bell Telephone System. The lines of propriety and ethics get blurred when an entire society is hooked on a particular form of technology. Creating a communication system upon which the world comes to depend is not just big business—it is a *big responsibility*. Do we see ourselves as 'customers' of the 'brands' called 'Twitter', 'Facebook', etc., or do we see ourselves as 'owners' of them? Who really owns social media? Who can decide which innovations and inventions can and cannot be made and sold to support social media platforms? Where do the lines of propriety begin and end in this situation?

And here we are, swimming (and hopefully not drowning) in this turbulent sea of unanswered questions. We are now being called to define a new set of ethics that not only preserves the integrity of these companies, but facilitates communication, protects free speech *and* protects free enterprise in the form of new technological innovation. In short, the Twitter versus Skootle dispute is much more than a minor backroom blip; it is a major event in the history of social media. The decisions made as a result of this litigation will define 'ethics' in a way that could extend to all social media interaction. One commentator on the Pro Twitter Forum offers his opinion that 'this lawsuit could be a big influence on the future of companies providing programs for people to use on Twitter as well. To be honest it would be nice to see a company win against a social network in a lawsuit to open the doors for future companies and growth here'.[12] Speaking for myself, I can only hope the honourable presiding US District Judge Susan Illston is given enough evidence to look beyond the surface of this case and into the long-term implications, lest the outcome open up a Pandora's Box that will change our world in ways not currently apparent. In my thinking, that evidence really needs to come from a canvas of regular Twitter users, not just from Twitter, Skootle and their attorneys.

I've said my piece on this matter, so let's move on. The bottom line is there are really only two things we must 'obey' when we enter the Twitterverse:

1. Twitter policy (as best we can understand it), and

2. Our own conscience regarding what is 'ethical' and what is not.

My primary hope is that this book will help marry the occasional differences that may exist between 'ethics' and 'policy', as well as give you the knowledge, skills and strategies to honour both, regardless of how events may swing in the coming months or years.

WHAT ARE THE 7 GRACES AND HOW DO THEY FIT IN?

While I respect the fact that each of us has a different outlook on the topic of 'ethics', for the purpose of giving focus and structure to this book, I am enlisting the aid of the '7 Graces' to serve as a starting point for discussion. The 7 Graces are a set of values that form the foundation of a new approach to marketing that focuses on ethics, responsibility and sustainability for the benefit of people, planet and the economy at a societal level. They are not meant to be 'dogma' but rather a kind of 'self-assessment system' to evaluate how congruently and effectively we are expressing our values through our marketing and our businesses in general.

While it is not necessary to have read my book *The 7 Graces of Marketing* before reading *Tweep-e-licious!*, I suspect those who have already read and absorbed the essence of that 400+ page book will more easily be able to understand the deeper purport behind many of the strategies I will be presenting within these pages. For the benefit of those who are unfamiliar with them (and as a quick 'refresher' for those who may already be familiar), on the next page, you'll find a chart of the 7 Graces alongside each of their corresponding 'Deadly Sins':

The 7 Deadly Sins of Marketing	The 7 Graces of Marketing
Disconnection	Connection
Persuasion	Inspiration
Invasion	Invitation
Distraction	Directness
Deception	Transparency
Scarcity	Abundance
Competition	Collaboration

Copyright Lynn Serafinn 2011
www.the7gracesofmarketing.com

This book will not focus so much on the '7 Deadly Sins' as it will the '7 Graces'. Here's a broad overview of what each Grace 'looks like':

1. **Connection** – to aspire to unity with Self, people and planet

2. **Inspiration** – to give value, express generosity and share wisdom freely

3. **Invitation** – to practice openness, engagement, hospitality and respect

4. **Directness** – to embrace simplicity and straightforwardness in our communication

5. **Transparency** – to use our businesses to express who we really are and what we value most

6. **Abundance** – to aim towards sustainable wealth through ecological and economic balance

7. **Collaboration** – to continually seek ways to create truly innovative projects together

In *The 7 Graces of Marketing*, I dealt mainly with the theory, history and sociological aspects of the 7 Graces. Because I want *Tweep-e-licious!* to be a practical book, we will not explore theory as much as the *practical application* of the 7 Graces within social media marketing, with particular emphasis on Twitter. Not every tip in this book will be referenced to a specific 'Grace'. Still, I think you will find it surprising how easily many of these tips render themselves to a discussion of the 7 Graces. By the end of this book, you will hopefully become an expert in utilising these Graces for your own self-assessment, and feel confident that you are creating a marketing platform that brings genuine value to your customers, your network partners and your business.

DO I HAVE TO FOLLOW ALL THE ADVICE IN THIS BOOK?

It goes without saying that each of us is different and has a unique communication style. To try to turn everyone into the same cookie-cutter type of marketer would not only be impossible, but pointless. If you (or your organisation) want to attract your ideal clients and customers, you have to 'show up' in your marketing as you truly are.

So, while you don't have to follow every single piece of advice in this book, it is my hope that the 7 Graces combined with the practical strategies I will share will help you forge your own Twitter identity with style, consistency and clarity.

I'VE BEEN USING TWITTER FOR A WHILE. DO I NEED TO READ THIS ENTIRE BOOK?

For those of you who might have already been active Twitter users for some time, I imagine the temptation will be to skip to the parts of the book you feel would be most useful to you. I have this image of 90% of readers jumping right to the chapter on 'monetising' before anything else, followed closely by the chapter on 'automation'. If leaping ahead in the book has already been running through your mind, I'd like to propose that you not assume you have necessarily covered all aspects of the basic elements on Twitter. For example, a great many new clients come to me and still have ineffective, ambiguous Twitter profiles even after having been on there for a couple of years. Others have never really learned the art of constructing a good Tweet that is likely to get attention from the right people. Fewer still know how to construct a body of Tweets for a marketing campaign, or how different kinds of Tweets are needed to speak to different types of people in your audience. Others have no idea how to find ideal followers most likely to become loyal fans and customers. And most new clients are clueless about automation and making Twitter work with other systems so they can concentrate on creating content and building relationships. But most of all, almost no one I have met seems to understand *the dynamic nature of relationship-building* on Twitter and the way these different degrees of closeness operate within your Twitterverse.

All of these topics and more are covered in this book. Even if you believe you know quite a lot about Twitter, I recommend you go through the book in order from the beginning, as there is a natural progression that gradually unfolds, illustrating not just a set of strategies for Twitter, but an entire *ethos and approach* to how we communicate and connect with our customers through our marketing—in whatever context.

TRANSPARENCY AND DISCLAIMER

The ideas presented in this book are wholly my own. While I have been careful to respect and abide by official Twitter policy as I personally understand it, this is not an 'official' Twitter handbook and this book has not been endorsed or approved by the owners of Twitter. I am not connected with Twitter in any way other than as an end user, just like you.

It's equally important to point out that I shall be talking about a variety of third-party applications throughout the text, and that in some instances the links I provide for them will be my affiliate links. This means if you decide to purchase any of these products via one of my links, I will make a commission on the sale. But don't be afraid that clicking the links will automatically bring you to a page where someone will ask you for money. Many of these products permit you to use a trial version of the product before buying. Many others also have a perfectly good 'basic' or 'non-pro' alternative that requires no purchase at all. The specific products for which I have used my affiliate link in this book are HootSuite, Tweet Adder, Social Oomph, 3 Essentials Virtual Private Server, My Private Proxy, WP Affiliate, iDev Affiliate, WP eStore, GetResponse, AWeber, 123rf.com, iStockPhoto, Blog Talk Radio and Interactive Life Coach. Titles of recommended books may also contain my Amazon Associates links. If you see a link to a product in this book other than those specifically mentioned above, it is either free of charge (such as TweetDeck) or I am not an affiliate for that product (such as 1ShoppingCart).

Please know that I will **never** use an affiliate link for a product unless I have personally used the product and feel it is of good quality and valuable to the end user. Please also know that I am not a member, owner or shareholder of any of these companies, nor am I connected with them in any capacity other than as an affiliate. Also, in the event that the current (or any future) legal dispute results in one or more of these products becoming again Twitter policy to use, I will cease recommending them and using my affiliate link for said products.

Due to the frequently changing landscape on Twitter, I also recommend that you regularly check the official Twitter blog and company policy, to stay on top of any changes and not accidentally violate their TOS.

IMPORTANT NOTE BEFORE WE BEGIN...

We'll be looking at LOTS of different software and technological resources throughout this book. To avoid clutter from too many footnotes, and to make Tweep-e-licious! a handy reference guide for you, I have organised these resources into categories in the **Resources and Useful Links** *section at the end of the book.*

You can also DOWNLOAD a free PDF file of all these resources, *with fully* clickable *links, PLUS a 90-minute audio class at http://the7gracesofmarketing.com/tweep-resources. When prompted, enter coupon code:* **TWITTERLOVE**

PLEASE DO NOT READ THIS BOOK IF...

- You're looking for a quick fix to help you 'get' followers

- You're looking to make a fast 'buck'

- You want to spam people on Twitter

- You're looking for a way to 'beat the system'

If any of those statements reflect your current mindset, I beg you to *please* put this book down right now. Return it and ask for a refund if you want. I'd rather refund your money than mislead you, because I'm not going to tell you how to do any of those things. Moreover, I do not wish to encourage anyone who has this kind of mindset. There are enough opportunists on social media as it is, and I'd like to think this book will help dissuade some of them, or maybe even 'convert' some of them to become ethical marketers.

PLEASE DO READ THIS BOOK IF...

- You are an established or aspiring writer, blogger, social entrepreneur or changemaker

- You are passionate not only about your own business, but about making the world a better place in some small way

- You are ready and willing to put in the time, care and attention into learning how to attract and cultivate genuine business relationships that are based upon authenticity, generosity and trust

- You are ready and willing to embrace the learning curve that may arise as you encounter new technological challenges

- You are ready and willing to think differently about how you communicate

- You are ready and willing to throw out a lot of things you might have been taught about marketing in the past

- You are ready and willing to learn how, when and why to use Connection, Inspiration, Invitation, Directness, Transparency, Abundance and Collaboration in your marketing

- You are ready and willing to have every molecule of your Twitter resistance challenged and transformed into delight

- You are ready to discover how writing a great Tweet can feel as satisfying as writing a great book, article or poem

If you can recognise yourself somewhere in this checklist, we've completed the first step in what some of us coaches call 'designing the alignment'.

So now that we're properly 'aligned', let's get started.

PART 1:
GET OVER IT!

TIP 1: GET OVER YOUR TWITTERPHOBIA!

7 Graces Checklist:
Connection; Transparency

Many newbies to Twitter are what I would call 'Twitterphobes': they are genuinely *afraid* of Twitter. When you get right down to it, it's just a matter of people fearing what they don't understand and what seems to go against the 'old paradigm' of social interaction. In my experience, Twitterphobes tend to feel panicked over the very act of Tweeting, worrying that whatever they Tweet will be visible to the whole world. And while *in theory* that is true, in practice the only people who will see your Tweets are those who either follow you or who may have seen you mentioned by someone else they follow. It's kind of like the old riddle of 'if a tree falls in the forest and no one is there, does it make a sound?' If you send a Tweet and have no followers, no one will see it.

Even after you start to gain a following, your Tweets are visible to far fewer people than you might imagine. Your followers are not watching Twitter every moment of every day. So if you don't Tweet very often due to fear of being too visible, your followers are likely to miss your Tweets altogether, especially if they follow a lot of other people. As of this writing, I am nearing 100,000 followers across four different Twitter accounts and I follow about 80% of them. This means my incoming data stream is continuously changing. It's true that if you 'bombard' me with non-stop Tweets, I'm likely to get annoyed and stop following you; but by the same token, if you play too small I'm unlikely to notice you are even there, as you will get lost in the cyber-soup.

So get over your Twitterphobia. Don't waste time being worried that everyone will see you. No one is likely to see you at all...unless you *make* yourself seen with courage and Transparency, and you make Connection your primary aim on Twitter.

> **SIDEBAR NOTE:** *If the idea of following tens of thousands of people made you gasp and panic, don't worry. We'll be addressing how to handle possible 'information overload' in* PART 12: Personal Sustainability.

TIP 2: GET OVER YOUR TWITTER DENIAL!

7 Graces Checklist:
Connection; Inspiration; Invitation; Directness;
Transparency; Abundance; Collaboration

Another typical complaint I hear from newbies (and even from those who have been on Twitter for some time) is, 'I just don't get all this hype about Twitter. It seems cold. It seems empty. I don't like it. I prefer Facebook.' Invariably when I take a look at their Twitter account, I see a plethora of 'Twitter *faux pas'* that make it really obvious why they have not reaped the wonderful benefits of Twitter. Most of these errors come in the form of:

- Not having an effective profile
- Not knowing how to locate and attract their ideal audience
- Not understanding how their communication style impacts their followers
- Not understanding the different kinds of Twitter relationships

- Not knowing how to write engaging and relevant Tweets

- Not Tweeting often or consistently enough

- Not knowing how to integrate Twitter with other systems and applications

- Not knowing how to preserve their own sanity on Twitter

- Not knowing how to monetise from Twitter

- Not knowing how to take their relationships to a deeper level

- Not knowing how to create collaborative partnerships through Twitter

All these *faux pas* boil down to the person not being fully committed to mastering Twitter as a valuable and vital part of their online marketing toolkit. As I point out 'the errors of their ways', these clients eventually release their Twitter denial and admit, 'Yes, I can see now that Twitter hasn't been working for me because I didn't understand how to use it.'

Yup.

Only when we admit the 'problem' is with us and not with Twitter can we start to make progress. My hope is that well before you finish this book, you will have overcome your 'Twitter denial' and become an informed and empowered Tweep.

TIP 3: GET OVER THE OLD PARADIGM!

7 Graces Checklist:
Connection; Inspiration; Invitation; Directness;
Transparency; Abundance; Collaboration

The traditional paradigm of business (and life in general) has been all about privacy. We have been conditioned to protect our intellectual property in a way bordering on paranoia. Even today, we worry about identity theft, invasion of privacy and stolen dreams. We also worry that if people see our work without paying for it, we will have nothing left to give them and we'll go broke. I agree everyone has a right to protect intellectual property. But I also think we have been suffering from something I call 'scarcity mentality'.

Social media is changing this. At the dawn of the digital age, musicians quickly had to learn not to be so 'precious' about their music, because there was no way to stop the world from sharing it online. These days, sites like YouTube, iTunes and Last.Fm make it possible for us to hear music without needing to buy it. But funnily enough, people DO still want to buy music despite it being so freely available. Over time, the music industry learned to roll with the punches and invent new ways to monetise on their music via iTunes, CD Baby, Amazon and other technologies.

In contrast, writers and the publishing world have only recently started to understand that they must also bend to the times. Like it or not, we cannot 'get seen' in this day and age if we cling to the old privacy/scarcity paradigm. Today, we need to be visible and transparent, and have faith that sharing our ideas with the rest of the world will not minimise people's desire to spend money on what we publish and the change-making work we offer for a living. Don't get me wrong; this doesn't mean we should allow people to use our work without our permission or misrepresent us by pirating or repurposing our intellectual property without our consent. But it does mean we should look for ways to share our ideas freely (and at no cost) with the public, for the purpose of the greater good of our work, rather than simply for profit. While this might seem financially counter-intuitive to those still stuck in the old paradigm, you'd be amazed at how much *more* profitable this kind of practice can be, when you get it right.

Why do we feel the need to be so private, anyway? In my observation, this need arises from fear. We fear something being taken away from us: we fear loss of profits, loss of respect, and loss of control of what we believe is legally and morally 'ours'. Ultimately, we fear a loss of our own freedom, creativity and potency. But if we continue to allow these fears to rule us as the world changes, we will only be contributing to an out-dated, disconnected, competitive world that will eventually die from the suffocating weight of its own self-imposed limitations.

Fear, disconnection, competition and scarcity are cornerstones of the old paradigm. If you are stuck in any of these mindsets, I guarantee you'll find the world of Twitter not only a challenge, but possibly a nightmare. And no number of technical tips will alleviate this discomfort. It's not just about what you do, but who you are.

'Getting over the old paradigm' does not mean we need to expose every last secret, pain, wrinkle or personal embarrassment to the rest of the world on social media. But in this new era of Transparency, those who will not *allow* themselves to be seen will simply NOT be seen. Even worse, they will be seen as someone who has something to hide. And that is not an auspicious start to building long-term online relationships.

PART 2:
BASICS, PROFILE AND SETTINGS

TIP 4: KNOW THE BASICS

I f you're like me, you probably hate memorising facts and figures. Nonetheless, it will be very useful for you to commit to memory a few of the basic Twitter parameters given below. If you forget any of them and need to look them up again, just remember to come back to 'TIP 4: Know the Basics'.

Twitter ID –15 characters maximum

Your Twitter ID is the 'handle' you use on Twitter. You have a maximum of 15 characters for your Twitter ID. Your ID can only include letters, numbers and underscores. While your ID is not 'case-sensitive', you CAN use uppercase letters to make it more readable. For example, here are my current Twitter IDs:

@LynnSerafinn

@SpiritAuthors

@GardenOfTheSoul

@7GracesMarketng *(that's NOT a typo!)*

When I say your ID is not case-sensitive, it means you can log in with or without uppercase letters, and that other people can locate you without having to enter any uppercase letters in your handle. It also means no one can make an ID that has the exact same spelling as yours. Choosing a good Twitter handle is important; we'll talk about how to do that in TIP 5.

Profile – 160 characters maximum

You have a maximum of 160 characters to create your profile. The wording of your profile is very important, as it will be instrumental in helping others find you and/or decide to follow you. We'll look at how to write a good Twitter profile in Tips 7, 8 and 9 later in this chapter.

Tweets – 140 characters maximum

Twitter is sometimes referred to as 'micro-blogging' because you are sending super-short messages, even shorter than a mobile phone text/SMS. The updates you send out on Twitter are called 'Tweets'. Every Tweet you send has maximum length of 140 characters, including spaces and links. Well be talking a LOT about how to write good Tweets throughout this book, especially in *PART 6: Creating Effective Content.*

SIDEBAR NOTE: *Incidentally, the full title (with subtitle) of this book, including spaces, is exactly 140 characters.*

People you can follow – 2000 maximum to start

Twitter have put some restrictions in place that help cut down on spamming and other 'predatory' behaviour. One such restriction is that you cannot follow more than 2000 people unless 2000 people follow you (it's actually more complex than this, as I'll explain later). Many people new to Twitter make the mistake of following too many people too quickly, only to find themselves stuck with a small following and no knowledge of how to move forward. I call this the 'Twitter wall'. In Tip 36 and Tip 37 we'll look at the 'Twitter wall' in greater detail, along with strategies for avoiding and escaping it if you get stuck.

Lists – 20 lists maximum

One of the most powerful tools on Twitter (if used correctly) is Twitter lists. You can create up to 20 public and/or private lists, and you can subscribe to other people's lists. We'll talk about creating and using lists to increase your following in *PART 5: Twitter Lists.*

List members – 500 people maximum

Each list you create can have a maximum of 500 people. While that might seem like a lot, it can fill up more quickly than you might think. Lists can also get out of date. We'll talk about managing lists and keeping them fresh in *PART 5: Twitter Lists*.

TIP 5: DON'T BE CUTE OR CRYPTIC WHEN CHOOSING A TWITTER ID

7 Graces Checklist:
Invitation; Directness; Transparency

I see so many people labour over what 'handle' they should use as their Twitter user name. Sometimes they get really 'cute' while other times they get downright cryptic, using some sort of weird 'code' or 'anagram' that only they understand. Please don't imagine that Twitter is akin to an online forum where everyone has an alias to hide their true identity. Twitter is a place where you WANT people to know who you are and what you do. It's the ultimate place for the 'Graces' of Invitation, Directness and Transparency. Everything about you has to be succinct, relevant and understandable. There is no room for ambiguity.

When in doubt, *use your real name.* After all, if you are looking to make a name for yourself (or if you are the main 'face' of your brand), your real name makes the most sense. If you have a name that other people in the Twitterverse share with you, try putting a word in the handle that identifies what you do, like @AuthorJaneSmith or @JoeJonesCSR. Failing that, try adding your middle initial, e.g. @JaneQSmith.

If you typically use your initials in your professional name or author penname (e.g. @JKRowling) go ahead and use those initials in your handle. But unless you don't *ever* want people to address you by your first name, I recommend including your first name in your Twitter profile (there's a place where it asks you for your real name). This way, people can call you by your first name when they engage with you in conversation.

Many authors ask me if they should use the name of their book as a handle instead of their personal name. You could, but what I generally recommend is to have at least one account in your personal name to start, and that you mention your book title(s) in your profile. After all, if you are an author, you will likely have many books to your credit over the years and these books may not have the same audience. Having a presence under your personal name establishes YOU as your brand, rather than one particular book.

You have a maximum of 15 characters for your user name and, unlike Facebook, you CAN change your user name later if you wish (how I wish Facebook would change their policy!). Also, while Twitter handles are not case-sensitive (but passwords are), it makes sense to use uppercase for the first letters of different words/names in your handle to make them more readable.

TIP 6: CHOOSE A COMPLEX PASSWORD

I know many people worry about forgetting their password, but here's the reality: if you make your password too simple, someone else is likely to guess it sooner or later. Your password should be COMPLEX. Complex means it should be a combination of UpPeRCaSE and lowercase letters, and it should include numerals. Also, do NOT use obvious things like your name, your date of birth, etc.

Twitter's passwords are case-sensitive, so make sure you remember any uppercase letters when you set yours up. You can only use alphanumeric characters in your Twitter password (i.e. letters and numbers) and the first character must be a letter, either upper or lowercase.

If you are worried about not remembering your password, here's a way to create something hard for others to guess but easy for you to remember. Think of a memorable phrase and translate the first letter of each word into a letter or numeral. For instance, if your memorable phrase were 'To be or not to be', your password could be something like: TBoN2b. I would put a few more numbers at the end, like a memorable date. Let's say it's the date of Shakespeare's death, 1616 (for some reason I always remember that date). This would make your password TBoN2b1616. Of course, you'd have to remember which letters you capitalised and which date you used. Choosing something as random as this, with varied capitalisation and numbers, makes it harder for an unscrupulous hacker to 'guess' your password.

Put your password somewhere safe, where no one else is likely to find it. And if you're like me (who cannot read her own handwriting), be sure it is typed!

TIP 7: USE KEYWORDS IN YOUR PROFILE

7 Graces Checklist:
Invitation; Directness

Once you have a Twitter ID, you need to create an informative and compelling profile. Again, your challenge is that you have a limit of 160 characters in which to do this. It's just as important to practise Directness when you write your profile as it is when choosing a handle. Get to the point in your profile, using relevant keywords, like 'writer', 'author', 'social entrepreneur', etc. If you write in a specific genre (e.g. self-help, spiritual, fantasy, health, transformation, etc.) be sure the relevant keywords are in your profile. If you have a particular passion or value (e.g. ethical, sustainable, holistic, transition, etc.) or speak to a particular audience (young adults, entrepreneurs, autistic, women, etc.) be sure these words are in there too. If you've written a book, mention the title.

The reason for having keywords in your profile is that most experienced users will use keyword searches to find targeted followers. In many tips later in this book, we'll be looking at how to use keywords properly to find ideal connections on Twitter.

TIP 8: MAKE EVERY CHARACTER IN YOUR PROFILE COUNT

7 Graces Checklist:
Directness

Because you are limited to 160 characters in your profile, it's important not to waste a single character on fluff. Don't use words like 'I am a' or something as elaborate as 'I am the author of the book "XYZ"'. Instead, say *Author XYZ* or *Editor XYZ* where 'XYZ' is the title of your book or publication. Similarly, if you are Founder or CEO of company ABC, say *CEO ABC* or *Founder ABC*. Then be sure to include keywords in your description of what you do and what you stand for.

Twitter does not let you use formatting in your profile, which means you cannot italicise titles. But don't waste characters by putting quotation marks around the title of a book, magazine, film or other product. If you capitalise your title and precede it with the relevant word (i.e. author, editor, Founder), it should be self-evident that it's a book, film, etc.

TIP 9: CHOOSE AND PREPARE YOUR PROFILE PHOTO CAREFULLY

7 Graces Checklist:
Connection; Invitation

Choosing the right photo allows you to practise the Graces of Connection and Invitation. Are you 'inviting' people or pushing them away? Are you engaging with them or sending the message that you don't really want them to know you? All too many times I see people make mistakes in their choice of profile picture (this also goes for Facebook). Common mistakes are:

- Using a grainy, blurry webcam photo.

- Using a shot of yourself taken on holiday in some exotic place; it might look great full-sized, but when shrunk down to Twitter size, it becomes impossible to see your face.

- Using a good headshot, but not taking care to centre it properly, resulting in your head being cropped out of the frame.

- Using your book cover or company logo, and having the same problems with visibility when it is shrunk down and cropped into a 150-pixel square.

- Using something irrelevant to either you or your business, like a picture of a butterfly or flower; this doesn't help people know you or remember who you are.

- Trying to be cute by using a photo of a celebrity or cartoon character; you may think it's amusing, but it says nothing about you and does not foster Connection with followers.

- Not bothering to upload a photo at all, leaving that annoying Twitter default image as it is. This sends the passive message to others that either a) you're trying to hide something or b) you really don't know what you're doing on Twitter. Neither of these is particularly inviting.

Just as I said, 'When in doubt, *use your real name*,' when in doubt, use a photo of YOU in your profile. Even writers for major newspapers and magazines will have an account with their own name and photo. This is my profile headshot for my primary Twitter profile @LynnSerafinn. I had a professional photographer take this. It is well-lit, closely cropped and I am recognisable even when the photo is shrunk down to quite a small size:

If you are Tweeting for your company, you can certainly use a company name and logo if it is strong and recognisable when shrunk down to size. If you are an author setting up an account for a specific book, remember your whole book cover will not show up after it is cropped, and it is unlikely to be powerful enough to make a good profile picture once shrunk. Instead of your whole book cover, use a 'logo' or 'symbol' from the book, so it is not only visible but immediately recognisable as your 'brand'. Here's one example from the @7GracesMarketng account (it looks quite striking and is easily identifiable in colour):

Whatever you choose, be sure to prepare the image so it is readable and visible when cropped and reduced in size, even at the level of a mobile phone viewer, which is yet smaller than how it appears on a computer screen. Download the Twitter app onto your smartphone and check what your profile image looks like in the upper right-hand corner of your screen. That will tell you whether or not the image is bold, strong and recognisable enough for applications.

TIP 10: PERSONALISE YOUR PAGE WITH A CUSTOM HEADER

7 Graces Checklist:
Connection; Invitation

Not everyone will visit your actual Twitter profile, but when they do, they should be able to see you've used some inspiration and put care into it. This creates a welcoming and congruent experience for your visitors. But customising your page also helps reinforce your brand identity and makes you stand out and be memorable. Two effective (and not very difficult) ways to achieve this are to create a custom background and custom header.

Twitter introduced the custom header feature in September 2012 (while I was writing this book). I think it's a terrific new innovation that permits Twitter users to express their unique brand, identity and creativity. If you upload a custom header, the design of your page is radically changed.

Getting your custom header onto Twitter is easy. Log into your account and click the 'gear' icon to access your account settings. Then go to 'edit profile' and click 'design'. Go down to where it says 'change header' and select 'choose pre-existing image'. Then just browse to locate your image and upload it. Some browsers might stall during this function. If this happens to you, don't give up; just try a different browser. I've found Firefox can sometimes be temperamental when I'm trying to upload images, but Google Chrome seems to work fairly reliably.

Creating your custom header image requires some basic skills in Photoshop or other image editing software. Your header image needs to be a GIF, JPG or PNG file, with recommended dimensions of 1252 pixels wide by 626 pixels tall (Twitter resizes it down after you upload it). The file size must be no larger than 5 megabytes. The image should be fairly dark, especially in the lower half, because your user name and bio will be superimposed in white font against it, beneath your profile picture. Here's an example of one I recently made for my @LynnSerafinn profile (I encourage you to view it online, because it really doesn't have the full impact in black and white):

Notice the following elements:

- I use my personal name.

- I don't waste characters by saying 'I am a'.

- I don't say 'author of' but just 'author'.

- I use & instead of 'and'.

- The profile is keyword-rich; in fact, nearly every word is a keyword.

- The profile gives a real overview of who I am and what I talk about.

- I use a closely cropped, professionally taken headshot for my profile picture that is easy to see and identify when viewed online.

- The custom header is unique to my brand *The 7 Graces of Marketing*.

- The lower half of the background is dark enough to make the white font readable.

- Finer detail: it took me a few tries to stretch and distort my image slightly so the 'eye' in the logo wrapped around my profile headshot and text instead of running through it. Take some time to ensure your custom header is working nicely on your page.

TIP 11: PERSONALISE YOUR PAGE WITH A CUSTOM BACKGROUND

7 Graces Checklist:
Connection; Invitation

Making a custom background is another way to strengthen brand identity and extend an inviting welcome to your followers. The most basic way to create a custom background is to use Twitter's design feature (under 'edit profile'). There, you can change the background colour of the page and the colour of your fonts and links. You can also opt to use one of their design templates. In a pinch, these are better than the default background settings Twitter gives you when you register your account, but if you have established a brand identity through a book or website, it's a much better idea to bring that identity onto your Twitter page. That is why most experienced Twitter users will create a custom background for their Twitter profile page. You can upload any GIF, JPG or PNG file under 800k to use as a background image. If the image is small, you can 'tile' it to make it fill the screen.

There are many options for your background image. You might already have some branded imagery you wish to use from your website. Alternatively, if you have written a book, a quick solution is to upload your book cover and tile it so it appears all over the screen behind your profile. If you have no background imagery, you can do a search for 'backgrounds' and your preferred colour on a royalty-free image sites such as 123rf.com or iStockPhoto (it's very important you do not use photos from other sites you do not own or are not royalty-free). Then you can upload and tile the image as you like.

If you want something more individual, many people on Twitter use third-party applications to make customised backgrounds. One popular application is called TwitBacks. There are many others available, many of which have a free option. Such applications permit you to include images, text, links, etc. in your background image. Bear in mind that the links in your background are NOT clickable, as a header on your website might be. Also, since Twitter introduced its new design layout, there is much less space for your background than there used to be.

If you know your way around the basics in Photoshop, you might prefer to create your own custom background from scratch, either to tile or fill the entire viewable background area. If you'd like to take this route, you will find some clearly explained instructions in this article and video called 'How to Create a Custom Twitter Background'[13] (it's a lot easier than you might imagine). If you want to fill the entire screen, the best size for your background image is 1800 pixels wide by 600 pixels high. Be careful not to make the resolution too high, as your image needs to be less than 800kb in size.

Many people put their logo and/or custom text on their custom background image. Note that your background image will be static (i.e. it won't 'scroll' when people scroll through your Tweets) so you'll need to make sure the dimensions of your logo/text will be visible when people land on your page. To do this, position your logo and/or custom text in the upper left-hand side of your background image, ensuring the total dimensions of your logo/text are no more than 150 pixels wide by 500 pixels tall. This might seem tiny when you're creating the image in your editor, but after the finished image is uploaded, your logo and text should fill the entire left side of *most* viewers' screens (it may be a bit too large for some smaller laptop screens). You can see an example of this on my @LynnSerafinn profile page.

Whatever custom background option you choose, even if you can only just about handle setting up your custom colour scheme, it's important to show you've put at least some effort into creating a nice environment for your Twitter visitors. Think of it as buying nice new throw cushions or arranging a bouquet of flowers before some special guests come to your house. It's a small touch, but it creates a welcoming atmosphere that shows you care. Apart from helping establish your brand identity, it also sends an unspoken message of welcome, connection and engagement.

TIP 12: PROVIDE A LINK TO YOUR WEBSITE

7 Graces Checklist:
Connection; Invitation

This may seem REALLY obvious, but you'd be surprised how many people do not include a link to their website in their Twitter profiles. You may also be surprised how many people don't make this link relevant to what they are actually Tweeting about, sending people to some out-of-date blog or business site that has nothing to do with them. If you don't have a website yet, send people to your Facebook or LinkedIn profile (or even your YouTube channel) until you get your website.

Perhaps you do have a website but it isn't quite 'finished' yet. Some may disagree with me, but I think as long as people can see something relevant, it doesn't matter if your website is still a work in progress. Even if your site isn't ready for launch, put a link in your Twitter profile that takes people to a special welcome page on your blog where you tell them what you are about and when they can come back to view some great content. In later chapters, we'll dive deeply into how you can use Twitter to drive traffic to your blogsite.

TIP 13: CONSIDER LINKING TWITTER TO YOUR FACEBOOK PAGE

7 Graces Checklist:

Connection; Invitation

As of this writing, Twitter has a feature in the profile settings where you can connect Twitter and Facebook. The 'signal flow' is FROM Twitter TO Facebook. In other words, if you enable this feature, whatever you Tweet will go directly onto Facebook. Some of you might say, 'Hallelujah! This sounds like a real time-saver. Sign me up for that!' And while I recommend using this function, I recommend it *with caution*, and bearing in mind the following caveats:

- I do NOT recommend connecting Twitter to your Facebook profile (your personal wall or 'timeline'). If you do this, it means all your Facebook friends will see every one of your Tweets. This is very likely to make you very unpopular on Facebook, as the two environments have completely different 'virtual cultures'. While it is perfectly acceptable on Twitter to post frequently throughout the day with links to your content, the same is not so for Facebook profiles. In most cases, it is advisable to keep your Facebook profile personal, with only a couple business references throughout the day.

- I DO recommend connecting Twitter to your Facebook PAGE, however. You will see this option when you connect your Facebook account to your Twitter profile. A Facebook page is a professional page meant to share information on a particular topic with your audience, and hopefully engage them in discussion as well. If someone 'likes' your page, they expect it to be about your business, your book, or whatever. While posting Facebook-specific messages is always preferable, even for pages, if you have neither the time nor staff to manage this for you, connecting your Twitter account to your page might be a good stop-gap option.

- Be advised that if you have more than one Twitter account, you will only be able to connect ONE of them to the same Facebook account, even if you're trying to connect to different pages. I tried to do this without success many times and Twitter confirmed it was not possible.

- As a safety measure, Twitter is 'smart' enough not to forward your '@' messages to Facebook (see *PART 3: Twitter Culture and Courtesy* for information about '@' messages).

- Be aware that your Facebook posts might end up including irrelevant information, such as people's Twitter IDs or hashtag keywords. This can sometimes be confusing for people on Facebook who do not understand Twitter.

- Good Facebook communication requires a greater level of interaction than simply posting your Tweets and links, so don't come to depend on this feature exclusively for your Facebook page content.

- Twitter will sometimes arbitrarily disconnect itself from your Facebook account. This seems to happen when either Twitter or Facebook perform an upgrade. It can also happen if you log out of Facebook on your computer, so it's best to stay logged in. In any case, be sure to check your page regularly (a minimum of once a week) to make sure your Tweets are actually posting, and reconnect your accounts if necessary.

To link your Twitter account to your Facebook page (*this information may have changed since this writing*):

1. Log on to Twitter

2. Click 'view my profile' under your Twitter icon in the upper left-hand side of the screen.

3. When the next window opens, on the upper right-hand side, select 'edit my profile'.

4. At the bottom of the page you'll see an option to connect Twitter to your Facebook account. Click the button.

5. A Facebook prompt will come up asking for your permission. Log into Facebook and allow Twitter to connect to your account.

6. After it says you're connected, UNTICK the box that says send Tweets to your Facebook PROFILE, and TICK the box for your Facebook PAGE.

7. Select the correct Facebook page, if you have more than one.

8. Now ANOTHER permission screen will come up, asking if you want to allow posts to that page. Click 'Allow'. If this screen does NOT appear, Twitter should have a message there with a link for you to click.

9. Save your changes in Twitter.

10. Send a test Tweet to see if it's working. If it is, the Tweet should appear within seconds on your Facebook page.

TIP 14: DO **NOT** OPT TO SEND YOUR FACEBOOK UPDATES TO TWITTER

Another big mistake many people make is they set up Facebook to send updates FROM Facebook TO Twitter. Again, while this might sound like a time saver, especially if you tell yourself you'd rather focus on Facebook more than Twitter, this strategy rarely, if ever, works, as it's like trying to bake an apple crumble using spinach instead of apples: what you get is something totally unrecognisable and unpalatable.

There are many reasons why sending Facebook updates to Twitter doesn't work. If you post a link on Facebook, for example, you don't always bother to put an explanation of what it is, because it will show up in your Facebook stream with a preview image and a description that Facebook extracts from the web page you are sharing. But if you post this link to Facebook and it gets sent to Twitter, all your Twitter followers will see is a link and no explanation. No one on Twitter is going to click that link because they have no idea what it is or what it's about. A bare link on Twitter makes no sense, and a series of 'naked' links can make you look like a spammer and no one will want to engage with you.

An equally counter-productive scenario arises when you post a long commentary to your Facebook wall and it goes to Twitter. Twitter will take the first 120 characters of your post and then a link back to Facebook. This 120-character message probably won't make much sense to your Twitter followers, as in all likelihood it will cut off in mid-sentence, mid-word and mid-thought.

Lastly, if you happen to have privacy controls set up on your Facebook account, even in the unlikely case that someone on Twitter does click your link, they won't be able to see your profile (and they won't be able to read the post).

I have never seen a case where the signal flow FROM Facebook TO Twitter works. My tip is: don't use this feature, ever.

TIP 15: KNOW THE RELATIONSHIP BETWEEN TWITTER AND LINKEDIN

Twitter and LinkedIn used to work together like clockwork, as you used to be able to connect the two accounts so Twitter updates would *automatically* post to your LinkedIn status updates (or vice versa). From 29 June 2012 this functionality was discontinued and, as of this writing, there is no way to set up any kind of automated delivery from Twitter to LinkedIn. If you happen to be reading this book long after that date, you might want to check whether this status has changed. Just for curiosity, you might like an article on the Mashable website called 'Twitter Drops LinkedIn Partnership'[14] for some possible 'political' reasons for this breakup. You can also read the 'official' announcement about this split from LinkedIn.[15] It doesn't say anything about why the partnership was discontinued, but it gives some suggestions on how to share your activity and updates with people on LinkedIn.

LinkedIn still allows you to send LinkedIn updates TO Twitter manually/individually, and you can still list your Twitter accounts on your LinkedIn profile (which you should, so people can find you). You can also schedule your updates via HootSuite or other third-party programmes, which we'll explore in *PART 9: Automation* later in this book.

TIP 16: DISABLE ALL THOSE ANNOYING EMAIL NOTIFICATIONS **EXCEPT** 'FAVOURITING'

7 Graces Checklist:

Connection

Something newbies complain about a lot when they first get going on Twitter is all the email notifications they receive when someone follows them, mentions them, etc. There's no need to get stressed about this. Just go into your Twitter account and turn them ALL off. You can find your 'mentions' easily on your Twitter homepage by clicking the link at the top of your profile that says '@ Connect' (I generally prefer to access them via my mobile application). You don't need to know every time a new person follows you, especially if you set up auto-follow, as we'll look at in *PART 4: Followers and Following.* You don't need to crowd your already crowded inbox with emails from Twitter.

In my opinion, the only email notification you *might* chose to keep on is the one that lets you know when someone 'favourites' one of your Tweets. I find this useful, as it helps me see who is reading my Tweets carefully and which Tweets they like best. It also gives me a chance to thank them personally for marking it as a favourite and ask them what they liked about it. It's a way to start a conversation and build ongoing rapport with the person.

TIP 17: DO NOT SELECT 'PROTECT MY TWEETS'

7 Graces Checklist:

Connection; Invitation

Many people new to Twitter have the mistaken impression that being 'private' will help them maintain integrity (if you still feel this way, please go back to *PART 1: Get Over It!*). If you want to reap the benefits of Twitter, please do NOT choose 'protect my Tweets' in your profile set-up.

Protecting your Tweets sends the unspoken message, 'I don't trust you and I don't want to engage with you.' If you really don't trust people on Twitter and you don't want to engage with them, spare yourself the time and frustration and delete your Twitter account right now. But, as you bought this book, I'm assuming you DO want to build a strong and vibrant network of real people through Twitter. If my assumption is correct, please embrace the Graces of Connection and Invitation, and don't protect your Tweets.

PART 3:
TWITTER CULTURE AND COURTESY

TIP 18: LEARN THE LINGO

Here are some simple translations of Twitter lingo that can help you understand Twitter as you start to use it:

- **Tweet:** The updates you post. Tweets have a maximum of 140 characters. 'Tweet' can also be a verb, i.e. the act of sending a Tweet to Twitter is called 'Tweeting'.

- **Tweep:** A person on Twitter; you can also pluralise it and say 'tweeps'. Some people also say 'peeps'. You might also see the word 'twits' but that tends to sound insulting!

- **Tweeple:** Twitter people; collective noun when talking about people on Twitter as a culture.

- **Twitterverse:** The world of Twitter; the Twitter culture and environment.

- **Twitterquette:** Twitter etiquette; the courtesy code on Twitter.

- **@:** This is the sign that comes immediately before your (or anyone's) Twitter user name. When you put someone's Twitter user name directly after it with no space in between, it becomes a clickable link that takes people to that person's profile page.

- **Replies:** A 'reply' is an open, *public* interaction between two or more tweeps. If you want to have a conversation with a specific person on Twitter, you can't just post a Tweet to your stream because the other person will not be able to tell that Tweet is intended for them. Instead, you need to start the Tweet with the Twitter handle(s) of the people you are addressing. For example, if you wanted to send a public message to me, you might say something like: *@LynnSerafinn Hey Lynn. Just wanted to say I really liked your article on the Triple Bottom Line.* You can include more than one person's handle in the message opening up the conversation even more.

- **Mentions:** Mentions are similar to replies in that they use the '@' sign before someone's Twitter handle, and are visible to all your Twitter followers. However, a 'mention' is not a discussion but a 'shout out' to praise, acknowledge or recommend someone to your followers. Although there is a difference in purpose and use between 'replies' and 'mentions', throughout this book I'll frequently refer to them both as '@ messages'.

- **DM:** A direct message sent privately from one tweep to another. Unlike an @ message, no one but the two tweeple exchanging communication can see the DM. You can only exchange DMs with someone who is following you. See 'Tip 27: Know How And When To Send DMs'.

- **Hashtag:** The symbol # followed by a word, set of words or code, used for tracking a specific topic (more in *PART 8: Using Hashtags*).

- **Trending:** Topics that are being Tweeted about a lot, usually identifiable by hashtags.

- **Follow Friday:** A Twitter 'tradition' where people recommend other people to follow on Fridays (see more in *PART 8: Using Hashtags*).

- **RT:** a 'ReTweet'. This is when a tweep reposts someone else's Tweet. See 'Tip 21: Send An RT At Least Once A Day'.

- **Follower:** If someone is following you, they are your 'follower'. Being your follower means they can see your Tweets on their Twitter homepage. Only your followers will see your activity, unless they happen to stumble across your profile via a link from somewhere else, like in the signature of your email, or in a mention by one of their followers.

- **Following:** If you are following someone else, you are their follower. Unlike Facebook, following and followers are not automatically reciprocal, so following someone does NOT necessarily mean they will follow you back. When you follow someone, you will be able see their Tweets on your Twitter homepage. These Tweets on your homepage are sometimes referred to as a 'stream'. More in *PART 4: Followers and Following.*

TIP 19: CHECK YOUR 'MENTIONS' AND SEND 'THANK YOU' MESSAGES DAILY

7 Graces Checklist:
Connection; Invitation; Transparency

Sometimes people will mention you on Twitter. They do that either by ReTweeting (RT) your posts or by 'mentioning' you (using '@') to someone else. They might also 'reply' to one of your Tweets using '@'. All of these kinds of mentions are easily findable by going onto your Twitter profile and clicking '@ Connect' at the top of your page. Then click 'mentions' or 'interactions' to see who is engaging with you.

Once you see who is talking to you (or *about* you), it's good Twitterquette to reply to these people. If they ReTweeted you, thank them for the RT. If they made a comment about your article, say something back, using an '@ reply'. When you use '@' to send a message, that message is public, so take care not to share personal information, private emails or phone numbers in this kind of conversation (use a DM instead for private contact details). But if you're not sharing anything private, DO keep the conversation public. This way, if others see what you are talking about, they might join in, check out your article, etc. Open conversations like this show you are a real, live person and not just an automated bot. They also show you are friendly, courteous and willing to engage. Keep your communications as open, inviting and transparent as possible, and be sure to engage like this at least once a day.

 TIP 20: SEND AN '@' MESSAGE AT LEAST ONCE A DAY

> *7 Graces Checklist:*
> *Connection; Invitation; Transparency*

The previous tip was all about replying to conversations and thanking people for sharing your content, but it's equally important to show your support and appreciation of your Twitter followers by *mentioning* them or *starting* conversations. Here are some ideas:

- If you meet someone new and they have an interesting profile, tell others about them with a 'mention'. Example: *Suggest you check out new tweep @AuthorMarySmith who has a great blog about health & fitness at [link to her website].*

- If someone wrote a great blog post, you could Tweet an '@ reply': *@AuthorMarySmith - loved your article on organic vegetables. Do you have any more info?*

- If you meet someone who has a lot in common with someone else you know, you could connect them. Example: *@AuthorMarySmith meet @WriterJJones. John's looking for health articles for his magazine. Mary writes about health. Synergy here?*

SIDEBAR NOTE: *If you have a smartphone, @ messaging and interaction is super simple using the free Twitter app. Since I've been using my mobile to access Twitter, my personal engagement with my followers has gone way up. We'll look at Tweeting by mobile in more detail in* 'PART 14: Expansion, Mobility and Influence'.

TIP 21: SEND AN RT AT LEAST ONCE A DAY

7 Graces Checklist:
Connection; Collaboration

One of the easiest and fastest ways to show your tweeps you are reading their content is to ReTweet their posts. If you are on your Twitter homepage online and you see a Tweet you think your followers might enjoy reading, just hit the ReTweet option below the Tweet and it's done. This sends the Tweet out to your followers, exactly as it was originally posted by the other person. The person you have ReTweeted will see your RT in their 'interactions'.

Sometimes you might wish to make a comment on a Tweet, as well as RT it to your followers. If that's the case, you should copy the Tweet first, and then paste it into the area that says 'compose Tweet'. Insert the letters RT and the author's name at the beginning. Example: *RT @AuthorMarySmith*. Then, put your comments at the end of the Tweet. Please note that if you RT this way, you may also have to edit the original Tweet if you go over the 140-character limit.

SIDEBAR NOTE: *If you are using the Twitter app on your mobile phone, when you select 'RT' it will also give you the option to 'quote Tweet', allowing you to edit it easily. HootSuite, BufferApp and other applications also allow you to edit your RT before sending it out.*

TIP 22: 'TAG' PEOPLE IN TWEETS WHENEVER POSSIBLE

7 Graces Checklist:
Connection; Collaboration

'Tagging' is when you use a person's Twitter handle in a Tweet rather than (or in addition to) their real name. Tagging is important because it will automatically put that Tweet into the other person's 'interactions' stream. If they see it, they are likely to RT it, or at least send you a 'thank you' message.

For example, if you are going to be on John Jones' radio show, don't Tweet 'I'll be on John Jones' radio show tonight'. Instead, Tweet:

> *I'll be speaking about donuts with @WriterJJones on the*
> *@DonutHour Radio Show at 9am EDT [short link to show].*

Here I've used two tags, which means both John and the producers of the radio show or network are likely to see the Tweet, and possibly RT it. This instantly increases the potential reach for this Tweet. If you don't tag people in your Tweet, they might miss your Tweet altogether, and that's a missed opportunity to show your desire to connect and collaborate.

TIP 23: DON'T START WITH @ UNLESS YOU ARE TALKING DIRECTLY TO THAT PERSON

7 Graces Checklist:
Connection; Directness

This is a subtle tip that warrants some explanation. If you want to comment on someone's Tweet and you hit 'reply', Twitter will automatically put their Twitter handle first, followed by your comment. Example:

> *@SpiritAuthors loved your article on Virtual Blog Tours. Could*
> *we talk sometime on Skype about setting one up?*

This is the *correct* way to have an open conversation *with* someone on Twitter. But what if you want to talk ABOUT that person? In such a case, it's best NOT to put their handle first thing in the Tweet. Let's say you want to tell people about an article @SpiritAuthors wrote on Virtual Blog Tours. This is the *incorrect* way to mention it on Twitter:

@SpiritAuthors article on Virtual Blog Tours
http://bit.ly/id3cxP

If you put the @SpiritAuthors handle first, your other followers will be unlikely to pay attention to it, as they'll think it's intended for @SpiritAuthors rather than for the public. So if you're intending to do a 'shout out' about someone, it's better to write a Tweet that looks something like this:

Enjoying article on Virtual Blog Tours by @SpiritAuthors. Great information for authors. http://bit.ly/id3cxP

TIP 24: DON'T ABUSE @ COMMUNICATIONS

7 Graces Checklist:
Connection; Invitation

While @ messages are great for connecting with people on Twitter, it's important to know what constitutes appropriate and inappropriate use of them. There are some unscrupulous people on Twitter who will use @ messages to send the same Tweet or link over and over to everyone on Twitter, regardless of whether or not they are following them. This kind of aggressive behaviour is called 'spamming'.

Simply put, spam is unwanted communications from other people. When you spam someone, it means you are sending them information, links, adverts, etc. they didn't request. Spamming on Twitter is likely to make others 'block' you and is highly likely to get your account suspended. In 7 Graces lingo, spamming is an example of the 'Deadly Sin of Invasion'.

Every now and then, a new person on Twitter will inadvertently 'spam' others without realising they are doing something against Twitter policy or they are at risk of losing their good name on Twitter. For example, a few years ago I had a client who was going on a book tour. One of her upcoming gigs was in Asheville, South Carolina. She started looking up people in that part of the world and sending them '@' messages telling them about her speaking gig. One of them very aggressively lashed out, called her a spammer and said he was reporting her to Twitter. This shook her up, but it was also a wake-up call for her, as she didn't know this kind of activity was spamming. Fortunately, she apologised to him and stopped sending out her '@' messages before anything ugly happened (she still has a large and loyal following on Twitter today).

While my client's offense was done quite innocently and came from lack of experience, please be warned that there are indeed professional spammers on Twitter. They often use keyword-generated software that shoots out an '@' message to you on a specific product or service if you look like a potential customer. Don't be tempted to buy or use any software that has this capability, no matter how many glossy adverts you receive. You will spend money on the software and your account WILL get banned, leaving you further behind than when you began. And to make it even more futile, none of those software programmes are discriminating enough to understand the context of the keywords, anyway, meaning the so-called 'targeted' leads are usually anything but targeted. In short, auto-spamming is not only unethical and against Twitter policy; it's also pointless.

Links posted to your stream are fine, but unless you want to get a reputation as a spammer, never use @ messages to send unsolicited links. If you really do want to share a link with someone specific, make sure it is in the context of a conversation:

@LynnSerafinn I notice you do book promotions. I'd love to get your input on an article I wrote on blog tours http://bit.ly/id3cxP

This kind of approach takes the aggressive, predatory edge off the Tweet, and it shows you put some thought into why you are sending the link to that person. You're also acknowledging the other person rather than promoting yourself. This strategy utilises the Graces of Connection and Invitation. It doesn't guarantee the other person will look at your article, but it makes it far more likely than if you just sent them a link without any personal touch.

If you have an upcoming event in a specific region, as in the case of my client above, and you want to get people's attention in that region, start your Tweet with the name of the town/city. Example:

LONDON: I'll be speaking at the #CSR MeetUp group Tues July 24th. Please join us. [link to event].

This way, you're not aiming a bullet at random strangers, but you have a good change of grabbing the attention of people who live or work in London.

If your event (including online events) is being hosted by a particular person or organisation, be sure to check if they are on Twitter and 'tag' them in your Tweet, so they will be likely to RT your Tweet. Example:

#ENTREPRENEURS: Please join us today for a FREE 1-hr class on 'The Dharma of Business' hosted by @Shaboom. http://bit.ly/Lo48Cr

TIP 25: DO **NOT** TOLERATE SPAMMERS!

7 Graces Checklist:
Connection; Invitation

While Twitter policy clearly states that abuse will not be tolerated, spammers still slip through the cracks despite Twitter's best efforts. I think it's important that GENUINE Twitter users become 'Neighbourhood Watchdogs' to help keep our online environment clean, safe and pleasant for everyone. We should not be passive when it comes to spammers, but REPORT them when we encounter them. If we are all vigilant together, we can help Twitter maintain the kind of social environment they want Twitter to be.

Of course, reporting someone can really mess them up if they don't actually happen to be a spammer. As shown with my unassuming client mentioned earlier, not all people who send you an '@' message with a link are spammers. Sometimes they are simply new to Twitter and very enthusiastic to make contact. So to help you tell who is a spammer and who is not, here are some ways you can identify them and get rid of them from both your stream and from Twitter:

- If someone sends you an @ message and you think it looks like spam, go to their Twitter profile page and see if ALL their Tweets look identical or very similar. If you see that they are repeatedly sending out '@' messages to other people with the same or similar message (with little or no other content), you can be pretty sure this person is a spammer.

- If you receive an @ message and a link, with no Tweet attached, it's more than likely it is spam.

- If you get an @ message with some sort of 'get rich quick' or 'get 10,000 Twitter followers in one day' type of scam, it's definitely spam. In fact, Facebook just recently shut down a whopping *80 million* bogus Facebook accounts, many of which were created solely for the purpose of selling 'likes' to Facebook business page owners. Unbelievable!

- Less commonly, you might receive an @ message that is a 'phishing' scam, but these tend to come via DM rather than @ messages. I'll explain how to recognise and handle the most common phishing messages later in this chapter.

If you are now certain they are a professional spammer and not someone making an innocent mistake, as my client did, you can report them to Twitter. To do this, go to the spammer's Twitter profile and click the downward arrow next to the little icon of a person in the upper right-hand corner of the page. Then, select the option 'report so-and-so for spam'. This will not only report them to Twitter, but it will also automatically block them from being able to communicate with you and vice versa.

Please don't be put off (or get too worked up) by the fact that there are some spammers on Twitter. 99% of people on Twitter are real people learning the ropes, just like you. I like to have an 'open door' policy and weed out the rubbish as I go along. If you become relaxed about this, you will find spammers are easy to get rid of and you can keep your Twitter stream full of good, interactive content from real people.

TIP 26: DON'T USE 'TRUE TWIT' (PLEASE!)

7 Graces Checklist:
Connection; Invitation

In the previous tip, I asked you to be vigilant but relaxed about having to deal with spammers. But because many people don't seem to be able to do either, someone out there invented a free programme called 'True Twit'. The alleged purpose of True Twit is to cut down on spam. It does this by requiring *every* person who wants to follow you on Twitter to 'prove' they're human by filling in one of those annoying 'captcha' forms.

While having people prove their identity may sounds like it's in your best interest, True Twit doesn't really work, and it can often backfire on you:

- Let's say you follow one of my Twitter accounts. I have my accounts set up so I automatically follow you back, but if you have True Twit, it will ask me to 'prove I'm human'. This is absurd because you are the one who followed me first.

- It's a huge time waster to those of us who have lots of followers. Many Twitter veterans don't bother to acknowledge True Twit requests anymore. That means if you are using it, you are losing *real* followers every single day, simply because you are trying to avoid a few spammers.

- It's sort of insulting to be asked to 'prove I'm human' when I've been on Twitter a lot longer than most people who ask me to verify my identity and I have tens of thousands of followers.

- It's a red flag that says, 'I don't trust you.' That's not a good start to a relationship.

True Twit might present itself as a service, but I feel it's just another platform for banner advertising. In my opinion, it does more damage than good, and I don't recommend using it.

TIP 27: KNOW HOW AND WHEN TO SEND DMS

7 Graces Checklist:
Connection; Invitation

The purpose of a DM is to exchange information privately with another Twitter follower. You cannot send a DM to someone unless they are following you. In other words, if you are following them but they are not following you, the only way to communicate directly with them is via an '@' message.

Sending a DM is useful when you wish to ask someone a private question or send them your contact information, such as your email address or Skype ID. Unless you are sharing this kind of private information, an open '@' message is preferable, as it is generally a GOOD thing to let other people see what you're talking about (and that you do talk to your followers).

While DMs might sound like a more intimate way to communicate on Twitter, the fact is that probably 99% of DMs these days are automated 'thank you' messages sent to you when you follow someone new. And because these messages do not warrant any kind of reply, many people don't bother to check their DMs as carefully or as often as they might check their email account. If someone has a lot of followers and their following is growing by the hundreds on a daily basis, they might miss your DM altogether.

Because DMs are so overlooked, if you do need to send one, my recommendation is that you also send an '@' message that says something like, 'I've just sent you a DM with my email address. Please watch for it.' That way, the person will know to check their DMs for a relevant message from you.

I also recommend using DMs for leads generation. While they are getting less effective than they used to be, I still get many new leads on my mailing list every week from this strategy, and several of my clients notice a real increase in their mailing list size when I employ this approach with them. See *PART 9: Automation* for more information on this.

TIP 28: KEEP AN EYE OUT FOR PHISHING DMs

I promise I'm not trying to scare you, but there ARE some people out there who manage to hack into other people's accounts and take them over. Please do not be too anxious about this, as a little vigilance will generally protect you from being affected.

Just as spam email scams will find their way into our inboxes despite our best efforts, new hacker/phishing attacks crop up regularly on Twitter. In a recent attack (2011-12) hackers got hold of (honest) people's accounts and sent out weird DMs to their followers that said variations of, 'Do you see what horrible things people are saying about you?' More recently, I've been receiving messages like, 'Hey, what are you doing in this video?' After this 'dig', there's a link. I've never been so gullible as to click these links, but according to several blogs I've read about these scams, if you were to click the link, it would take you to a page that looked like Twitter, and it would ask you to sign in with your user name and password. If you do this...BANG...your Twitter account is hacked. Now armed with your user name and password, the hackers can log into your account and do whatever they want with it. Typically, they'll just set it up so it sends out the same DMs to other people, so the cycle of hacking goes on and on, preying upon innocent victims.

This particular typed of hacking is called 'phishing', as its sole purpose is to 'fish' for your password and thus gain access to other information, such as your email address, etc.

Please be assured: *there is no need to get paranoid about phishing attacks.* You cannot get 'phished' just by accidentally clicking the link. You would have to *log into* the bogus Twitter homepage for that to happen. And as long as you are informed, aware and careful, you won't accidentally do that...right?

So what if you forget or aren't paying attention and you do accidentally log into a phishing site without realising it? Well, unless you are checking your 'sent messages' in your DM box, you probably won't know anything is wrong until other people start saying, 'Hey! What's up with this message you just sent me?' If that starts happening, log into your REAL twitter account at http://twitter.com and RESET your password right away. Be sure it's COMPLEX (see 'Tip

6: Choose A Complex Password'). This will stop the phishing immediately.

To ensure your account hasn't been compromised, be sure to check your DMs at least once a week (I glance at them every time I log in). Make sure the 'DMs you have sent to your followers are the ones you actually intended to send. If you see anything coming FROM you that looks suspicious, it means your account has been compromised. Again, don't panic, just change your password. And you might also want to send a DM or @ message to those people who got bogus messages from you, explaining the situation.

Lastly, if you RECEIVE any of these bogus DMs, don't just ignore them. And also, do NOT automatically 'report' or 'block' the person who sent it, because *it probably didn't come from them.* 99 times out of 100, it came from someone whose account got hacked. So be a Good Samaritan and send an @ message to the person who sent it, telling them you think their account has been hacked. Assure them that it has happened to many other people on Twitter and advise them to change their password right away. If they were the unwitting victim of a phishing scam, they will be very grateful to you, I assure you.

Just as I advised with spamming, don't let the 'threat' of phishing scare you off social media. It is usually avoidable or fixable if you keep your 'inner antennae' on alert.

TIP 29: CHANGE YOUR PASSWORD FREQUENTLY

Bearing in mind all I have just said, make a habit of changing your password once every few months (or even more frequently). Do this as part of your routine and you shouldn't have to worry about all the scary stuff I've been talking about. Amen.

TIP 30: DON'T SHARE ANYONE'S PERSONAL CONTACT INFO PUBLICLY

7 Graces Checklist:
Invitation

This morning I read a blog post about a British journalist who got his Twitter account suspended because he was urging people to write to someone at NBC to complain about their coverage of the London Olympics. The 'offense' was that he Tweeted the NBC executive's email. Sharing someone else's email is a violation of Twitter policy, so don't do it, ever. The journalist countered that the email he shared was a publicly available company email and not the executive's personal email, but trying to 'prove' the ethics or legality of this technicality is an argument you are not likely to win. While free speech is sacred on social media, Twitter do reserve the right to draw the line if they think someone has turned 'free speech' into a 'hate campaign'. If you wish to encourage people to contact someone, try using hashtags to start a trending conversation (see *PART 8: Using Hashtags*), or provide a link taking people to a blog post you have written or a petition to sign.

And I hope I don't need to remind you not to share your OWN email address publicly on Twitter, unless you really enjoy getting spam mail. Be sure to share your email, Skype ID, address, etc. via private DM only.

SIDEBAR NOTE: *I always encourage my clients not to publish their email address on their website, but to use a contact form instead. Similarly, if someone wants to contact you on Twitter and you don't really feel comfortable sharing your email address, you can give them the link to your contact form instead. If you have a WordPress blog, there are several free plug-ins for contact forms. Just do a search in the plug-ins area for 'contact form' to see what is currently available. Two of my favourites are* **Contact Forms by Contact Me.com** *(free and paid versions) and* **Gravity Forms** *(not free, but well worth the price if you need a more complex form). Contact Forms by Contact Me.com also have an app you can install on your Facebook business/fan page.*

PART 4:
FOLLOWERS AND FOLLOWING

M any people join Twitter with the mistaken impression that it's all a numbers game. While quantity of followers is certainly a factor in your Twitter success, *quality* is far more important. For that reason, please pay careful attention to Tips 31 and 32 as we start this chapter. While at first they may not seem like they have anything to do with Twitter, they are nonetheless THE most important tips you can get from *any* marketing book. Taking ample time to reflect upon the personal enquiries in these two tips can help you establish a solid and effective Twitter marketing platform that connects the real 'you' with your ideal audience.

TIP 31: KNOW THYSELF!

7 Graces Checklist:
Connection; Transparency

While 'knowing thyself' has been a major philosophical tenet at least as far back as Socrates, it is of particular importance for marketers because:

- If you don't know who YOU are in your business and marketing, you will never be able to communicate it to your audience (especially in 140-character bytes).

How well do we marketers know ourselves? How well are we communicating from the core, rather than from the surface? A good way to find out is to ask some reflective questions:

- Who am I REALLY as a writer, blogger, changemaker, business owner, etc.?

- What is the real message I want to share with the world through my work?

- If I were truly transparent, what would show up?

- How willing am I to allow that 'transparent me' to be seen?

- How can I communicate that 'transparent me' to others?

- Where am I still afraid to be fully transparent?

- How willing am I to work on addressing those fears?

Allow yourself time to absorb these questions before you begin your Twitter journey, and again over time as your business grows and you invariably grow and change as well. *Do not* let the fact that you cannot necessarily find all the answers right away stop you from beginning your journey. These questions are never 100% answerable and the answers will change every day. But the simple act of asking the questions will put you in the right frame of mind to know how you want to create your profile on Twitter (or anywhere else, for that matter).

> **REMEMBER:** *The journey towards true Transparency is a life-long process, so if you're waiting for 'the right time' you'll be waiting forever. Get started NOW, no matter how tentative you might feel about it. The more transparent you become, the more easily your ideal customers/ clients will 'see' you. In other words, if you want the 'right' people to find you, first you have to make yourself visible.*

TIP 32: KNOW THY AUDIENCE!

7 Graces Checklist:
Connection; Transparency

For a marketer, the all-important flipside of 'knowing thyself' is to 'know thy audience':

- If you do not know your AUDIENCE, you will be drifting around in No Man's Land until you find yourself surrounded by strangers shouting about things of no interest to you.

Here are some personal enquiry questions that can help you get a better idea of how well you know your audience:

- Who are your 'low-hanging fruit', i.e. the people you seem to attract naturally without effort?

- What are the beliefs and values of this group?

- How 'congruent' are you with their beliefs and values?

- What vision of the future do you all have in common?

- How in tune are you with the 'culture' of this group?

- How do you feel when you think about this group?

- What do these people *really* want (to have, to know, to feel, to experience)?

- What do you have or know that might address that want?

You will notice that I began by asking you about the 'low-hanging fruit' rather than asking you to define your 'target audience'. That's because I've learned from experience that this is really where we all must start. In 'old school' marketing, companies bombarded the public with the same message, hoping the wide-angle fire would 'hit' enough targets to make their marketing effective. However, in the new paradigm, and most particularly in social media, if you are not congruent with your audience, it will become evident very quickly.

Start with the 'low-hanging fruit': the audience that can easily 'recognise' who you are. Over time, it is possible to expand your audience organically. This happens when you reach enough of a critical mass in your 'low-hanging fruit' audience that many of them 'cross over' into other niches. When this happens, and you have started to build credibility in other areas, you can start to create marketing materials to address those audiences as well. But if you do this too soon before that critical mass has been reached, you are likely to confuse your audience with mixed messages. This is a mistake I've made a few times in my career, but I think I've 'got it' now. It's really a matter of patience. You plant the seeds and need to let them take root. If you try to rush the process, you are likely to kill off the crop you already have.

In any case, when it comes to defining and cultivating an audience, stay focussed on the first of the 7 Graces: Connection. Without congruence and relevance, there will be no Connection. Without Connection (within yourself, between you and your business, between you and your audience) you will be swirling helplessly in that No Man's Land I mentioned earlier. Remember that you DO have control over who comprises your audience. Define yourself. Define your audience. Then start following people who appear to be part of the 'low-hanging fruit'. Many of them will become your followers in turn. Watch your followers closely and, with time, you will have grown a 'tribe' of people who 'get' both you and your work easily.

TIP 33: DON'T FALL INTO THE TRAP OF FOLLOWING EVERYONE FAMOUS!

One thing newbies often do when they first join Twitter is follow all the 'big names' in their 'dream' category. I cannot count how many of my mind-body-spirit authors immediately follow New Age celebrities like Oprah, Deepak Chopra, Eckhart Tolle, etc. Perhaps you *are* genuinely interested in what they have to say, but if you are following them because you imagine they might follow you back or you might somehow get their attention, forget it. The chances of that happening are pretty much zero. As of this afternoon, Oprah has almost 13 *million* followers; she follows *59* people. Let's get real here. It's not so bad if you follow a few celebrities to satisfy your curiosity, but if you flood your dance card with people who will *never* follow you back, you are going to hit the dreaded 'Twitter wall' pretty fast and pretty hard (more on this in the next few tips).

If you want to succeed on Twitter, don't be a spectator. Follow your *audience* and give them reasons to follow you. If you want to follow 'popular' people on Twitter, follow useful people like @MariSmith (one of the leading experts in social media) and @Mashable, and keep them both in your private 'VIP' list (more on this in *PART 5: Twitter Lists*). Mari is just about the perfect model of a 'social media maven' and is likely to follow you back. Mashable are a great resource on social media innovations, strategies, etc. but are unlikely to follow you. Regardless, the information you'll receive about social media from these two sources (and others like them) is some of the best you'll ever get and you *should* follow them, especially if you are interested in expanding your social media knowledge and skill.

SIDEBAR NOTE: *If you follow any of my Twitter accounts (listed way back in 'Tip 4: Know The Basics'), I will automatically follow you back. The only way I'll stop following is if you spam me (which you won't, right?) or you become inactive for more than six weeks, as I'll assume you have quit. I hope this book will help ensure that never happens!*

TIP 34: FOLLOW BACK THOSE WHO FOLLOW YOU

7 Graces Checklist:
Connection; Invitation

It is my policy to follow back anyone who has followed me. I've had a few clients disagree with me on this, but let me present my case. I believe 99% of people on Twitter are good, honest people who are genuinely seeking to connect with others. The other 1% is (unfortunately) comprised of spammers, scammers and pornography. Personally, I'd rather save myself the time of having to vet 200 new followers a day so I can follow 198 of them, just to spare myself from the 1% I don't want to follow. Instead, I'd rather follow them all and un-follow them when they give me good reason to do so.

I believe this practice of following back strengthens the 'Grace of Invitation'. Having an open door policy says 'welcome' and exhibits graciousness to others. When we show goodwill, trust and a collaborative spirit by following people back, it not only sends the right 'message' to them, but in some energetic way it makes the world a better place. That's just my personal perspective, of course, but if you're at least willing to try it on for size, I suggest you give it a shot.

The 'slow' way to do this is to follow your new followers manually. You can do this by logging onto your Twitter account and clicking 'followers'. The newest followers will be at the top of the page. From there, you can follow them (or not) and add them to lists. You can also block them if they appear to be spammers.

Of course, if you have a large following, doing this manually every day can be a real chore. That's why I suggest using *automation* to perform the task of following back for you. Later in *PART 9: Automation*, we'll look at various third-party applications you can use to do this.

Tip 35: Don't Follow Too Aggressively

7 Graces Checklist:
Invitation

The majority of people who use Twitter regularly tend to auto-follow back when someone follows them. This is because it's often easier to weed out the undesirables than it is to vet and follow back every 'desirable'. As this is so widely practised, some not-so-scrupulous people will try to boost their follower numbers by following lots and lots of people very quickly. To help protect users from such abuse of the system, Twitter have both a technical limit as well as a carefully guarded 'algorithm' that helps them track people who become too 'aggressive' in following others. The technical limit is that you cannot follow more than 1000 people a day. However, that is NOT to say you can (or should) go ahead and follow 1000 people in a single day. This is because Twitter's algorithm will kick in, possibly resulting in suspending your account if you are deemed to be following too 'aggressively'. And even if the algorithm doesn't get you, the dreaded 'Twitter wall' will (as we'll explore in the next two tips). I've seen such scenarios happen many times.

While the exact algorithm Twitter use to determine what is 'aggressive' is a closely guarded secret (to prevent spammers from trying to trick the system), I think any intuitive person can get a sense of what 'feels' aggressive by how we respond to Twitter users whose accounts feel 'out of balance'. For instance, if people visit your profile and see that you are following 1000 people while only 10 are following you back, it sends the message, 'This person isn't worth following.' It may also say, 'This person doesn't know their way around Twitter and is likely to quit.' And, of course, it can say, 'This person is really aggressive. Better stay away from them.' However, if you are following 75 and 40 people are following you back, it sends the message, 'This person is just getting started,' which has a completely different impact. We are likely to take a chance on a newbie; we're unlikely to want to engage with someone we sense is a predator, a bore or a quitter.

How you *follow* people on Twitter communicates just as loudly to potential followers as how you engage with them. If you are starting from scratch, don't begin by following 500, 1000 or even more people right off the bat (I've even seen some people follow 2000 people on their first day!). If you do, you'll find yourself stuck with no way to grow, and you might even get your account suspended. Here are some guidelines I use with my clients *(note: these guidelines are my own, and are in no way 'official' Twitter figures):*

- If you are an absolute beginner, start by following 10 people a day.

- When you reach about 100 followers, increase this to 20 new people a day.

- When you reach 500 followers, go ahead and increase this number to 30.

- When you reach 1000, you might start to follow about 50 people a day.

- Gradually increase this number in increments of 10 for every 1000 followers you gain. By the time you reach 10,000 followers, it's usually fine to follow around 100 new people a day

- It's NOT a good idea to keep on increasing this figure forever, however. I wouldn't ordinarily recommend following more than 200-250 new people a day (this does not include follow-backs), even if your following exceeds 50,000. My reasoning is this: as you grow you will start to appear on many Twitter lists and, if your content is compelling and relevant, it will be shared by your ever-increasing 'tribe' of followers. This means you will probably be following *back* many new followers every day, who reached out to you without you having to seek them out. These 'follow-backs', along with a steady flow of 200-250 new tweeps a day, will keep your account growing without the need to increase your follows.

- As a basic 'target', always ensure your following-to-follower ratio is no wider than 1.1 (following) to 1 (follower). If it is wider than that, you may be flagged as 'aggressive' by Twitter. An ideal would be either a 1:1 ratio or one in which you have slightly more followers than those you are following.

These figures are not 'cast in stone'. They are relative to the ratio of follow-backs and new followers you receive compared to the number of new people you follow each day. Generally, I have found that if you are regularly following X number of people a day and after a couple of weeks your daily new follower ratio averages less than 35% of that number, it means you're doing something wrong. If this happens, it's time to ask yourself these questions:

- Are you following too many people a day in proportion to your current following? (For instance, following 100 or more people a day when you have fewer than 2000 followers is probably counter-productive.)

- Are the people you are following are truly in your target audience?

- Are you giving your followers enough *relevant* content to sustain their interest?

- Are the people you are following likely to follow you back?

- Are the people you are following still active on Twitter?

Regarding the last point, if you've been following people based upon a particular Twitter list, it's important to check how 'fresh' the list is. Sometimes people will have been put on lists a long time ago, but they have since left Twitter. Also, if a list was auto-generated sometime in the past (as with the now defunct programme 'Formulists'), it's not uncommon for the people on the list to be less than 100% relevant to the topic, as they were assembled automatically using keywords, which can produce odd results.

Bear in mind that the rate at which you follow people on Twitter must *always* be relative to the quality, relevance, frequency and diversity of your *content,* because these are the factors that influence people to follow you. If you are not Tweeting *many times a day* with diverse, relevant, high-quality content, and you rarely or never come online to interact with your followers, you might wish to follow people at a slower pace than I suggested until you build up that steam. In *PART 6: Creating Effective Content,* we'll look at what 'relevant, high-quality content' means and how to deliver it with impact on Twitter.

TIP 36: BEWARE OF THE 'TWITTER WALL'

Earlier I mentioned the 'Twitter wall', but now let's take a closer look at it. To review, Twitter has a rule that prevents you from following more than 2000 people until at least 2000 people follow you. The actual rules are slightly more complex than this, but every time I try to explain them to people, they stare at me blankly. So let's keep it simple and stick with the number 2000. Once you have over 2000 followers, you are fairly free to follow others at will, as long as you don't hit the alarm bells of Twitter's elusive algorithm.

Until you exceed 2000 followers, it's important to watch your numbers carefully—and monitor the *ratio* between your followers and following. If the number of people you follow is approaching the 2000 mark (say, above 1700) and you still only have 500 followers, you're in trouble. If you find yourself in this situation, you've probably been making one or more of the mistakes listed in Tip 35. If the Twitter wall is looming ever closer, stop whatever you're doing on Twitter immediately and move on to Tip 37 to find out how to reverse the damage.

TIP 37: KNOW HOW TO ESCAPE THE 'TWITTER WALL' AFTER YOU'VE HIT IT

If you've found yourself hitting the Twitter wall, and you're MILES away from getting your required 2000 followers, don't panic. The road back to 'health' is a three-step process

1. Get rid of dead wood

2. Un-follow your non-followers

3. Rebuild s-l-o-w-l-y

Below are some suggested methods you can use.

STEP 1: Get rid of the dead wood

'Dead wood' refers to 'stale' Twitter users who don't log on very often. The best tool for this is programme called 'UnTweeps'.

Log into UnTweeps using your Twitter account and ask it to list everyone you follow who hasn't Tweeted within the past 30-40 days. You might be surprised to find 500 or more of the people you follow are 'dead wood'. In all likelihood, many more than those 500 might be dead wood, but UnTweeps will only identify about 500 at a time. Click the boxes next to the accounts you wish to un-follow and hit the 'un-follow' button at the bottom of the screen. In a few minutes, you should see a screen that shows you how many un-follow requests were sent out. In my experience, UnTweeps rarely manages to un-follow all 500 accounts, but it might get rid of a good 250 of them. You can then come back another day and perform the whole process again until you have brought your numbers down and there are no more 'stale' Tweeps to un-follow.

Currently, you can use UnTweeps three times a month for free; alternatively, you can purchase unlimited access for a single month, or set up a recurring monthly subscription. The free service is sufficient for most people, but if you need to use it more frequently or if you want to be able to log into multiple Twitter accounts using a single UnTweeps account, the rates for the paid options are reasonable. Also, the owner Randall is very helpful if you get into any difficulty.

There is another (quite good) programme called Manage Flitter that can help you identify inactive tweeps. Unlike UnTweeps, it has many other kinds of filters you could use to locate people you would like to un-follow, such as non-reciprocal follows, accounts that use the default Twitter image, and people who don't Tweet in English (I'm not sure whether they have similar filters for speakers of other languages). They also let you search for people with a disproportionate followers-to-following ratio (typically people who have hit the Twitter wall!). Manage Flitter currently have a 100-un-follow limit for free, but you can raise the limits significantly (and still use their service without paying) by following them on Twitter, sending out a Tweet about them or signing up for their mailing list.

Another programme that can help you get rid of inactive tweeps is JustUnfollow. JustUnfollow has a free and paid service; their free service limits you to a maximum of 25 un-follows a day. They also have a very economical paid plan, which is (currently) $9.99 per year for a single Twitter account, giving you unlimited follows/un-follows for inactive tweeps, tweeps who do not follow you back and/or people who follow you but you are not following.

SIDEBAR NOTE: *You will note there is no 'select all' function on any of these programmes. This is because Twitter has a rule against 'bulk un-following' and a 'select all' feature is deemed in violation of Twitter policy.*

STEP 2: Un-follow everyone who does not follow you back

Once you've got rid of the dead wood, it's time to un-follow your non-followers. There are several tools you can use to do this. The easiest solution I've found is Tweet Adder, which allows you to automatically and gradually un-follow non-reciprocal follows after a specified number of days. If you're flat against the Twitter wall, I suggest you set this value to '0' days (be sure you have turned off any automated following you may have set up before you do this). It won't actually show your non-follows right away, but you should see them on the second day. Do NOT un-follow them all at once, as this is in violation of Twitter policy. Instead, eliminate perhaps 10% of your non-followers per day (spread throughout the day) until your ratio is close to 1:1.

If you'd rather not use Tweet Adder, you can use either Manage Flitter or 'Just Unfollow' as mentioned earlier. Other programmes for this purpose are Refollow and Social Oomph. You can read an overview of all of these products in *Automation – Follower/Following Management* in *Resources and Useful Links* at the end of this book.

SIDEBAR NOTE: *Twitter's official policy states they do not permit automated follow or un-following. However, I have to admit there is some ambiguity as to what this means. Twitter does not seem to have issue with software programmes running analytics about your followers, only about un-following them in bulk. The grey area remains as to whether or not un-following them automatically but not 'in bulk' (i.e. gradually over time) is a violation of policy. In all honesty, I have not been able to find a definitive answer to this. When in doubt, use the analytical tools to identify who to un-follow, but un-follow manually.*

STEP 3: Rebuild s-l-o-w-l-y

Once you have come back to roughly a 1:1 ratio of followers to following, you can start rebuilding *gradually*, using the guidelines above. As you rebuild, be sure to go back to the beginning of *PART 4*, and give some serious thought to the kind of audience you wish to attract and the kind of relationship you wish to build with them.

TIP 38: BREATHE NEW LIFE BACK INTO A 'DEAD' TWITTER ACCOUNT

7 Graces Checklist:
Connection; Inspiration

Many new clients will come to me after having used Twitter for some time, saying their account feels 'dead' and they don't know how to resurrect it. Perhaps they haven't even reached the point of hitting the 'Twitter wall' but have been stagnant with a very low number of followers (and following) for a long time. When someone's account feels 'dead', it is invariably because they are making the same mistakes I highlighted previously:

- They don't have a clear idea of their audience

- They haven't had a clear plan for finding their audience

- They aren't being pro-active about following and engaging with their audience

- They aren't creating enough relevant Twitter content for their audience to take interest in them

Whatever you do, do NOT make the additional mistake of quitting Twitter because you think it 'doesn't work'. If you think your account is 'dead', it's because you haven't been feeding it the right 'food'. Like anything else malnourished, it shrivels up and dies with time. In the case of Twitter, you'll end up with a list of followers with whom you have little, if anything, in common. If this sounds like you, read all of *PART 4* again (and maybe even earlier chapters; perhaps your profile is not strong enough).

Reflect on who you are, who your audience is and what your message is. After you have a clear idea on all three of these key components, clear out the dead wood and non-followers from your account and start looking for your ideal Twittermates. Then create some fabulous content for your potential new followers and rebuild your following slowly, until you start to see people taking a genuine interest in your content and showing a desire to interact with you.

TIP 39: REGULARLY UN-FOLLOW 'STALE' TWEEPS

I've already discussed un-following stale tweeps as a way of getting around the 'Twitter wall', but weeding out stale tweeps should also be part of your *regular* Twitter operations. Instructions for how to do this can be found back in Tip 37 under 'STEP 1: Get rid of the dead wood'.

Why should this be a part of your regular routine? There are countless people who come onto Twitter and leave it. They may have become bored with it, changed their line of business, or quit because they never really got the hang of it. If people don't show up for a month on Twitter, perhaps they went on holiday. But if people don't show up for 6 or 8 weeks or more, it's likely they've left Twitter. Regardless of their reasons, there's no point in continuing to follow someone on Twitter who is no longer there. So I always suggest that my clients make it a practice to un-follow tweeps who have been inactive on Twitter for more than 6 weeks.

Sometimes when my clients first see their 'stale' tweeps, they feel unsure about un-following them. They say, 'So-and-so are good personal friends/family members/clients. Won't I offend them if I un-follow them?' Think about that. If they've quit Twitter, they're hardly going to know or care whether you're following them, are they?

But then they ask, 'Can't I just leave it *in case* they come back? It can't hurt anything, can it?' Well, yes it can. As already discussed, if you're getting close to following 2000 people and you don't have 2000 followers, you'll need to clear out stale accounts to bring your numbers down right away. But apart from the Twitter wall, it's also important to remember that Twitter is not like a 'friends' list; it's meant to be a place where people share content. Following people who are not delivering any content serves no purpose. Also, if you follow lots of 'dead' accounts, it's possible that some of your other followers will start to follow them too, in which case you are helping create a ripple effect where many people are following inactive accounts. Un-following stale tweeps help keeps Twitter vibrant and active. It also helps you get a clearer picture of the activity on your account.

TIP 40: REGULARLY UN-FOLLOW (MOST) NON-FOLLOWERS

Just as it's important to weed out stale tweeps, it's also a good idea to make a regular practice of un-following people who don't 'get' that Twitter is supposed to be a 'social network' and do not bother to follow you back, even after adequate time has been given for them to do so. What is 'adequate time'? It depends upon your own activity and level of content. If you're a newbie at Twitter, you might give people a wide berth and wait 30-60 days before un-following them. But if you are an active Twitter user who Tweets often and shares lots of rich content on a daily basis, you should expect to see people follow you back within 10 days or sooner (unless they are 'celebrities' as we discussed earlier). If you don't see people following you back, try to get their attention by favouriting or ReTweeting some of their Tweets, or by starting a conversation with them. Ask them a question, make a comment. If they are active on Twitter, they will probably come around to following you with time.

Instructions on how to un-follow non-followers are in Tip 37, under 'STEP 2: Un-follow everyone who does not follow you back'.

TIP 41: DON'T BE TEMPTED TO PARTICIPATE IN TWITTER GROWTH SCAMS

7 Graces Checklist:

Invitation; Transparency

Just as there a lot of 'get rich quick' scams in the world, there are also a lot of 'get lots of Twitter followers fast' scams (the same goes for Facebook). Some of these scams 'sell' you followers. Unfortunately, these so-called followers are bogus accounts the scammers have set up solely for this purpose. Other scams operate in much the same way as pyramid schemes, except the 'commodity' is followers instead of money. This variety of scammers will ask you to give permission to auto-generate Tweets through your account about their 'get followers quick' programme. In exchange, they promise a certain number of followers (and you will end up following a bunch of people also hooked into the scam). Basically, you all end up becoming part of a big ring of spammers.

Here are some very good reasons why you should NOT participate in such a 'get followers quick' scam:

- Even if you do get more followers, they will either be random people who are not in your target audience OR 'fake' followers, i.e. from fake accounts.

- Many of these scams involve you having to Tweet 'spammy' stuff to your followers without your knowledge, which is likely to lose your legitimate followers.

- Twitter are very tuned into these scams and they routinely suspend accounts that make ANY claims to 'get 1000s of Twitter followers fast'.

- It's just plain unethical. Do you really want that kind of 'Tweeputation'? (Credit to my daughter, Vrinda, for thinking up that one).

As an example, the other day I was doing a search on the topic of 'proxies' (which I'll explain in *PART 14*) and I found a pitch on a techie forum from someone who wanted to find people willing to run multiple Twitter profiles via proxies for the purpose of one of these scams. The guy making the pitch admitted 'you are likely to get your account suspended, so you will need to know how to move through this using proxies'. In other words, he was openly seeking Twitter 'mercenaries' who were fully aware of the unethical and illegal nature of the work, but who would do it anyway because it was for pay and a technical challenge. Please don't be naïve and fall prey to such unscrupulous people. And ironically, if you check their Twitter accounts, most of those people who claim they can get you 5,000 to 10,000 followers in a day have far fewer than that number of followers themselves, for the simple reason that their accounts regularly get suspended.

The only real way to 'get' followers is to 'invite' them into your space. They only way real people will enter that space is if you are transparent and genuine. Let the real you shine through your content and you will attract the right followers, even if it isn't as fast as some of these scam artists claim is possible. Be patient. Have faith in your own power to attract followers through your naturally gracious demeanour.

PART 5:
TWITTER LISTS

TIP 42: GET TO KNOW YOUR WAY AROUND TWITTER LISTS

7 Graces Checklist:
Connection; Invitation

One of the most powerful features of Twitter is the ability to create and subscribe to Twitter lists. Using third-party software and applications, you can also track these lists and even follow the members of a list. In this section, we'll be exploring the various ways you can utilise the list feature on Twitter to connect with more people in your 'tribe'. But before we do that, let's review some basics, so you have a working knowledge of what lists are and how they work:

- PURPOSE: The purpose of making a Twitter list is to help you and others identify Twitter users who share a common interest, expertise or other defining parameter. See more info in 'Tip 43: Make Some Great Public Lists'.

- NUMBERS: You can create up to 20 lists on your Twitter account; each list can have a maximum of 500 people on it.

- TYPES: You can create 'public' lists and 'private' lists. Public lists are visible to everyone. Private lists are visible only to the person who created them.

- <u>ACCESS</u>: No one but the list creator can add or remove people from a list, whether public or private. In other words, you cannot add yourself to someone's list, but you CAN send them a Tweet to ask them to add you, if you think you would be a good match for the list.

- <u>MEMBERS</u>: If you are a 'member' of a public list, it means someone has put you on their list. To look up what lists you might be on, see Tip 45.

- <u>SUBSCRIBING</u>: You can 'subscribe' to other people's lists. This is more like a bookmark than anything else, and it does NOT mean you are following everyone on the list.

Those are the basics. Now let's look at the strategies that make lists so powerful.

TIP 43: MAKE SOME GREAT PUBLIC LISTS
Making a Twitter list is easy:

- Log into your Twitter account.

- Select 'view my profile page'.

- On the left, select 'lists' from the sidebar menu.

- On the upper right, select 'Create List'.

- Make sure you select 'public' list.

- Enter a name for your list that makes it clear what the list is about.

- Optionally, enter a short description. For example, if the people all come from a particular company or marketing campaign, you might want to state this in the description, as the name of the list might not be self-evident.

To add people to (OR remove them from) your list:

- Go to their Twitter profile.

- In the upper right-hand corner, click the downward arrow next to the little 'person' icon.

- Select 'Add or remove from lists'.

- Assuming you have already created a relevant list, check the box next to the list to which you want to add them (or uncheck to remove them).

- If you haven't yet made a relevant list, you can select 'create list' from this window also.

The best and most useful lists are **public lists** that clearly define what people have in common with one another. Here are some examples of how you might group people together:

- People who all Tweet about a particular topic (e.g. yoga, autism, health, politics, business, etc.)

- People who all live in a specific geographic location (e.g., California, London, Australia, etc.)

- People who all share a common profession (e.g. writers, marketers, filmmakers, accountants, NGOs, etc.)

- People who share a common vision or cause (e.g. environmentalism, social justice, CSR, world peace, etc.)

Don't worry about having loads of people on your list to start. Just add them as they come along. All lists start with a few people and then grow with time. Just remember to add new people to lists as you follow them whenever possible. If I see someone in my stream consistently Tweeting on a particular topic, I click on the little arrow next to their Tweet and add them to a list whenever I get the chance.

If you're concerned this all seems a bit too 'organised' for you, be assured that you CAN change the title and description of the list if you decide to broaden or narrow its focus. You can also remove people if they are no longer relevant to the list or if they have left Twitter. Lastly, you can delete a list if you don't think it's useful anymore (especially if you have hit the 20-list maximum and you want to create a newer, fresher list).

Don't be tempted to make 'pointless' lists that say things like 'my followers' or 'people who un-followed me'. These are of no real help to anyone. Good public lists should be useful not only to you, but also *to your followers.* They show you are a good networker and someone with good connections. Your lists also provide your followers with a good resource to find contacts (and their lists provide a good resource of new contacts for you, too).

Unlike mailing lists and email lists, Twitter lists are something people actually WANT to be on. This is why they are most useful when they are shared publicly. Later in this section, I'll show you many different ways you can use public lists (both yours and those of others) to your advantage.

> **SIDEBAR NOTE:** *Over time, the people on your lists (and even the lists themselves) will change. Using Twitter's interface to keep your lists current is very tedious. At the end of this chapter, we'll look at some useful third-party applications that can make your lists management easier.*

TIP 44: MAKE ONE OR TWO PRIVATE LISTS

7 Graces Checklist:
Connection; Collaboration

I'll share a secret with you. I have a private list of about 200 people I call 'My VIPs'. Because this list is private, I'm the only person who can view it. Who do I put on this list? Well, a combination of people, who are all on the list for different reasons.

- Some of them are on there because they are major resources of information I want, such as new software, CSR, sustainability, etc. They're on the list because I want to make sure I don't miss the information they are sharing.

- Others are personal friends, clients or network partners. They're on the list because I want to make sure I can find their updates easily so I can ReTweet them to my followers.

- Others are people who commonly Tweet inspiration or interesting trivia. They're on the list because they are a source of quick and easy ReTweet content to share with my followers.

- Others are tip sharers, such as other book marketers or social media experts. They might seem like the 'competition' to you, but they often have new things of interest to me. They're on the list so I can read their blog posts or perhaps leave a comment, which is a win-win scenario for both of us.

- Other people are 'targeted' authors and media people who don't know me yet, but with whom I'd like to cultivate a friendship. Perhaps they seem like a prospective collaboration partner or guest on my radio show. They're on the list so I can watch for ways to share their content or start a friendly conversation. This strategy has worked very successfully for me.

Maintaining a private VIP list is good because it doesn't have to have a particular theme. It's just a bunch of people you want to follow every day. Sometimes I get tired of them and take them off the list. Because it's private, no one knows they're on in the first place, so no one gets offended if I remove them. Basically, whenever I see someone I'd like to keep an eye on, I put them on the VIP list. Maybe I'll get lucky and you'll put me on yours. ;-)

In Tip 49 I will tell you **how to track activity** on both your public and private lists, and how this can help you build better relationships with people on Twitter.

TIP 45: FIND TARGETED FOLLOWERS ON LISTS WHERE YOU ARE A MEMBER

I'm always surprised when my new clients, even those who might have been on Twitter for some time, don't realise they are on a number of their followers' Twitter lists. It's important to check what lists you are on because you can often FIND great followers from these lists. If someone has placed you on a list that says 'green thinkers', 'writers', 'spiritual' 'marketers', 'business advice' or whatever, and you happen to be looking for people interested in that same topic – bingo!

You've just tapped into a goldmine of potential partners and/or readers.

To find out what Twitter lists you are on:

- Log onto Twitter.

- Click 'View My Profile'.

- Click 'Lists' on the left-hand side of your screen.

- When the main window opens up, click the link that says 'member of'. This will show you the lists where other people have added you as a member.

Look at the names of the lists. If the person has named the list appropriately, you can probably tell whether or not a list is relevant to your ideal target audience. If you suspect it might be, click on the link to the list and when the new window opens, click the link that says 'members' on the left-hand side of your screen. From here, you can manually follow anyone you like on the list (and add them to one of your own lists, if you like). You can also check out their profiles first, if you want.

> **SIDEBAR NOTE:** *For a quick check of how MANY lists you are on, log onto TweetDeck and click on your own Twitter handle in one of your Twitter streams. On the right-hand side of the screen you will see how many public lists you appear on. I checked my own accounts today and I'm on over 2400 lists in a wide variety of categories. If you've been on Twitter for some time and you're not on lots of lists, it means you are probably making one of the following mistakes: a) you are not delivering specific enough content for your followers to identify what you are about; b) you are not reaching the right audience; c) you are not Tweeting frequently enough to be noticed; d) your content is not diverse enough to be interesting; or e) you are not engaging with your followers. You will find various strategies for rectifying all of these 'errors' elsewhere in this book.*

TIP 46: FIND TARGETED LEADS ON LISTS ON WHICH INTERESTING PEOPLE APPEAR

You can also find fantastic leads by checking out lists on which other people appear. Remember I talked about your VIP list? Well, what about checking out the public lists your VIPs are members of? If they've been on Twitter for a while, they're apt to be on many relevant lists. I'm on thousands of lists in various subjects from 'marketing' to 'writers' to 'coaches' to 'spiritual' to 'ethical' and so on. Say you are looking for people in these kinds of categories. Checking out where I am listed would then be a logical starting point. From there, you'll find more people with more lists; and so your network starts to grow. Taking a look at the lists of a single Twitter influencer in your niche can be one of the biggest bonanzas you can find.

You can check out these lists the same way you checked out your own: go to a person's profile, click 'lists' on the sidebar menu, and then browse either the lists they have made or the lists on which they appear. Very often, people who have been on Twitter a long time have learned how to create good lists. Occasionally the lists go stale, but sometimes you hit a 'vein' of gold. Look for lists that seem to include people in your ideal audience, and start following and connecting with those people who are a good match for your interests and audience.

TIP 47: FIND TARGETED LISTS ON LISTORIOUS

Another rich source of lists is a site called 'Listorious'. Here you can search for lists using keywords. You can peruse the lists and see which ones you'd like to subscribe to or whether you would like to follow any of their members. You can (and should) also add your own lists to Listorious, as this will drive more traffic to your lists and, ultimately, your Twitter profile.

TIP 48: SUBSCRIBE TO OTHER PEOPLE'S LISTS

If you were doing a lot of research on the Internet and wanted to be able to find your way back to certain pages, you'd probably bookmark the pages you wanted. Similarly, if you stumble across a list on Twitter that you'd like to refer to again, you can 'subscribe' to it. As mentioned at the beginning of this chapter, subscribing to a list is like 'bookmarking' it, and it does NOT mean you are following the *people* on the list. If you do want to follow the people on the list, you have to click 'follow' next to each name.

When you subscribe to a list, it will appear in your Twitter lists as a list you 'follow'. If you want to view the activity of the list, you can click the link to the list from your Twitter profile, or create a stream for the list in either HootSuite or TweetDeck, which we'll look at next.

SIDEBAR NOTE: By now, you might be thinking that manually following everyone on lists that contain hundreds of people can be extremely time-consuming. There are ways to automate this action but, strictly speaking, they are not currently permitted within official Twitter policy. We'll take a look at this in PART 9: Automation.

TIP 49: TRACK ACTIVITY OF LISTS WITH HOOTSUITE OR TWEETDECK

7 Graces Checklist:
Connection

One way to stay on top of the activity in a particular list is to set up a custom 'stream' (also called a 'column') for it in HootSuite or TweetDeck. Both programmes operate in a similar way, but of the two, HootSuite lets you organise your streams more precisely than TweetDeck. In TweetDeck, all your columns are on a single screen and you click through them via a navigation bar at the top of the screen. In HootSuite, each of your social media accounts is shown on a separate tab, and within each tab you can create 10 different streams. Your 'core' streams include your main stream (all the Tweets from everyone you follow), your private messages (DMs), your mentions, your sent messages and your pending (scheduled) messages. Once you have your core streams set up, you should also up streams for some of your lists, such as your VIP list or specific topic lists.

Creating streams for specific lists helps you stay on top of what your closer contacts are doing, and it makes it super easy to share their content with your other followers. It's also a great way to avoid getting overwhelmed by 'information overload' when using Twitter. We'll look at this in more depth in *PART 12: Personal Sustainability.*

> **SIDEBAR NOTE:** *You can also set up streams for specific keywords and/or hashtags. We'll be looking at this in* PART 8: Using Hashtags.

TIP 50: DEFINE AND TRACK YOUR 'TRIBE' IN A LIST

7 Graces Checklist:
Connection; Invitation; Collaboration

One thing I do when I run a marketing campaign such as a book launch is create a list of all the joint venture partners (JVPs) who are supporting the campaign. This could include people who are offering a bonus gift, radio show hosts, blog tour hosts, etc. You can also create a list for all the people involved in a particular project or business. We can call this our 'tribe' list. If you create a 'tribe' list, be sure the members of your 'tribe' know it exists, and educate them a bit on how to make it work as a collaborative tool that will benefit everyone:

- Make sure you announce the list to your tribe.

- Give everyone in the tribe the link to the list.

- Ask everyone in the tribe to be sure they follow everyone else in the tribe.

- On #FollowFriday (#FF) be sure to recommend people from your tribe by sending out #FF Tweets about them (more on this in *PART 8: Using Hashtags*).

- Track the tribe list on HootSuite or TweetDeck and regularly RT Tweets from members of your tribe.

- Tell your tribe how to set up streams on HootSuite or TweetDeck and ask them to do the same.

- Set up a 'virtual newspaper' for your tribe list (see next tip for info on how to do this).

I've used this strategy in all my clients' book launches and I've found it really helps build a strong network, and makes campaigns more 'buzzy'. The key to making it work is that the 'tribe leader' (you or whoever made the list) creates the buzz by exemplifying the Graces of Connection, Collaboration and Invitation amongst the members of the tribe.

Tip 51: Create A 'Daily Newspaper' For Your Tribe

7 Graces Checklist:
Connection; Inspiration; Collaboration

There's a neat little social media application called Paper.li that can help spread the message of your tribe. Paper.li allows you to create an auto-generated online daily 'newspaper' of top stories from specified tweeple. It will only draw stories from Tweets that contain links. If, for example, a Tweet links followers to a blog post, you will see the title, featured image and first few lines of the article in the paper, with a link to read more on the original source. If someone has Tweeted about a YouTube video, you can click to play the video from the paper. Paper.li likes rich content, so if it sees images and videos they are more likely to be picked up as 'top stories'.

While the actual headlines you get are sort of hit-or-miss, the parameters from which the application draws the content are completely customisable. For example:

- You can specify that your 'daily' draws stories ONLY from a specific list. I always create dailies from the lists I make of partners for a specific marketing campaign. If you have created a list for your 'tribe', use your Paper.li daily to draw the content from that list.

- You can also set your Paper.li daily to draw content from a particular hashtag. This doesn't have to be a hashtag you have created. It can be on a particular trending topic or on a topic related to your niche. This way, your daily can have a wide variety of stories on that subject. Before trying this, I suggest you read *Part 8: Using Hashtags* very carefully, so you obtain the best result.

- You can also set the daily to draw content from specific keywords. I do NOT recommend using keywords, however, because keywords are often used in a completely different context within an article, and the resulting content in your daily paper can be irrelevant (or even weird).

- Some people set their dailies to draw content from ALL their followers. **Please don't do this!** It's pointless, as there is no niche or focus to the subject matter.

- You can also set your daily to draw content from specific tweeple, but if your lists are targeted well enough, this shouldn't be necessary.

Once you set your content parameters, you can specify the categories of the 'stories' (e.g. business, sports, entertainment, education, etc.). Then, give your 'daily' a custom name. It's best to call it something that tells what it's about. PLEASE don't be silly and call it something like 'The Mary Smith Daily' (i.e. don't name it after yourself). Also, when you create your paper, be sure to customise the 'editor's note' area, where you can explain the purpose of the daily (who the people are, what the paper is about). This area accepts HTML code, so if you mention your website, remember to insert the code; if you include a web address, make sure it is hyperlinked.

Your daily will come out every 24 hours (you set the time you want it to come out) and it will automatically Tweet an announcement to your list. Typically it says something like this:

7 Graces Global Community Daily is out! Top stories today by
@WholeSelf @HealingForum @JanHaley96
http://bit.ly/uJCPQG

Bestselling Mind-Body-Spirit Authors Daily is out! Top stories
by @BrightMichelle @SpiritAuthors @AlphaChickBook
http://bit.ly/excPuo

Notice that it mentions specific people (usually two or three) whose Tweets have been included as 'top stories'. This is useful because the people mentioned in the Tweet are likely to ReTweet this to their followers when they see their name mentioned (especially if they have read this book!).

You can also embed a widget for your daily on your website. It doesn't show all the stories, but if people click on it, they will be taken to the online version for that day. People can even subscribe to the daily to receive updates via email.

Like many other applications discussed so far, there is a free version and a paid version for Paper.li. The key difference between them is that the paid version is devoid of advertising. I believe it also opens up other options for content, such as Facebook.

> **SIDEBAR NOTE:** *While this application is very cool, there are a LOT of people who use it on Twitter and it doesn't always get quite as much attention as you might hope. The best advice I can give you to try to stand out in the crowd is a) make sure the title clearly identifies what your daily is about; b) make sure the editor's note gives a full explanation of what the daily is about; and c) make sure the content actually IS about what you say it's about! The best way to ensure congruence is to use one of your lists or custom hashtags as your content source.*

TIP 52: USE REFOLLOW TO HELP MANAGE YOUR LISTS

While Twitter lists are one of the most powerful tools on Twitter, when it comes to managing your lists, using Twitter's interface can be a nightmare. Right now, the only way to add or remove people to/from lists through your Twitter profile is to go to each person's profile individually and select 'add or remove from lists'. This can take forever, especially if you have a lot of followers. If you're new to lists, you might not see this as such a big issue. So far, you've been adding people to your lists as you meet them on Twitter and it all seems pretty easy. But over time, you'll notice that your Twitter landscape has changed. Some people will leave Twitter. Others you may not follow anymore. Still others will have changed their brand. Maybe you have also changed your brand. As your Twitterverse changes, your lists should change too. Unless you have a way to keep your lists up-to-date, there's really no point in having them. But how can you keep your data current if you have to add and remove people from your lists one at a time?

I've tried and tested many third-party applications for Twitter list management. A programme called Refollow is the only one I would currently recommend using, as all the others I have tried are nearly as cumbersome as Twitter's own list management.

What 'sold' me on Refollow was how it helped me do something I'd been trying to do for the previous six months. Some time back, I made the mistake of using a (now defunct) programme called 'Formulists'. This programme used to auto-generate 'dynamic' lists according to a variety of interesting parameters you could set, such as keywords in Tweets, or making composites of other pre-existing lists on Twitter. 'Dynamic' meant that they were updated at certain intervals. While using Formulists seemed liked a great idea at the time, the results were practically useless. I ended up with constantly changing lists of people I wasn't even following and who often had little relevance to the topic of the list. Then, in January 2012, Formulists announced that they had folded and I found myself stuck with half a dozen dreadful lists and no way to sort through them, short of going through them manually. I started to try to rectify this by copying some people onto new lists, but this was not only painfully time consuming, but also utterly confusing. I almost reached a point where I was resigned to deleting all my old Formulists-generated lists and starting from scratch.

Then I found out about Refollow, which is not promoted specifically as a 'list management tool', but as a 'Twitter relationship manager'. To cover their costs, there is a monthly fee if you wish to use Refollow to follow and un-follow people on Twitter, but as of this writing there is no fee if you simply wish to use it to *sort and manage your Twitter lists*.

To use Refollow's list management feature, log into the application via your Twitter account. If you scroll down the right-hand side of the screen, there is an option to see the members of any of your current Twitter lists. Then you can apply a number of different filters to the results. Once you get the results you're looking for, you can either select all of them or select them individually. You can then remove the selected accounts from your list and/or add them to another one of your lists.

I successfully used Refollow to clean up and merge a couple of particularly messy lists. It set the filter to show me all the people I wasn't following and I removed them from the list (I figure if I'm not following them, there's little point in having them on a list). I also removed people who hadn't Tweeted in more than a month, as well as people who were not following me. Then I selected everyone remaining on this nice 'clean' list and copied them onto the new list I had created when I had tried to sort the mess manually. Refollow recognised if people were already on the list and didn't copy them. Now, all my contacts were on one good list. When that was done, I deleted the old list. This process only took me about 15 minutes. Perhaps you'll think I'm really geeky, but I have to say it got me really excited to see two useless, messy lists become one nice tidy, relevant list. It also meant I had room in my Twitter account for a new list (as I had already maxxed out my 20-list allowance). Now I can load my nice new list into a stream in HootSuite or TweetDeck and stay connected with active tweeple who speak about topics in which I'm genuinely interested.

Refollow has another great feature for list management: it lets you view, follow or add people to your lists from *other people's lists*. For example, if you log into Refollow and put one of my Twitter IDs @LynnSerafinn into the menu, you will be able to see my lists. Then, you can add all or some of the list members to one of your own Twitter lists. On the next page is a screenshot of what that would look like:

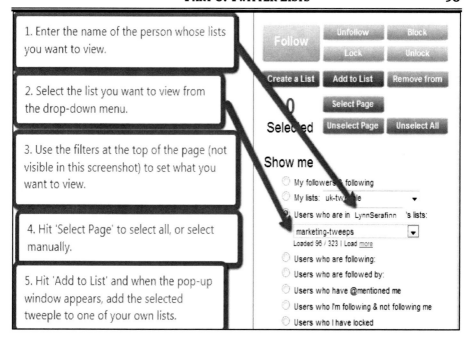

1. Enter the name of the person whose lists you want to view.

2. Select the list you want to view from the drop-down menu.

3. Use the filters at the top of the page (not visible in this screenshot) to set what you want to view.

4. Hit 'Select Page' to select all, or select manually.

5. Hit 'Add to List' and when the pop-up window appears, add the selected tweeple to one of your own lists.

SIDEBAR NOTE: *There are many other companies working on Twitter list management applications, but as I said, Refollow is currently the only one I would recommend. However, these kinds of applications are always coming into and going out of existence, or they may increase their price and become an impractical option for some people. If this happens and you find yourself without a way to manage your Twitter lists, the best thing to do is run a Google search for 'Twitter list management tools' and see what's currently being recommended by reputable social media bloggers.*

PART 6:
CREATING EFFECTIVE CONTENT

TIP 53: MEMORISE YOUR TWITTER MANTRA

The most common question beginners ask me is, 'What's the purpose of Twitter?' The answer to this question should become your Twitter mantra:

The purpose of Twitter is to attract people to your content.

Let me explain a bit more. The *ultimate* purpose of Twitter is to find and build *relationships*. But all relationships begin with a single encounter; on Twitter, that encounter is a Tweet. If a Tweet is to open the door to a new relationship, it must hold the promise of compelling, valuable content. When someone feels inspired enough to click one of your links, it is your responsibility to deliver on that promise. Through this process, you come to be trusted by your followers, which is essential to any relationship, whether personal or professional. When you understand this process implicitly, this mantra will guide you in the construction of all your Tweets as we go along.

What is the 'content' you want people to consume? In my opinion, at least 95% of your Tweets should take people to:

- Your blog posts

- Your info articles in your newsletter

- Your info articles on someone else's site

- Your info videos on YouTube or Vimeo

95

- Your info audios

- Your free offers

- Articles and offers from friends and partners that you feel are valuable and interesting

If you've been reading carefully, you will probably have noticed something is conspicuous by its absence on this list...*sales pages.*

TIP 54: NEVER LINK TO A SALES PAGE (WHAT, NEVER? WELL...HARDLY EVER)

7 Graces Checklist:
Connection; Inspiration;
Transparency; Abundance

(Apologies for the shameless 'homage' to Gilbert and Sullivan.)

At this point, you might be scratching your head and asking, 'Hmmm...I thought Twitter was supposed to help me promote and sell my book, product, business service, etc. How can it do that if I 'hardly ever' send people to my sales page?

Unlike many Internet marketers who will talk about conversion rates and sales pages, I believe Twitter is all about GIVING – giving value, giving information, giving free stuff. For that reason, rarely do I send people to an actual 'sales page'. Typically (probably 95% of the time, if not more), I send them to a blog post, a radio broadcast, an informative article or video, or a free offer of some kind. Because people know they 'get' stuff from me, and I'm not bugging them for money, they have a good relationship with me. Having that good relationship means that when I DO have a book, course, conference or other product for sale, they are more likely to take the time to check out what I have.

Remember that the vast majority of your Twitter followers don't know you that well. Always plant the seeds for greater Connection, and trust the process rather than zoom in for the 'kill'. Being generous and helpful to your followers is practising the Grace of Inspiration. If your Inspiration is coupled with the Grace of Transparency, it leads people to trust your integrity and the quality of your expertise, products or services. Once you have built trust and shown your worth to your audience, making sales is easier than you think. Trying to sell to your audience before they trust you, however, is not only difficult, but almost *requires* that you practise the 'Deadly Sins' of Persuasion, Deception and Scarcity, and will ultimately backfire on you.

Throughout the rest of this chapter (and indeed the rest of this book), we'll be looking at many ways to build a stronger Connection with your followers. If you focus on Connection rather than on sales, you will find your sales increasing with time even though the vast majority of the time you are not asking your followers to buy anything.

TIP 55: GIVE PEOPLE WHAT THEY WANT, NOT WHAT YOU WANT TO GIVE THEM

7 Graces Checklist:
Inspiration; Invitation

This is possibly THE most important content creation 'rule' for Twitter success.

My clients are all experts in their respective fields and they have plenty to say about their niche topics. When I help my clients build their following, we always start by creating *compelling* content on their blogs. We aim to make their posts rich in information on their specialty subject. If they choose to make videos or audios rather than just depending upon the written word, they can show their followers how to do things, or inspire them in some way. The key to creating compelling content is to ask the question, *'What do I have that other people want?'* Then, when you know the answer, *give* it to them. Giving people what they want does NOT mean you artificially or manipulatively create a desire within them through your marketing; it means you understand where they already are and you address their genuine need. This is practising the Grace of Inspiration. It is the opposite of 'The Deadly Sin of Persuasion', which is so widely taught and practised in traditional 'old school' marketing.

But while the 'old school' might be attached to their persuasive marketing tactics, in the Twitterverse, Inspiration is king. Why? Because *it works*. The reason why Inspiration works on Twitter (and indeed, anywhere on social media) is simple. If people see a Tweet that promises them good information on a subject they are interested in, they will click that link. If your Tweet looks like it will take them to a sales page, they are unlikely to check it out. Also, if you get a reputation for sending people only to sales pages, you are likely to lose followers. And if you lose followers, you ultimately lose sales.

Put yourself in your followers' shoes. Let's say you are trying to find out information on hypothyroidism. If you were on Google, you might do a keyword search. If you are on Twitter, you can also do a keyword search OR you might just see a Tweet mentioning hypothyroidism. You click the link on the Tweet. What do you *want* to see? Well, you probably want to read a carefully written article on the subject, or watch an informative video. What you do NOT want to see is someone in big, bold letters selling you the latest 'cure' for hypothyroidism (and if you do, all I can say is *caveat emptor!*). If you can bear this example in mind, you will begin to master not just the Grace of Inspiration, but also the Grace of Invitation (as opposed to the 'Deadly Sin of Invasion'). Leading someone to a sales page when you implied you had valuable information to share is just as invasive as cold-calling.

'But, but, but,' you say, 'if I never tell people about my products, how can my business possibly benefit from being on Twitter?' That's another good question, and it leads us to our next tip.

Tip 56: End EVERY Blog Post With Your 'Call to Action' (CTA)

7 Graces Checklist:
Connection; Inspiration; Invitation;
Directness; Transparency; Abundance

Only after you have given rich and valuable content to your audience in your blog post should you ask your readers for something back. That 'something back' is your opportunity to ask your readers to *do* something. Marketers refer to this as a 'call to action' or CTA. By 'call to action', most marketers mean 'get people to make a decision to buy something'. But in this book, a CTA is when you 'reach out' to your readers by *asking them to stay connected* with you.

You first do this by inviting your readers to share their thoughts in the comments box at the bottom of your article. Remind them that you have a lot more good content to share with them and they can sign up to receive your blog updates. Then invite them to share the article with their social network, as well as follow you on Twitter (and wherever else you might be).

Below these CTAs, you should put your headshot and a short bio. Either within your bio or at the very end of it, you can also include things like:

- Links to your book(s) (on Amazon, your shop page, etc.)

- Link to your company (where they can request a consultation, etc.)

- Links to any free offers (where they sign up to your mailing list)

- Link to an upcoming event (be sure to include the YEAR, as people may read your article after the fact)

- Links to your social media profiles

- Links to anything else you would like them to know about

As your Twitter followers become your blog readers and/or mailing list subscribers, they will become increasingly open to the idea of doing business with you *in their own time*. Continue to give them great content. Show you are an expert and that you are GENEROUS. Show them that you always have more to give and you have no fear about sharing your wisdom. These behaviours demonstrate nearly every one of the 7 Graces: Connection, Inspiration, Invitation, Directness, Transparency and Abundance. When your readers sense these Graces *authentically* emanating from you and your work, they are much more likely to become long-term, loyal followers and customers.

> **FICTION AUTHORS:** *I often get asked by fiction authors how they can write blogs that give value to their readers. Consider getting your audience involved in your process. Pitch ideas and ask for comments on ideas you have for characters, plot lines, book covers, etc. Create a 'tribe' around certain characters by letting your audience co-create scenarios with you. You might even write blogs as if they were written by your characters and encourage your audience to talk back to them. Discuss your research process, especially if you do any kind of historical fiction or sci-fi. Get your readers involved in the creative process of your book, as much as a year before it is published. You will be amazed at how easily they will want to buy your book when it comes out, because they will feel like they have been a part of its development. And don't forget to thank your readers in your Acknowledgments when the book is published!*

TIP 57: MAKE SURE YOUR TWEETS MAKE SENSE!

7 Graces Checklist:
Directness; Transparency

I find it astonishing how many writers find it challenging to compose a Tweet that actually makes SENSE. The trap many fall into is the use of their own professional jargon that requires too much explanation. Others get way too philosophical and verbose, filling their Tweets with all kinds of 'therefores' and 'howevers'. As an example, here's a paraphrase of a really AWFUL Tweet I came across a few years ago (please note that these are not real brand names; I chose random words so I could demonstrate a point):

Auriga consciousness is shadow energy, i.e. ego, temporary.
Therefore Orion practice, i.e. permanent, is used. [link]

If you just said, 'Huh???' you're not alone. Apart from being wordy, it uses indecipherable jargon, clumsy sentence structure and ambiguous grammar. It's everything a Tweet should not be.

Think of a Tweet as a kind of headline that must stand on its own. Its purpose is NOT meant to inform, but to give people an idea of what they will find if they click the link to a blog post, article or media file. After they click the link and land on your site, that's when you can share all the explanation, jargon and philosophy you want.

The example above used unusual, specialised terms for its various healing methodologies. If the writer had wanted to use these branded terms in a Tweet, he would have done better to say something like:

ARTICLE: The difference between 'Auriga' and 'Orion' consciousness [link]

What is 'Auriga' energy and how does it affect us? Article here: [link]

How can our inner 'Orion' energy help us be happier and healthier? Article here: [link]

OR...he could have taken out the specialised jargon altogether and written something like this:

ARTICLE: How can we move from 'shadow' consciousness into our light? [link]

HEALING TIPS: Two different kinds of energy that affect our health and happiness. [link]

Simple tips on how to heal painful emotions and memories: [link]

Now these Tweets make *sense*. Unless and until your brand is a household word like Oprah (and even then), my advice is that you NEVER presume your readers know anything about you or your methodology. Every time your write a Tweet, *assume people are hearing about you for the very first time.* Make your Tweets understandable to everyone, and write them in such a way that readers know exactly WHY they should click your link. If you really don't know what makes sense and what does not, have someone (not connected with your company) read your Tweets before posting them.

TIP 58: SIMPLICITY IS KING

7 Graces Checklist:
Directness; Transparency

Mastering the Grace of Directness means learning to 'tell it like it is', without succumbing to the alluring traps of filling our marketing with gloss and fluff. I've seen too many people fall into these traps, thinking it makes their marketing 'pretty'. Really, it only makes it ambiguous and evasive. And I don't know about you, but when things are ambiguous and evasive, I tend not to trust the person behind it. Ambiguity and evasion are often first-alert indicators of a deeper deception going on beneath the surface. And 'Deception' is one of the '7 Deadly Sins' of marketing. Its opposite is the Grace of Transparency. Both Directness and Transparency are necessary if we wish to build trust. If you want to create a trustworthy public image for yourself on Twitter, the first thing you need to learn is how to be SIMPLE.

As you know by now, your Tweets are limited to 140 characters, including your link. While many people might find this restrictive, I find it positively liberating. Twitter is like a playground for the arts of simplicity and Directness where we can leave complexity behind. I feel a certain sense of achievement when I make a really good Tweet that is under 100 characters. And from a business level, I find the shorter, simpler and more direct my Tweets are, the more people seem to click the link. Of course, the content in those 100 characters has to be compelling (which we'll look at shortly).

Try to look at the art of composing Tweets as a creative meditation for learning simplicity. This important ability will impact everything you do. The simpler and more direct you become in your verbal communications, the cleaner, clearer and closer your relationships will be—in the Twitterverse and beyond.

TIP 59: ALWAYS ASK 'YEAH...SO WHAT?' BEFORE POSTING YOUR TWEET

7 Graces Checklist:
Connection; Invitation

All too often I read Tweets (or, even worse, DMs) from people saying things like:

You can buy my book on Amazon [link]

Please check out my website [link]

Sign up for my newsletter [link]

Are these Tweets simple and direct? Yes. Do they make sense? Yes. So, are they good Tweets?

No way!

Why not? Because they fail the 'acid' test of a good Tweet: the **'Yeah...So What? Test'** (I'll call it the 'YSW Test' for short). What is the 'YSW Test'? Read these Tweets again and you'll see what I mean:

YOU TWEET: 'Read my new blog post [link]'
YOUR FOLLOWERS THINK: 'Yeah...so what?''

YOU TWEET: 'You can buy my book on Amazon [link]'
YOUR FOLLOWERS THINK: 'Yeah...so what?''

YOU TWEET: 'Please check out my website [link]'
YOUR FOLLOWERS THINK: 'Yeah...so what?''

YOU TWEET: 'Sign up for free my newsletter [link]'
YOUR FOLLOWERS THINK: 'Yeah...so what?''

The 'YSW Test' is a measure of *relevance* and, ultimately, the strength of your Connection with your audience. If you are telling people what YOU want them to know, rather than what THEY want to know, you are going to fail the YSW Test. I cannot tell you how many times a week I receive such messages on Twitter. And whenever I read them I think, 'Yeah...so what?' and forget about them almost instantly.

If your readers do not KNOW the answer to the 'so what?' it's not their fault; it's YOURS. If you are not telling them *why* they should have a look at something and *how* it is relevant to their needs or interests, you are failing the YSW Test. And while there is no way to craft a Tweet that is 100% foolproof from failing this test, there are some basic guidelines (which we'll look at in the next few tips) that can help you pass it the vast majority of the time.

SIDEBAR NOTE: *The YSW Test extends to when you make first contact with someone via email. For instance, I might receive an email from someone who would like to be on my radio show that reads, 'I'd be a great guest. Check out my website and contact me if interested.' If you send an initial contact message to someone like this, they'll just think, 'Yeah...so what?' and ignore you. Please remember that when you send someone a message (whether by email or Tweet), the ball is in your court to establish the relevance of your communication with them. If you do not provide them with adequate (but not too much!) information, you are unlikely to get a response. Your contact has no obligation to 'check you out' and is not likely to be motivated to do so without a good reason. Establishing relevance is crucial to the Grace of Connection. Only once Connection is established can you build towards the Grace of Invitation, with the likelihood of people accepting your offer to connect.*

TIP 60: NO, PEOPLE WILL NOT SEE YOUR TWEETS IN A SEQUENCE

So many times people have asked me, 'Will people see my Tweets in a sequence?' The answer is 'No, they won't.' Your Tweet is one of thousands people will receive every day. Furthermore, no one has their eyes glued to their Twitter stream 24/7 (not even me!), which means NO one will see ALL your Tweets. So unless your Tweets stand up on their own as full statements, ideas or messages, they will not make sense to your followers.

TIP 61: DO NOT TRY TO TWEET YOUR WHOLE BOOK!

If you are an author, do not even DREAM that Tweeting your book one line at a time is a really clever idea. Trust me on this one. I know because (I confess with some embarrassment) I tried to do this back in 2008 when Twitter was still fairly new to me. One day, I got the great idea to Tweet my book The Garden of the Soul one line at a time. It took me about three days to realise this idea was sheer lunacy. Trying to Tweet a book one line at a time is pointless, time-consuming and near impossible. You'll either come up with sentences that make no sense, or you'll spend hours and hours trying to make your sentences 'fit' into Twitter. And because your followers will not see them in a sequence, your Tweets will be cryptic at best. For all your effort, it is unlikely many people will click your link to find out what the heck you're talking about.

I still occasionally see some authors (especially fiction authors) Tweeting their books one line at a time. Please take my advice and don't waste your valuable time doing this.

TIP 62: DON'T TWEET ABOUT YOUR BOOK (WHAT?!)

OK, let's say you've just written your book. You're excited and want to get the word out about it. Maybe you even bought THIS book to help you learn how to market it. But now, here I am telling you NOT to Tweet about your book. What gives?

The keyword here is 'about'. Tweeting 'about' your book is boring and likely to fail the 'YSW Test'. Posting Tweets that say things like 'Find my book xyz on Amazon' or 'Read my book xyz' are almost certain to go unnoticed. Equally ineffective are Tweets that hype up your book, like quoting from reviews. Why would someone be interested in reviews of a book without knowing what the book *is* and why it is *relevant to them*?

The key to getting attention for your book through your Tweets is to allude to your book without actually talking 'about' it. Let's look at some ways to do that.

TIP 63: DO TWEET GREAT QUOTES AND IDEAS <u>FROM</u> YOUR BOOK

7 Graces Checklist:

Inspiration

While Tweeting your book one line at a time is a mad idea, Tweeting strong quotes and key ideas from your book is a great idea. Some of my most frequently ReTweeted Tweets (that's a tongue twister!) are these kinds of Tweets. If you do this, here are some guidelines:

- Make sure they are *complete statements or ideas* and are not dependent upon other Tweets in order for people to make sense of them.

- Remember that people will not see your Tweets in a sequence.

- Try to make them provocative and original.

- Cite your book title as the source (not just your name).

- You don't always have to include a link, but if you do, send people to a page where they can find out more about the book (and/or purchase it).

Below are some examples of quotes and ideas I have used from my book *The 7 Graces of Marketing* that have received a good response from my followers:

Abundance: Knowing true wealth is Absolute & not subject to our ever-changing opinions. ~7 Graces of Marketing http://bit.ly/uIDOtt

Thoreau dared us to march to the beat of a different drummer – the rhythm of our values. ~7 Graces of Marketing http://bit.ly/uIDOtt

Collaboration: knowing what we create together is always more than the sum of its parts. ~7 Graces of Marketing http://bit.ly/uIDOtt

You may have even found this book as the result of some Tweets I (or a partner of mine) sent out on Twitter. What do you think I used for most of my Tweets for *Tweep-e-licious*? Yup. The 'tips' themselves. I combined the tips, so key ideas, a hashtag and a link to come up with Tweets like these when I started promoting this book:

Twitter is a playground for learning the art of simplicity.
http://bit.ly/RDhD0t #Tweepelicious

A Tweet can open the door to a new relationship when it holds
the promise of valuable content. http://bit.ly/RDhD0t
#Tweepelicious

#Tweepelicious Tip 59: Always ask 'Yeah...So What?' before
posting your Tweet. http://bit.ly/RDhD0t

#Tweepelicious Tip 55: Give people what THEY want, not
what you want to give them. http://bit.ly/RDhD0t #ethical

Tip for authors: Don't Tweet ABOUT your book; Tweet ideas
FROM your book instead. http://bit.ly/RDhD0t
#Tweepelicious

Twitter Tip 64: the best Tweets are those that arouse
curiosity. http://bit.ly/RDhD0t #Tweepelicious

Notice how these Tweets have value *even if people don't click the link.* Hopefully, these will give you some examples of how you can extract ideas from your book that will arouse enough curiosity for people to check it out.

TIP 64: THE BEST TWEETS ARE THOSE THAT AROUSE CURIOSITY

7 Graces Checklist:
Connection; Invitation

There are a lot of people on Twitter who will Tweet little quips of inspiration. When I have a client who does not have a lot of content to share, I often advise them to start this way, with short statements that uplift, inform or in some way send their message. However, once you develop content, especially in the form of blog posts, I find the best Tweets are those that arouse curiosity.

How do you arouse curiosity? Well, for one thing, the topic has to be relevant to your followers. In my case, my followers include thousands of authors, so I send out a Tweet that promises some useful information that is hard to find elsewhere. This way, they are likely to click my link to check it out. Here are a few examples:

What Is a Virtual Blog Tour and How Do You Set One Up?
http://bit.ly/id3cxP

FAQ: What eBook formats are there? Which format should I use? http://bit.ly/rCpFQE

What can marketers learn from the ancient Greeks?
bit.ly/n1itco via @7GracesMarketng

If you happen to visit the links above, you will see that they take you to one of my blogs. The articles 'deliver' the content promised in the Tweet, and they also contain the 'call to action' discussed earlier. If your content is well-written, informative and (most of all) relevant to your audience AND you demonstrate a relaxed, inviting style of communication, your readers will want to remain connected with you. Mind you, in this day and age of data-overload, you've got to write some pretty useful information on your site to inspire people to stay with you. That's where the next tip will come in handy.

TIP 65: TWEET ABOUT FREE STUFF (BUT MAKE SURE IT ACTUALLY IS FREE)

7 Graces Checklist:
Invitation; Abundance

Another way to arouse curiosity and give value is with the promise of something free, such as a free audio download or video access, or a free trial of something substantial:

#Social #entrepreneurs: 1 hour FREE audio on the 'dharma' of business. No email sign-up required. http://bit.ly/Lo48Cr

Ready to BE the Change? Watch 90-min video from 7 Graces Conference FREE. No sign-up required. http://bit.ly/Nf1Q8i

The links in these Tweets take people to a page where they can get a free offer of some kind. In this case, there is no email sign-up required to access the content. The hope is that people will listen to the audio or watch the video and sign up to receive more blog posts, or purchase the rest of the videos in the series. If they don't, no worries. They are following me on Twitter and they got something valuable from me at no cost. If they like my content, they are likely to stay connected.

Here's a slightly different approach:

Authors: Have you downloaded these 5 FREE podcasts on writing, publishing and book marketing? http://bit.ly/NUeVco

FREE: Download 68 pages from #1 bestseller 7 Graces of Marketing by @LynnSerafinn #CSR #ethical http://bit.ly/O5rewE

FREE eBook: 'Why NICE People HATE Marketing' http://bit.ly/O5rewE

These Tweets bring people to a landing page where they must enter their name and email to get the free offer. If it is compelling, relevant and valuable enough to them, they are likely to sign up for the offer. This way, you are building a mailing list to which you can send more complex content, like a newsletter. To create these kinds of offers, you will need an email delivery service (a.k.a. auto-responder) such as GetResponse, AWeber or MailChimp. As this is a book about Twitter, I won't be going into how to set these up, but if you click the links above you can read about the programmes and get a free trial of them.

There's great sense in sending someone to a free download page. Once people are on your mailing list, you can communicate with them again. You can also include a CTA at the end of the download, inviting them to check out something else you have (for sale) such as a book, course, event, service or product. However, if you choose to do this, please be sure you have actually *delivered* the promised content for which they signed up, and that the content is of high quality. Don't try to 'trap' your followers with free offers.

By 'trapping' your followers, I mean the practice of trying to 'sell' to your new subscribers right away by blasting them with emails or taking them to a sales page immediately after they sign up to get your so-called 'free' offer. 'Free' should MEAN 'free'. It should NOT mean, 'Ah ha! You've been stupid enough to give me your email to get this cheap piece of rubbish and now I'm going to sucker you into buying something.' I know an awful lot of people do this (and teach others to do it), but I personally can't stand it and it's completely against my ethical code as a marketer.

As a new follower, I want a chance to READ or listen to your free download first before I receive further requests from you. Asking me to buy something from you before I've even consumed the free offer is actually *worse* than taking me to a sales page in the first place. It makes me feel like I've been snookered. I feel exploited and it does nothing to strengthen our Connection.

And if I feel that way, your Twitter followers will feel that way too. Don't spoil your fledgling relationships on Twitter by taking this tactic.

> **SIDEBAR NOTE:** *If you're curious, I've used GetResponse since 2007 and I've been pretty happy with their features and service throughout that time. While I've only used MailChimp on a few occasions, I have used AWeber quite a lot when working with client accounts. AWeber is great and is widely regarded as the favourite with many people. Nonetheless, I prefer GetResponse primarily because they are more helpful when it comes to transferring lists obtained from other databases. AWeber (in my experience) has a blanket policy of requiring all imported subscribers to opt into your list, which can result in a huge loss of subscribers. In contrast, any time I have had to import a large list into GetResponse, as long as I call their customer support in advance and I can show them the list is of valid subscribers from a reputable source, they will help me import them without any additional opt-in. This alone makes GetResponse my first choice.*

TIP 66: SEND PEOPLE TO YOUR NEWSLETTER, NOT A SIGN-UP PAGE

7 Graces Checklist:
Inspiration; Invitation; Abundance

Many people will send out Tweets or DMs asking people to sign up for their 'free' newsletter, or 'e-zine'. In my experience, this is pretty pointless. People are already saturated with email and if you send out a Tweet that says something like, 'Subscribe to my FREE e-zine [link]' it's destined to fail the 'YSW Test.' Even worse is when your Tweet simply sends them to a subscription page, where all they see is a form telling them *about* your newsletter.

So how *do* you get people to sign up for your newsletter? After all, you've had your sign-up form on your website for donkey's years and very few people have signed up. Well, what has worked for me is to use Twitter to bring people TO my newsletter, not a boring sign-up page. Here are some examples:

NEW issue of Creative Spirit now online: Marketing tips, events & broadcast guide for mind-body-spirit authors http://bit.ly/RchkQF

Info for Authors: 3 Tips When Seeking Partners for Your Book Launch http://bit.ly/L94YPC #promotion #marketing

True Story of How One Author's Luck Changed When She Mastered the Art of Invitation http://bit.ly/L94YPC

How web ring can bring together businesses and bloggers with the same vision and values http://bit.ly/L94YPC

As simple an idea as this is, I see very few people on Twitter using this strategy, probably because they are making two crucial errors:

- They don't post their newsletter online, thinking it is something 'private' only their mailing list should see

- Even if they do post it online, they don't typically put a SIGN-UP box in the newsletter itself

Both of these errors are easily fixable, especially if you use a good email delivery service such as the ones I mentioned earlier. Because I employ these two strategies, I get new sign-ups to my newsletter every day via Twitter. So if you're looking to get more people on your list, try this strategy and see how it changes things for you.

SIDEBAR NOTE: *To help encourage sign-ups to my list, I also have a link to the latest issue of my newsletter in the navigation bar on my Spirit Authors blog.*[16] *For those of you who worry you are 'giving too much away' by doing this, I ask you to consider where this 'scarcity' worry may be coming from. Remember that we live in a world of information overload. The best way to inspire someone to join your newsletter mailing list is to let them read the latest issue without obligation.*

TIP 67: DON'T GET STARS IN YOUR EYES IF YOU'RE ON THE RADIO

7 Graces Checklist:
Connection; Invitation; Directness

I've been hosting a radio show on Blog Talk Radio (BTR)[17] since January 2009. If any of you reading this also use their service, you'll be familiar with their dashboard. One nice feature BTR has is integration with Twitter and Facebook. When you log into their dashboard, it lets you send a Tweet to announce your show. You can also send this announcement to your followers.

It sounds like a great idea, but unfortunately it is ineffective if you use BTR's 'default' message, which is:

I'm broadcasting live on the air! [link]

To me, this has all the appeal of an over-enthusiastic puppy barking wildly and jumping up and down as soon as you enter the house. And you should now be able to see that this Tweet DEFINITELY fails the 'Yeah...So What?' Test. Please do yourself (and your followers) a favour and never, ever Tweet this. It makes you look unprofessional, and it gives no one (except maybe your mother or best friend) any incentive to click the link to listen to your show.

Before you Tweet about your show, put a little care into saying what it's about. Then, when people visit the show page, make sure there is more information there for them to see the name of your guest(s), what you'll be talking about, the day/time of broadcast, etc. Here are some examples of what I think are more engaging Tweets about radio shows:

On the air: Guest @JoyfulPaws tells how #authors can get speaking gigs at schools & libraries on @GardenOfTheSoul http://ow.ly/aIBuY

What is an 'enlightened divorce'? #Author @FarhanaDhalla tells all on @GardenOfTheSoul Radio http://ow.ly/9vWJB

Fantastic show! NY Times Bestseller @MarthaBeck shares lessons from African shamans on @GardenOfTheSoul Radio http://ow.ly/8Geqs

The same holds true for when you are a *guest* on a radio show. If possible, don't just say, 'I'll be on such-and-such show today,' in your Tweet. Tell your followers what you'll be talking about AND be sure to 'tag' the host, if he/she is on Twitter.

> **SIDEBAR NOTE:** *Be sure to make it easy and obvious for your followers to figure out how to tune into the show. All too many times I've clicked a Twitter link wanting to check out a radio show and either the host hadn't listed the episode yet, or it was impossible to figure out where to tune in.*

TIP 68: 'SHOUT OUT' ABOUT PARTNERS AND SPECIAL OFFERS

7 Graces Checklist:
Abundance; Collaboration

During an online launch for a book or other product, it is common practice for your JVPs to offer free gifts as bonuses when someone makes a purchase. If you are running such a campaign, it's a great idea to create Tweets for each person offering a gift, giving them a 'shout out'. You might say something like:

FREE 1-hr audio book from @LynnSerafinn when you buy 'The
Destiny Discovery' by @BrightMichelle [link] #Destiny2011

FREE video series on forgiveness from @BrendaAdelman
when you buy Mal Duane's new @AlphaChickBook [link]
#AlphaFeb14

The link in the Tweet should take people to the launch page where they can make their purchase and claim their gifts. The hashtag should be something you have created to track your campaign (more on this in *Part 8: Using Hashtags*).

This is one of those occasions when you *should* send people to a 'sales page'. Don't hit people over the head by bringing them to a page where you're trying to sell them a $1000 product. Make sure your Tweets are light and fun and that the offer on the page is worth much more than the asking price. When the product is something reasonably priced (as most books are), relevant to their interests (which it will be if you choose the right partners) AND you are offering them loads of other goodies, it will be exciting and interesting instead of invasive to your followers.

The positive, collaborative energy your JVPs bring to your campaign is key to its success on Twitter. When you distribute a list of Tweets like this to your network of partners and they start Tweeting them to their followers, you create a viral motion. If people see their name being mentioned in a Tweet, they are likely to ReTweet it to their followers. But also, I have found that good JVPs enjoy supporting other tweeple. It creates a generous vibe in cyberspace because it takes the spotlight off the people doing the Tweeting and shines it on someone else. The person being 'shouted' about is also likely to follow the people doing the shouting. While a well-run JVP campaign depends upon having a strong network, it can also help strengthen an existing network and create many new connections within it.

TIP 69: MAKE COMPELLING TWEETS FOR A VIRTUAL BLOG TOUR

7 Graces Checklist:
Inspiration; Invitation; Collaboration

One marketing strategy I use in my book launches is the Virtual Blog Tour (VBT). If you're unfamiliar with VBTs, I'll be talking about the 'how to' of Virtual Blog Tours on Twitter later in Part 13: Marketing For Monetisation. But as we're currently exploring the topic of creating content, let's now take a look at how to create effective Tweets that support your VBT.

Twitter is a vital component of a good VBT, and nicely written Tweets can drive a lot of traffic to these interviews. In crafting these Tweets, it's very important you run them through the 'YSW Test'. They're bound to fail if they say something like, 'Check out my interview on so-and-so's blog.' Instead, whenever possible, tell people what you're *talking about* in the interview. Here are a few examples:

Why is Collaboration better than Competition? Top business ethics author @LynnSerafinn on @gallagherPOC 's blog http://bit.ly/NYMQgl #7GoM

Can a new paradigm help biz owners who hate marketing? Author & marketer @LynnSerafinn on @charlyjl 's blog http://bit.ly/Mk76Gm #7GoM

7 Marketing Principles for Your Coaching Business. Author @LynnSerafinn on @parent_coach 's blog http://bit.ly/um4hd7 #7GoM

Do we have a 'relationship' with marketing? @PaulaTarrant interviews bestselling author @LynnSerafinn http://bit.ly/rsb8Z1 #7GoM

How can we avoid the '7 Deadly Sins' in marketing? Author @LynnSerafinn on @MemoirGuru 's blog http://bit.ly/vUzQYS #7GoM

Let's consider the qualities of these Tweets and why they are effective:

- They are simple, clear, understandable and direct.

- They are written in a way to 'arouse curiosity'.

- They do not take people to a sales page, but to an article of interest.

- They are targeting specific needs to specific audiences.

- They have keywords that will help show up in search results.

- They include a unique hashtag, so people can check out related content.

- They tag other tweeple who are likely to ReTweet them to their followers.

In just a few words, these Tweets are practical demonstrations of several of the 7 Graces:

- **Connection:** They connect not only with the person tagged in the Tweet, but also with the specific, relevant interests of your readers.

- **Inspiration:** They are not persuasive 'buy this book now' Tweets, nor do they link to persuasive sales pages (although mention of the book and how to buy it is included on the page).

- **Invitation:** Even if people don't click the link, they are inviting engagement and conversation with your Twitter followers.

- **Directness:** They are simple, clear and not filled with fluff or hype.

- **Collaboration:** The Tweets are not directly promoting your book, but rather your colleagues' blogs and Twitter handles.

Of course, it's not always possible to create such elaborate Tweets for every stop on a VBT if your blog hosts do not send you their content in a timely fashion. But try to give as much care and attention to creating these Tweets as you can, because if they are compelling enough, they can also be used for a long time after the tour has taken place.

TIP 70: GOOD RETWEETS ARE ALSO GOOD CONTENT

7 Graces Checklist:
Connection; Collaboration

Maybe even after all these content creation tips, you still can't think what to Tweet. Or maybe you haven't set up your blog yet (or you are not able to blog as often as you'd like), but you really want to start building your following on Twitter. Well, don't forget that ReTweeting other people's Tweets is also good content, as long as they: a) are from people you know; b) contain high-quality content; and c) are relevant to your audience.

Sending out the occasional RT is easy if you are on Twitter, Twitter mobile, TweetDeck or HootSuite. If you see something you want to share, just hit 'RT' and it's sent. But sending RTs manually means you have to be *on* one of these applications in order to send your RT. Furthermore, it means your RTs will all go out in very close proximity to each other. It's a much better idea to find your RTs and spread them out over time. This also gives your posts a better chance of being seen, as they will appear at various times throughout the day.

There are several ethical ways to pre-schedule your RTs in compliance with Twitter policy. One is to use the scheduling feature in either TweetDeck or HootSuite. HootSuite even has an 'auto-schedule' feature where it will choose a time for you. I also really like a programme called BufferApp for this kind of thing. When you sign up for a free BufferApp account, you get up to 3 social media accounts and 10 spaces in your 'buffer' for free. Then, from your Twitter home stream, whenever you find some Tweets you'd like to RT you just click the 'buffer' link and it will spread out your RTs very nicely without having to specify a time. Using one of the above strategies means you can find a handful of nice RTs in the morning (check your list streams for the ones most relevant to your followers), schedule them, and forget about them until you come back online.

SIDEBAR NOTE: *There are ways to set up fully automated RTs, which means you don't have to search for content at all. These automation systems locate RT material based upon keywords, hashtags or specific Twitter accounts. Be warned that these kinds of automation systems are against official Twitter policy. Moreover, they do not tend to produce useful results. We'll look at this more in* PART 9: Automation.

TIP 71: DON'T USE ALL 140 CHARACTERS – USE 120 CHARACTERS OR FEWER

7 Graces Checklist:
Directness; Collaboration

Back in the 'old days' (2008) all savvy Twitter freaks knew it was important to leave at least 20 empty characters in your Tweet to make it easier for people to RT your Tweets. This is because back then, when you hit 'RT', Twitter would insert the words 'RT @YourTwitterID'. Twitter has since changed its system so this no longer happens. But while the new system has made it much easier to share someone's Tweet with your followers, it makes it tougher to leave comments after a Tweet or strike up a conversation with the person who sent it out.

That's why it's still a good idea to make your Tweets as short as possible. Plenty of us 'old school' tweeple like to copy and paste your Tweet rather than just hit 'RT' so we can make a comment on it. If you construct (most of) your Tweets with this possibility in mind, it will help people engage with you on Twitter.

Using no more than 120 characters also makes it easier and faster for readers to scan visually. As I said earlier, when I'm writing Tweets for a campaign, I try to make them under 100 characters each.

TIP 72: USE BIT.LY OR OW.LY FOR SHORTENING LINKS

On that same note, remember it is important to economise on the length of your URLs (links). While Twitter now has its own integrated link shortener, there are many occasions when you will want to prepare Tweets with the links already shortened (such as when you want to upload a batch of Tweets to a third-part programme, or when making Tweets for a marketing campaign). For such occasions, my two recommended link-shorteners are Bit.ly and Ow.ly. Both of these shortening services are free. Bit.ly is a stand-alone service; Ow.ly can also be used as a stand-alone service, but is more widely used as the shortener incorporated into HootSuite.

There are several reasons why I recommend these above many others. First, they tend to produce the shortest links. They also seem to be the most stable of shorteners I have tried. Many links I've made with other services in the past have suddenly and inexplicably become invalid. Lastly, these two services seem to be considered 'safe' by Twitter. Every now and then, Twitter 'decides' it doesn't like a particular link-shortening service, possibly because their security is questionable and they feel too many viruses or scams are being cloaked by them. So far, both Bit.ly and Ow.ly seem to be compatible with Twitter and just about any other application. So my advice is to stick with one of these.

Bit.ly also has an API key. The term 'API' refers to 'Application Programming Interface'; API enables different software programmes to communicate with each other. Bit.ly's API lets you do a lot of handy things. For example, some WordPress plug-ins allow you to incorporate the API key into their settings, so if people Tweet about your blog post, the link will be automatically shortened. This means you can *track* the activity of the link on Bit.ly. Bit.ly API can also be used within Tweet Adder, meaning you can shorten your links right inside the programme without having to go online. Tweet Adder also stores your shortened links so you can grab them when you need them for a new Tweet.

Ow.ly also has some excellent analytics within HootSuite. If you want to view reports showing you which of your Tweets are getting the most attention and other important data, Ow.ly is fabulous.

> **SIDEBAR NOTE:** *Some people worry about not having 'branding' in the links they send out if they use link-shorteners. If it's obvious that your content is sound and relevant, few people are going to pay attention to the actual URL on Twitter. Remember: Twitter is fast, furious and cluttered. People are NOT reading the address of the link; it is the Tweet that informs their decision whether to click or not.*

TIP 73: BE CAREFUL NOT TO USE 'UNRECOGNISABLE' CHARACTERS

If you use Microsoft Word for your typing, you might also use it to compose your Tweets. The problem with Word is that it has many proprietary text styles that do not easily translate to other applications (including WordPress, Tweet Adder, Twitter and Kindle). This means certain characters that look fine in Word will often come out as 'unrecognisable' in Twitter, showing up as empty boxes, black squares or question marks.

The main 'unrecognisable' characters that can create problems in Twitter are:

- <u>Curly quotes (also known as 'smart' quotes):</u> 'Smart' or 'curly' quotes are quotation marks and apostrophes that 'know' which way they are facing and 'curl' around the letters like little hands holding the word between them. It looks great in Word, but unfortunately hardly any other programmes out there are compatible with them. If you don't know how to change these, look up 'change smart quotes to straight quotes' in your Word help.

- <u>'En' and 'em' dashes:</u> Have you ever noticed that sometimes Word will take your single or double hyphens and turn them into really slick-looking dashes? In Word, these are called 'en dashes' (formed from a single hyphen with spaces on either side of it) and 'em dashes' (formed from double hyphens with no spaces on either side of them). Again, these look great in Word, but they are cryptic to most other programmes. For the purposes of Twitter, the best thing to do is replace them with two hyphens.

- <u>Ellipses:</u> Ellipses are the three...little...dots you might put into your text to indicate something has been omitted (or that you're thinking about something...). Word will often change these ellipses into a single character. As with the other auto-correct elements above, if your Tweets have ellipses, replace them with three separate dots OR consider not using them at all. For the most part, ellipses are usually not particularly useful in a Tweet anyway.

Once you have made all your corrections, save your work into a plain text file (*.txt).

SIDEBAR NOTE: *If you're unsure whether your Tweets have unrecognisable characters, you'll find out easily enough if you upload your Tweets to Tweet Adder as a plain text file (not Word document).*

TIP 74: USE '&' AND OTHER SHORT-CUTS TO ECONOMISE ON CHARACTERS

Sometimes when you're making a Tweet, you just can't seem to make it short enough. If that happens to you, here are some tips:

- Try replacing the word 'and' with an ampersand ('&').

- You can also say 'U' or 'U R' instead of 'you' or 'you are' (although I avoid this unless *absolutely* necessary, as it's a bit too casual and looks like a text message).

- Use 'thx' instead of 'thanks' or 'thank you'.

- Look for 'filler' words that can be removed without changing the meaning of your message. Cliché filler words are things like 'really', 'actually', 'very', 'truly' or any kind of repetition (like 'very, very').

- Be SURE you have shortened your link with either Bit.ly or Ow.ly.

- Be sure you have no double spaces (especially after punctuation).

- Check to see if you really need all that punctuation. Sometimes punctuation is not so important in Twitter, especially right before a link.

Tip 75: Don't Be Tempted To Use Auto-Generated Tweets

7 Graces Checklist:
Connection; Transparency

Sometimes it can be tempting to use shortcuts that seem to save time and effort. There are a number of software programmes on the market that offer 'auto-generated' Tweets. To set the record straight, I'm going to talk a little bit about what these programmes do, but I'm *not* going to name the software programmes that perform Tweet auto-generation because I don't recommend using them and don't want to encourage anyone to try them.

One type of auto-generated programme will spit out spam messages to people whenever it detects certain keywords. At this point in the book, I hope you've already come to the conclusion that this kind of activity will not only make you unpopular on Twitter, but it is also likely to get your accounted suspended. And be warned: the folks at Twitter will rarely reactivate an account suspended for spamming, unless the spamming was caused by hackers who got into your account.

Another kind of auto-generated Tweet software will compose Tweets for you by 'spinning' your selected keywords. 'Spinning' entails randomising the order of words and using synonyms. Notionally, the idea is to: 1) save you time having to make up Tweets, 2) 'outsmart' the Twitter system, which is always on the lookout for accounts that Tweet the same content over and over without change, and 3) give the illusion that these computer-generated Tweets are written by a human being. To those of you who have not yet come to love Twitter as I do, this kind of auto-generated Tweet software might sound like a gift from heaven. But in my opinion, it's pointless and rarely produces Tweets you would want to use. Besides, if you are a writer or any kind of creative person with your own ideas you want to share with the world, why in the world would you NOT want to compose your own content?

My tip regarding auto-generated Tweets is this: don't bother. Make genuine, original, human content that speaks YOUR message clearly, in such a way that it will connect with other real human beings. With time, you will come to love the creative challenge of writing your own Tweets.

It's sort of like composing a Haiku...with a link.

PART 7:
FREQUENCY AND REPETITION

TIP 76: DON'T BE AFRAID TO TWEET A LOT

Typically when new clients come to me, they have many misconceptions about the impact of their Tweets. I told the story at the beginning of this book about how a single Tweet from @TonyEldridge changed my life. But it's important to bear in mind that this particular Tweet came from someone who Tweeted lots of high-quality, relevant content every single day to a clearly defined niche audience. A single Tweet from someone like this has tremendous potential to get noticed (or may even go viral). But a Tweet from someone who Tweets sporadically and has a few hundred ambiguous and 'unengaged' followers is likely to go unnoticed by most of their audience.

I mentioned this earlier, but it bears saying once again: Twitter is not like Facebook. Things don't 'stick' to the wall. They get swallowed, absorbed, forgotten and lost. Let me say it in plain words:

Do NOT be afraid to Tweet a LOT.

If you are not Tweeting regularly and frequently,

people will NOT see your Tweets.

Paste those words over your desk, please!

But before I send you off into the big wide world of Twitter with this as your 'mantra', there are some very important guidelines you must follow. You must understand what I mean by 'regularly' and 'frequently'. You should also know that there is not a 'one size fits all' formula for how often you should Tweet, and that it is completely dependent upon your content and relevance to your audience. In other words, Tweeting regularly and frequently does NOT mean Tweeting the same message over and over every five minutes. If you do this, your account will get banned within days. Trusting that you have read the previous chapters on Twitterquette and the process of creating good content, let's explore *legitimate* ways to build your Twitter 'muscle' so your frequency increases over time until you have a steady flow of content that is serving your followers nicely.

TIP 77: DON'T JUST ANNOUNCE NEW BLOG POSTS—RECYCLE THEM

There are several ways to automate your blog to 'announce' new posts on Twitter (to be discussed in *PART 10: Integration*), but what a lot of people forget is how *saturated* Twitter is with information. This means that sending out a single Tweet when your new blog post comes out is not enough. In order for your blog posts to get noticed, you have to talk about them many, many times, over a long period of time, in a 'drip-feed' kind of way. This is, of course, assuming that your posts contain relevant information that is useful to your audience over that period of time.

Some of my current Tweets bring people to articles I wrote as long as two or three years ago. The reason for this is primarily that my network is continually growing and changing. Many of the people who follow me today were NOT following me back when I first published the articles. If a blog post you have written has 'back catalogue value' (meaning the information contained within it doesn't go out of date), be sure to recycle Tweets about it. You might take a look at the post to check whether your bio and call-to-action are current, and make edits as needed. But if you've put time and energy into creating a great article, it only makes sense to keep sharing it with new followers. This is how you build content over time.

TIP 78: MAKE A VARIETY OF TWEETS (NOT JUST ONE) FOR EACH BLOG POST

7 Graces Checklist:
Inspiration

Many people make the mistake of composing a single Tweet for each blog post they write. Usually that one Tweet is the title of the article plus the link. But what you may not realise is that for every blog post you write, you can probably extract a good 5 to 10 Tweets, all of which have a different 'feel'. One of the easiest and most obvious ways to break your article into different Tweets is if your article happens to have a specific number of points, tips or FAQs. For example:

FAQ: How do I get my book into digital format for Kindle and ePub? http://bit.ly/rCpFQE

FAQ: How do I price my book, and what kind of royalties will I receive per sale? http://bit.ly/rCpFQE

But how can you make Tweets from articles that cannot be broken down so easily? In these cases, look for sentences that can be extracted to make a 'curiosity-arousing' statement. For example:

If profit is our only measuring stick, we might believe we cannot afford things vital to the future of our world. http://bit.ly/KfADlk

We cannot afford to stay in our boxes and think, 'The problem is too big. There's no way to change it.' http://bit.ly/KfADlk

What could YOU gain from the world if everyone lived according to the Grace of Connection? http://bit.ly/OHjaUk

Click the links and have a look at the original articles to get an idea of how I've extracted the content from the articles to make compelling Tweets. Then, get creative. Go through all your relevant blog posts and set yourself the challenge of creating up to 10 unique Tweets for each one. Once you've composed them, set them up to recycle over time and watch the traffic to your blog site start to increase (we'll talk about the mechanics of recycling them in *PART 9: Automation*). If you have constructed each blog post carefully according to the guidelines we talked about earlier (including a good bio and call-to-action), you should see a steady increase in your Twitter following and blog subscribers, and hopefully your mailing list and book sales.

TIP 79: YOUR FREQUENCY SHOULD BE RELATIVE TO THE DIVERSITY OF YOUR CONTENT

While I advised you not to be afraid to Tweet a LOT, you also need to be sure to space out your recycled content over time. It's not good Twitter form to repeat the same content over and over within a short space of time. Twitter doesn't like it, your followers don't like it and it certainly doesn't look very enticing to your potential followers. Here are some guidelines I give my clients who are just starting to build their content:

- Never Tweet more than 10% of your total content *per day*. If you have only 10 (or fewer) Tweets in your repertoire, Tweet one of them a day, and make up for lack of content by ReTweeting and mentioning others. If you have 200 great Tweets, you can Tweet up to 20 of them a day. However, learn to draw the line so you're not going overboard; having 1000 great Tweets does not automatically mean you should be Tweeting 100 times a day, unless you happen to be a syndication channel for many different news outlets (which most of you reading this are not likely to be). If you have hundreds of good Tweets, spread them out over a longer period of time. Please note: I'm not including *conversational* Tweets (replies and mentions) in these figures. Apart from Twitter's mechanical limit of 1000 Tweets a day, you shouldn't need to worry about how many times a day you are communicating directly with your followers.

- Try not to allow your content to repeat itself more frequently than every 10 days (less frequently, if possible). The exception, of course, would be if your Tweets are leading up to a major launch day.

- If your content is getting stale or too repetitive, stop using it. You can bring it back in a few months if it still has 'shelf life'.

- One way to increase your content is to get lots of guest contributors for your site. My friend Gail Lynne Goodwin has used this model for InspireMeToday.com to get around 2 million readers daily. Major Twitter players like Mashable have so many contributors and so much fresh, new content that they can afford to Tweet three or four times an hour without any danger of becoming 'stale'. Look for ways to diversify your content by *creating collaborative projects* and you will soon find you have the ability to increase the frequency of your Tweets, and get more attention overall.

PART 8:
USING HASHTAGS

TIP 80: HASHTAGS – THE BASICS

On Twitter, a hashtag is a single 'word' preceded by a 'hash' sign (#). Some of you may refer to this as a 'pound' sign. When you put this # sign *before* any word on Twitter (making sure there is no space between the # and the word), it will turn that word into a clickable hyperlink. If someone clicks that hyperlink, a search stream will pop up on Twitter, showing all the Tweets that have recently used that hashtag. This makes a hashtag a very powerful Twitter tool for identifying trends and tracking your own promotional campaigns.

There are trending hashtags for anything from a celebrity or TV show to a major event or natural disaster. When singers Amy Winehouse and Whitney Houston died, hashtags spread the news. When the US Presidential elections took place, people shared results and opinions via hashtags. Twitter users shared their experiences of the recent London Olympics using hashtags like #London2012 and #Olympics. Over the past few years I've clicked hashtags that brought me updates, news, eye-witness accounts and videos of the earthquakes and tsunami in Kobe, Japan, the Australian floods, the London riots, Hurricane Sandy and many other global events. Hashtags make the news spread. They can even help disaster victims locate (and call for) help.

But hashtags can also be used as a means of *creating* news:

- You can invent your own hashtags to create a buzz around a particular topic or campaign.

- You can use hashtags to get your Tweets noticed amongst a certain 'tribe' who are already talking about a particular topic.

- You can use hashtags to get your Tweets ReTweeted by larger Twitter entities.

- You can also use Twitter-specific hashtags like #FF and #WW to find more followers.

- During a launch or special event, you can use hashtags to track who is saying what about your book, event, product, etc.

Hashtags are very simple in concept. Following existing hashtags to find out what's trending (or join in the conversation) is simple enough, but making a good hashtag for your own purposes requires a bit of forethought and creativity. Throughout this chapter, we'll be exploring the wonderful world of hashtags so you can learn how to create and use them effectively.

TIP 81: FOLLOW HASHTAGS FOR TRENDING TOPICS IN YOUR AREA OF INTEREST

Before you get started making your own hashtags, it's a good idea to get familiar with them by checking out existing hashtags you might see on Twitter. Notice how when you click on any hashtag you will see a stream of Tweets on a particular topic. If the hashtag is comprised of common keywords, you'll probably see a lot of diversity without much focus. But if the hashtag is on a more specific topic, such as a big event or name in the news, you are likely to find a much more focussed stream of comments and perhaps links to relevant articles or videos. This morning when I logged onto Twitter, a trending hashtag was #earthquake because there was a Magnitude 4.4 earthquake in Los Angeles (which, based upon the comments in the thread, most southern Californians seem to have met with a pretty blasé attitude).

Spend some time getting to know how to utilise hashtags to find information you need, or people interested in a particular topic with whom you would like to connect. You can locate existing hashtags by doing a Twitter search. You'll find the search box at the top of the screen on your Twitter homepage. Note that when you do such a search, it will show you results for instances of that keyword with and without the hashtag.

TIP 82: LEARN HOW TO CREATE GOOD HASHTAGS

From a strictly mechanical point of view, making a hashtag is dirt simple. Put a # sign and follow it with a *single* word, ensuring there is no space between the two. Remember that your 'single word' doesn't actually have to *be* one word; it just has to be joined together as one word. An example of this is the hashtag #LawOfAttraction. Technically it's three words, but as there are no spaces between the words (nor between the # and the first letter of the word 'law') it becomes a clickable link. Put that tag into Twitter's search and see what appears in that stream today. Note that the results you find might include the keywords 'law of attraction' and not just the hashtag. They might also include tweeple who use that hashtag or keyword in their *profile.*

But while making a hashtag is easy, knowing *what* your hashtag word should be can present a challenge. If you just want your Tweets to appear in searches amongst others who are talking about the same broad topic (examples: #money #business #spirituality) then it's a simple matter of using those words. That can be a great way for people to find you who share your interests.

But if you want to *create* a trend or use your hashtag for tracking purposes (explained in the next tip), you'll need to select a hashtag that isn't used by anyone else. That often means not using 'real' words, but rather creating a unique code or combination of words. For example, one of my clients had a book called *Messages from the Angels of Transparency* that was launching on March 20th. I wanted the keyword 'angels' but I knew that would be way too common (and besides, it also brought up Tweets for the Los Angeles Angels baseball team!). So I made up the hashtag #AngelsMar20. This hashtag was not just perfect for tracking, but it also contained subtle information for the reader, as it included the main keyword from the title of the book plus the date of the launch. I tend to use this formula whenever I create a launch campaign.

I've seen many of my colleagues make hashtags for their campaigns that are not properly researched, resulting in them choosing hashtags that are shared by other trending topics. Thus they find it difficult to track the activity of their promotional partners and marketing team. Give some real thought to your hashtags before you commit to them for a campaign. DO try to make them as short as possible so they don't take up valuable characters in your Tweets but DON'T shorten them at the expense of effectiveness.

TIP 83: TRACK YOUR MARKETING CAMPAIGN WITH A HASHTAG

7 Graces Checklist:
Collaboration

Just as hashtags can provide you with an easy way to find out information on trending topics, they are also very effective in helping you track activity during a promotional campaign. One way you can use your campaign hashtag is to set up a 'stream' for that hashtag in HootSuite or TweetDeck. Below is a screenshot of a HootSuite dashboard. You can see an 'add stream' option in the upper left-hand side. Click it and this window will appear:

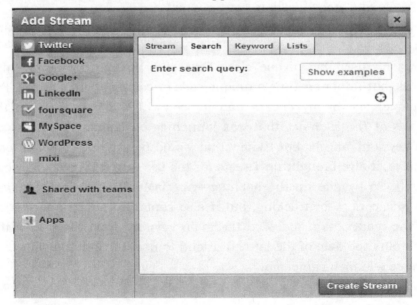

Select the tab that says 'search' and enter your hashtag (you can also enter a search for any keywords you'd like to follow on a regular basis). When you click 'create stream' you will see a continuously updated stream of all the Tweets that have used that hashtag. This tool can help you see who amongst your partners is actively helping with promotions and who is not. Sometimes it's a matter of offering help to those who aren't 'showing up'. This stream can also help you see which of your Tweets are getting the most attention in the form of ReTweets. It also helps you identify new people who have shared your Tweets, so you can thank them, follow them and engage with them.

TIP 84: USE TOPSY TO SEARCH FOR HASHTAGS IN OLDER TWEETS

Twitter's search capability is extremely limited. It will only search for Tweets that have been posted within the last week, and it is unable to perform multiple search commands (for example, you cannot look up a hashtag that was Tweeted by a particular Twitter user). So what do you do when you are in need of more advanced searches, or if you want to track a campaign after the one-week window on Twitter?

There are several third-party applications available, and most of them include some sort of free search option. I recommend reading an excellent article entitled 'All the easiest ways to search old Tweets' on the 'Tweet Smarter' blog as an introduction to the resources currently available.[18] I use a free service called Topsy. Their 'Advanced Search' feature[19] allows you to search for Tweets using your hashtag between a specified set of dates or other parameters. It's very useful for assessing the reach of a particular campaign, including how many RTs you might be generating, etc.

Keeping track of activity around a particular hashtag can provide you with a lot of useful information, such as which Tweets are generating the most interest, which of your partners are the most active, and whether there are new people appearing in your stream who might be worth checking out and connecting with.

TIP 85: GROW YOUR TWITTER NETWORK WITH THE AID OF HASHTAGS

7 Graces Checklist:
Connection; Invitation; Transparency

One of the most important elements in growing a network is *relevance*. Relevance is also one of the keys to the Grace of Invitation. When you 'knock' on someone's 'door' by connecting on Twitter or any social network, in order for them have a sense of wanting to engage, they need to know you share some sort of point of convergence. Hashtags can be extremely helpful in this regard because they make it easy to identify that point. When you click on a hashtag that seems to 'fit' the profile of the kinds of network friends and partners you are seeking, you are likely to find many good potential connections in the stream. If you want to follow the history of that hashtag a bit further, you can use the free Topsy Advanced Search as suggested above.

But once you tap into a 'vein' of Twitter gold like this, how do you extract its value? I usually begin the process of engagement by various means:

- I start following several of the most interesting and active people I see in the stream.

- I add these people to a public list, either one I already have or a newly created one, which brings them together with other people of similar interest.

- I put a few of them on my VIP list to keep a special eye on them.

- I immediately RT a few of the most interesting or useful Tweets I find in the stream.

- I mark a few more interesting Tweets as 'favourites' so I can read and RT them later.

- I send a few @ messages saying hello; as an 'icebreaker', I tell them I found them via the specific hashtag.

- I might also mention that I put them on the list (be sure you give them the link to the list) and I ask if they can recommend anyone else for the list.

Through these practices, you are displaying relevance, engagement, courtesy, respect and a collaborative attitude to your new connections. You are not only opening the door, but giving people *reasons* to check out what is inside. Do this with sincerity and authenticity (the Grace of Transparency), and you will likely find that many of your new connections will be happy to follow you back.

TIP 86: PAY ATTENTION TO RTS YOU RECEIVE FROM OTHERS VIA HASHTAGS

Hashtags are a great way to identify yourself as a thought leader in a given topic of interest, even if you and your readers don't know or follow each other. This is because if people are following a particular tag, they'll see your Tweets amongst the stream for that tag. If your Tweets contain good, relevant information, they might decide to ReTweet you to their followers even if they do not follow you. For example, if you Tweet about cause-driven topics like #CSR, #sustainability or #socent (social enterprise) and include these hashtags in your Tweets, you're bound to be ReTweeted by other like-minded people who are tracking these hashtags. This is a wonderful, organic way to extend *beyond* your current circle of followers. You're also likely to pick up some new followers along the way, who share this common interest with you.

Some Twitter accounts are set up to RT any Tweets that use a particular hashtag *automatically*. For example, the hashtags #YouTube and #BlogTalkRadio used to result in these companies' respective Twitter accounts auto-generating RTs to their streams. However, I notice they are not doing this anymore. I can only speculate this practice was stopped due to recent changes in Twitter policy and/or because people were intentionally abusing the system, resulting in too many irrelevant Tweets appearing in the stream.

'Abuse' of hashtags occurs when people include a hashtag in their Tweet just because the tag is popular, even though it has no relevance to what they are Tweeting about. Their hope is they will be seen in popular streams, or get ReTweeted by 'robots' for that tag, as described above. This kind of behaviour is deemed 'abuse' by Twitter and is against Twitter policy. It's also like 'gate-crashing' someone else's party (which is a perfect example of the 'Deadly Sin of Invasion') and it will gain you no points for popularity on Twitter. Ethical use of hashtags means ensuring your tags are relevant and current to the Tweet you are posting.

TIP 87: TWITTER CULTURE 1: #FF (#FOLLOWFRIDAY)

7 Graces Checklist:
Connection; Invitation; Collaboration

I've mentioned the hashtag #FF (or 'FollowFriday') a few times, but now let's look at it in detail. There is a 'tradition' (as traditional as you can be on Twitter, given the fact it is only a few years old) where people recommend other followers on Fridays. Back when I was new to Twitter in 2008, this was the day when EVERYONE would be online sharing their favourite contacts with one another. I notice nowadays it has become a lot less personal and a lot of people are blasting generic, automatic recommendations (sometimes about nearly all of their followers) rather than taking time to craft them with care. As a result, many #FF recommendations are of little value. But I still believe #FF is a great opportunity to create great recommendations that give value to your followers. This is how to do it *right*:

- Think about the people you follow on Twitter and consider who has been the most supportive, engaging or interesting over the past week or month. Then narrow them down to a select few, maybe up to 20 people.

- Group them into categories as best you can, such as 'authors', 'marketing gurus', 'social entrepreneurs', 'ethical business leaders', 'changemakers', 'spiritual', 'coaches', 'healers', 'eco tweeple', 'great accountants' or whatever characterises them collectively.

- Write some Tweets recommending each group (you might need to make more than one Tweet for each group if you have a lot of people). You can also include a few other hashtags if you think they are something people would be tracking. Here are some examples of how you could do this:

Follow #bestseller #spiritual #authors @BrightMichelle
@WeR1NSpirit @CharleneProctor @GaetanoVivo
@GardenOfTheSoul #FF

Follow enlightened #media #film tweeps @RoadToPeaceFilm
@MediaForTheSoul @Stuparich @LionHeartWoman #FF

Follow #ethical #business #leaders @GallagherPOC
@ecoSuperman @SpiritusShelagh @wholeself @ethicalvalue
#FF

Don't go too overboard with the hashtags, as it might result in your Tweets not showing up in Twitter searches, which would defeat the purpose of the recommendation. Notice that the longest Tweet above is only 118 characters. This is to give room in case someone wants to RT and add a comment. But more importantly, take note of how the Tweet gives a basic idea of who these people are and why people should follow them.

Sometimes I have one special person I'm trying to help build up (or just say 'thank you' to) that week and I'll dedicate a whole Tweet to them. If you have someone special you'd like to recommend through a #FollowFriday Tweet, here's what that might look like:

Follow my good friend @VanessaMilan21. Passionate about
#ethical #marketing. Speaks Italian, English, Spanish. #FF

In contrast, consider a how useless a Tweet like this would be both to the people being recommended and to your followers who are looking for good recommendations:

@RoadToPeaceFilm @MediaForTheSoul @Stuparich
@BrightMichelle @WeR1NSpirit @CharleneProctor
@GaetanoVivo @GardenOfTheSoul @ethicalvalue #FF

This Tweet fails the 'Yeah...So What? Test' because it gives me no reason to check out or follow these people. I see #FF Tweets like this every week and none of them prompt me to follow any of the people being 'recommended', because they aren't really *being* recommended!

Make Fridays a day to say 'thank you', 'I see you', 'I appreciate you' and 'I support you' to your followers. Make your #FF Tweets an exercise of love that reinforces the Graces of Connection and Collaboration. Make them clear and relevant to your other followers so they feel the draw of 'Invitation' to come follow those people you are recommending. Be selective and specific. Not only will your recommendations will have more value, but your followers will come to trust your word when it comes to whom they should follow.

TIP 88: TWITTER CULTURE 2: #WW (#WRITERWEDNESDAY)

7 Graces Checklist:
Connection; Invitation; Collaboration

Another Twitter 'tradition' of particular interest to writers is 'Writer Wednesday', which is designated by the hashtag #WW. Much like #FF, this is a day of recommendation, but these recommendations are focussed solely on writers or people who support writers. Much in the same form as #FF, here are some examples of useful #WW Tweets:

Fabulous #spiritual #authors to follow @AsiaVoight
@TambraHarck @BrightMichelle @HelenaMahatey
@CMRbyLuisDiaz #WW

Self-reflective journal & memoir #writers to follow
@MemoirGuru @MoonlightMom @NAMW @moonpoppy
@AlphaChickBook #WW

Because I work with so many authors, I follow lots of people based upon #WW recommendations. Just like #FF Tweets, it's a good idea to be as specific as possible in your #WW Tweets. I am much more likely to follow other authors who write in a genre relevant to my tastes or professional dealings. Rarely do I see #WW Tweets identify the genre of the authors they are mentioning. For me, saying someone is a 'writer' isn't specific enough to know whether I'd like to follow them, which means I have to check out all the recommendations one at a time. The more information you give your followers in your #WW Tweet, the more helpful it will be.

There are more writers on Twitter than you can possibly imagine. Not all are published authors; some are journalists, professional bloggers and aspiring authors. If you are also a writer, you might ask,

'How in the world can hooking up with other writers help me sell my own work?' Well, first of all, most writers are tremendously supportive of other writers and they like to help spread the word. Secondly, most writers I know have a favourite pastime—READING! Writers are great potential customers, if they are fans of your genre. And lastly, other writers can help you find valuable information on publishing, printing, promotion, etc. Sometimes it's as simple as studying how *they* do it. Treat other writers as your mentors and (as we said before) never see them as 'the competition'. Connecting with your peers can be the most powerful way to learn what you need to know and find the support you need.

TIP 89: TWITTER CULTURE 3: #AMWRITING #AMREADING

The two hashtags #amwriting and #amreading are also commonly used by writers and lovers of books. If you're writing a new book, start making people aware of it by using the tag #amwriting. If you're reading a great book, support you follow authors by giving it a great 'shout out' by using the #amreading tag. It's a simple way to get your Tweets seen by people who do not follow you.

PART 9:
AUTOMATION

TIP 90: WHAT'S POSSIBLE VERSUS WHAT'S PERMISSIBLE

One of the most frequent concerns I hear from clients who are new to Twitter is that they will have to spend all their time sitting at their desk posting Tweets. This might have been true when Twitter was first created, but fortunately there is now a wealth of clever third-party applications that support Twitter (and other social media platforms) in various ways through automation. Many people are surprised when I tell them how many ways your Twitter activity can be automated:

- You can automate your outgoing Tweets.

- You can automate your 'thank you' messages when people mention you.

- You can automate your DMs when people follow you.

- You can automate your 'follow-backs'.

- You can automate searches for new people to follow.

- You can automate your 'follows'.

- You can automate your 'un-follows'.

- You can automate Tweets from your RSS streams.

- You can automate RTs you want to send from specific people or topics.

'Wow,' you might be thinking, 'suddenly my whole world has changed. I can't believe I don't have to spend my whole life on Twitter. Hallelujah!'

But then you may ask, 'Hey, wait a minute. If everyone on Twitter is automating all of their activity, who's actually *reading* my Tweets? Is anyone actually *there?*'

And then you might add, 'I thought this was supposed to be a *social* network. What am I supposed to *do* on Twitter if I'm automating all this stuff? How do I interact with people and make connections?'

Well, Twitter evidently asked themselves the same questions. That's why they published their *Automation Rules and Best Practices*.[20] If you take a moment to read it, you'll see that **many of the types of automation listed above are in violation of Twitter policy.** This may come as a shock to many honest Twitter users reading this who may have used some (or all) of these types of automation practices. There is indeed a difference between what is *possible* and what is *permissible* on Twitter. Throughout this chapter, we'll be examining that difference.

TIP 91: THE BLACK, WHITE AND GREY AREAS OF FOLLOWER AUTOMATION

By 'follower automation', I am referring to the act of using third-party automation software to follow or un-follow people on Twitter. This topic has been the *most* challenging one of all for me to address, and I confess I've written and re-written this part of the book several times. I've also discussed it with a number of colleagues. Because it is a controversial subject that potentially infringes upon official Twitter policy, many of them felt 'nervous' about discussing this subject in a book; some even suggested I didn't mention it at all. But after much reflection, I came to the conclusion that the reason why we are all finding this topic so challenging is because it is so *ambiguous*. While, in writing, Twitter policy 'seems' to be black-and-white, in practice their relationship with various third-party programmes sends somewhat confusing messages to the end user. As a result, this topic remains a grey area for many Twitter users (including myself), even if Twitter believe their policy is crystal clear. I felt it was important to address that greyness in this book, not only so you may be informed on this important topic, but also to bring it out into the open in hopes greater clarity will eventually emerge.

There are many third-party applications that enable you to automatically follow or un-follow people on Twitter, according to a variety of parameters you select. One of those programmes is Tweet Adder. Tweet Adder has some very clever features, including the ability to enter the name of a specific Twitter list (found via Twitter, Listorious, etc.) and save all the people on the list to a 'to follow queue'. The idea is not that you would necessarily follow everyone at once, but gradually over the course of anything from a few hours to several days. The software also lets you search, save and 'queue up' people who follow (or are followed by) a particular user, or keywords contained in people's bios or Tweets. On the flipside, Tweet Adder allows you to automatically un-follow people who do not follow you back after a specific number of days.

The advantage of using these tools is that they would save you a lot of time by not having to manually click 'follow' or 'un-follow' many hundreds of times every day. While this may sound wonderful, we have a problem: Twitter states clearly in their official policy that **the only kind of automated following/un-following they permit is automated follow-back** (which we'll look at in Tip 93).

While Twitter policy *seems* very clear, ambiguities arise when you look at it in practice. Twitter is currently engaged in a lawsuit with Tweet Adder. The major issue seems to be the exploitation of the software by spammers to create multiple accounts for overlapping use (whether or not the software company itself can be held accountable for the actions of spammers is really the crux of the legal debate). It could also be speculated that Twitter may see Tweet Adder's follow/un-follow automation to be in violation of official policy. However, if that's the case, why are UnTweeps, JustUnfollow, Refollow and other widely used programmes that perform similar automation tasks *not* being cited as being in violation of official Twitter policy?

To add to the confusion, UnTweeps specifically states on their website that they do not use the 'check all' feature because that *would* be in violation of Twitter policy, which says you cannot bulk-un-follow. The unspoken implication of this is that programmes like UnTweeps and JustUnfollow are compliant with Twitter automation policy *just because* we have to click all the boxes ourselves, rather than set up a 'task queue'. But is that the case? And if not, why haven't Twitter come out on their blog and said these programmes are 'officially' in violation of policy and users should not use them?

Furthermore, programmes that seem to be 'within' Twitter policy can actually result in actions that are potentially 'aggressive' (a violation of policy), whereas these same actions are non-aggressive in Tweet Adder. For example, UnTweeps, JustUnfollow and Refollow will un-follow selected tweeps 'in bulk' (over a few minutes), while Tweet Adder's un-follow function can be set to happen much more gradually, over the course of many days. Also, Tweet Adder allows you to un-follow people only if they haven't followed you back after a specific number of days (or even months), whereas the other programmes may highlight people you recently followed and who simply haven't yet had a chance to follow you back. The same conflict arises when you compare the auto-follow features of these programmes. So how are we supposed to interpret Twitter policy in such scenarios?

If you're confused, so am I. I am confused as to why some automation programmes are seemingly 'OK' with Twitter while others are not. I am not sure how (or if) they distinguish between 'automated' and 'bulk' following and un-following. I don't know why it's seemingly OK to bulk un-follow with UnTweeps, JustUnfollow or Refollow while un-following automatically over many days with Tweet Adder is not. It's small wonder why talking about this subject makes people nervous. I could (and would) take Twitter's policy at face-value if I did not see so many inconsistencies in how they themselves seem to be applying and interpreting it.

For now, I guess the only choice we have is to work within the ambiguity. Thus, my 'official' suggestion is NOT to use the auto-follow/un-follow features of automated programmes like Tweet Adder at present, until Twitter bring us a greater sense of clarity. I strongly suggest you read Twitter's latest version of their afore-mentioned *Automation Rules and Best Practices* and *About Twitter Limits*[21] before embarking on any kind of automation practice, and I kindly ask you to **take personal responsibility** to cross-check the accuracy of this information (as it may have changed since publishing this book) before using or purchasing any products I may mention, and always to **make Twitter policy the final word** in what is permissible.

Finally, in the interest of creating *consensus* (not just defining policy), I also encourage all conscientious Twitter users to blog about this issue (and send a Tweet to @Twitter asking them to read it), so we can open up the dialogue as a community to help shape the future of third-party applications in the Twitterverse. There are undoubtedly many more than '50 shades of grey' to the subject of automation, and my opinions are not necessarily the same as yours. So let's speak openly about the pros, cons and everything in between, rather than remain nervous, confused or fearful about the subject. I believe an open dialogue about these issues can only result in a stronger, better Twitter.

TIP 92: NEVER LET AUTOMATION REPLACE INTERACTION

7 Graces Checklist:
Connection

As we begin our exploration of automation, I cannot stress heavily enough the importance of not allowing automation to replace YOU. If everyone were to do that, there would be no more 'social' in 'social media'. Think of automation as something akin to using a washing machine to clean your clothes. The washing machine should allow you to do *something else* while your clothes are getting washed. Maybe you're cooking a delicious gourmet dinner. Maybe you're chatting to your best friend on the phone.

Similarly, while automation is busy delivering your content, you should be doing *something else,* such as: a) creating more good content for your followers to consume AND b) giving attention to building relationships with your followers. Most simply put, the basics of the 'when' and 'why' of automation are:

- Use automation to *deliver your content.*

- Use interaction to *build relationships.*

Finding the balance between automation and interaction can be a bit of a learning curve for many new Twitter users. Those who depend upon one and fail to implement the other tend not to reap the results they seek. Regardless of how tempting it might be to automate ALL your Twitter activity, please trust me when I say that if you do not balance automation with the tips we will explore in *PART 11: Building Relationships*, you will most likely be disappointed in what Twitter brings to you. But if you hold this mantra as a guide as we progress through this examination of the automation possibilities for Twitter, you should be able to find your own personal communication style and begin to harness the true power of Twitter as a business-building tool.

TIP 93: AUTO-FOLLOW BACK THOSE WHO FOLLOW YOU

7 Graces Checklist:
Connection; Invitation

Back in Tip 34, I recommended that you adopt the practice of following back those who follow you. Doing this manually can take up a lot of your precious time, especially as your following grows. Twitter understands this, and using a third-party application to follow people back automatically is acceptable within their official policy. In fact, **it's the ONLY type of automated following Twitter *officially* permit**, assumedly because there's really no way to become 'aggressive' by following back those who follow you.

There are two applications I recommend for this purpose: Tweet Adder or Social Oomph. These programmes allow you to do a lot more than just auto-follow back, so in Tip 95 and Tip 96, we'll look at the pros and cons of each, along with the various kinds of automation they offer, and how these features fit in with Twitter policy and ethical practice.

TIP 94: USE AUTOMATED LEADS-GENERATING WELCOME DMs

7 Graces Checklist:
Connection; Invitation

When you set up either Tweet Adder or Social Oomph to follow back your new followers automatically, you should also set up an automated welcome message for them. This message is delivered to them via Direct Message (DM). There are a number of key elements that should go into this DM to make it effective:

- You need to say 'thank you' for following you.

- You need to assure them you are following them back (or will be very soon).

- When possible, you should offer them a free gift that is genuinely useful to them.

- You might use the opportunity to generate new leads for your list or members of your Facebook group.

You might be asking, 'How the heck can I do all that in only 140 characters?' (Social Oomph actually limits the welcome DM to only 130 characters). Well, I admit it's a bit of an art, but it can be done:

Thx! I'm following U back. Please enjoy free 90min video on ethical marketing. NO email sign-up required.
http://bit.ly/Nf1Q8i

Thx! Following U back. Enjoy 10+ hrs of audio free with #1 bestseller The 7 Graces of Marketing http://bit.ly/uIDOtt

Thx! I'm following U back. We're growing a new generation of ethical entrepreneurs. Be part of the buzz
http://on.fb.me/OfQrGZ

Thx! I'm following U back. Here's where to find free tips for authors & ethical marketers http://bit.ly/RchkQF

Thx 4 follow! Following U back. Would love to share these 5
free podcasts on writing & publishing. Hope U like them.
http://ow.ly/1dBSw

Thx! Following U Back. Tune In & Turn On at the 7 Graces
Hour Talk Radio show. Wednesdays http://bit.ly/svFLot

You may recognise some of these free offers from Tweets I shared
earlier in the book in 'Tip 65: Tweet About FREE Stuff'. The only thing
I have changed about them is the addition of thanking people for the
follow, and assuring them I will be following them back.

---

*SIDEBAR NOTE: To be fair, these days nearly everyone who is
experienced at Twitter does this, which means there are an awful lot of
DMs being sent out automatically and not everyone reads them
anymore. Twitter do not prohibit this practice, but in their* Automation
Rules and Best Practice, *they say they 'don't recommend' it either, as
they feel it 'might be annoying to some users'. Nonetheless, I still get
many new subscribers every week using automated welcome DMs. I
feel the key to making them work (and not be 'annoying') is to keep
your leads-generating offers* **relevant** *and* **valuable** *to your specific
audience.*

TIP 95: SOCIAL OOMPH – PROS AND CONS

Social Oomph is a web-based programme that has many good
automation features. There is a free version and a 'pro' version, as well
as what you might call a 'light' version that falls somewhere in
between:

- The free version of Social Oomph supports multiple Twitter
  accounts and allows you to schedule up to 12 Tweets an hour
  and save Tweet drafts for later use. When this programme first
  came out, I used it all the time for this feature, but since then
  I've changed over to other programmes like HootSuite,
  TweetDeck and Tweet Adder that are much easier to use for this
  purpose.

- A much more desirable feature is what they offer in their 'light' version (I'm calling it that; they don't actually have a name for it). For a fee of $3.97 *bi-weekly* ($103.22 per year) you can 'unlock' their automated follow-back feature so it will automatically follow back all new followers. You can also set up a 'welcome' message to your new followers, and even use their 'spin' feature to randomise your welcome messages. If you still prefer to vet your followers before following them back, you can set up granular conditions so you don't end up following spammers or inactive accounts. For instance, you can set it to wait three days before it follows back so you can check out your new followers first. I use this service, but I have to confess it's because I have a 'legacy' version of Social Oomph (because I signed up for it when they were brand new), which means I get this service for free. I've found it to be a good, reliable service over the years I've used it, and something worth considering if you have no other means of automating your follow-backs.

- Social Oomph Pro gives you many additional Twitter features, plus quite a long list of features that support other social networks. The cost is currently $17.95 bi-weekly (a hefty $466.70 per annum).

The primary advantage of Social Oomph is that, being web-based, it runs 24/7 even if you are not online, which means it stays active even if you are on holiday. Web-based also means you can access it from any computer, making it easy for your Virtual Assistant (if you have one) to manage it for you. The primary disadvantage, obviously, is the cost of the pro version. The pro version does a lot, but is quite a bit steeper than other products available, so be sure to weigh up the benefits of their added features carefully before going 'pro'.

TIP 96: TWEET ADDER – PROS AND CONS

Tweet Adder is a downloadable software programme, purchased for a one-time fee. Like Social Oomph, Tweet Adder supports multiple Twitter accounts. It also enables you to auto-follow back, auto-un-follow, send automatic welcome messages and schedule Tweets (although you don't set specific times for the Tweets to go out in Tweet

Adder). Both Social Oomph and Tweet Adder allow you to set up RSS streams. But beyond these similarities, Tweet Adder is a completely different animal, and it has a many automation features I've not found in any other programme.

The main features of Tweet Adder are:

- It allows to you to set up a queue of people you'd like to follow, and limit the pace for that following so it doesn't grow too quickly.

- It allows you to un-follow people if they don't follow you back after a certain number of days.

- It allows you to import and export your Tweets, your 'to follow' queue, keyword searches, members of Twitter lists, etc., with a single click.

- It allows you to send out your Tweets (either in sequence or in random order) according to timing parameters you set.

- It lets you manage multiple accounts, and turn individual accounts and functions on and off, making it easy to do maintenance and make changes to the account.

- From a visual/graphic interface point of view, it is extremely easy to navigate, make changes and watch what's happening in 'real time'.

The main disadvantages of Tweet Adder are:

- As useful as it can be, its auto-follow/unfollow feature is in violation of current Twitter automation policy.

- Because it is not web-based, it runs only when your computer is turned on and the programme is booted up. There is a way around this, however, by using a virtual server (more on this in *PART 14: Expansion, Mobility and Influence*).

- Unless you use a virtual server, if you've been running the programme on one computer and want to run it on a different one, you'll have to transfer all your data files over to the second computer first. This is because Tweet Adder stores all your automation settings locally; if you just boot up and run the programme on a different computer without having the latest data files on that computer, you are likely to undo (or redo) some of the work the other computer has already done. This is fine if you intend to use the programme on only one computer, but if you have a Virtual Assistant or you do a lot of travelling and require frequent access to the programme on multiple computers, you're going to have to consider getting a virtual server.

- It has a few 'bugs'. For one thing, it has an annoying habit of bringing up a screen that says the programme has crashed and needs to be closed. However, if you move the 'crash' screen out of the way rather than click on the 'close programme' button, the programme will frequently continue running.

- Tweet Adder currently has no capability to integrate with other social media platforms besides Twitter (but you can get around this by using it in combination with HootSuite Pro).

When you buy Tweet Adder, it's a one-off payment with unlimited software upgrades. The cost depends upon the number of Twitter accounts you want to run on the programme. As of this writing, a single license (i.e. a single Twitter account) costs $55. Purchasing 5 licenses will run you $74; 10 licenses are $110. You can also purchase an unlimited license for $188. The unlimited license is especially good if you manage Twitter accounts for clients.

TIP 97: HOOTSUITE AND GREMLN – A BRIEF COMPARISON

The reason I am combining HootSuite and Gremln (formerly called 'Twaitter') is that they bear a great deal of similarity in both pricing and features. When I wrote *Social Media on Autopilot* in January 2012, Gremln had not yet come out, and I had sort of fallen out of love with Twaitter because of many cumbersome aspects of its design. Gremln bears little resemblance to Twaitter apart from the ability to schedule 'recurring' Tweets. Otherwise, Gremln Plus looks and acts an awful lot like HootSuite Pro.

Like Social Oomph, both HootSuite and Gremln are web-based applications, meaning you do not have to download them and they are accessible via Internet anywhere.

HootSuite supports Twitter, Facebook, LinkedIn, Foursquare, MySpace, Mixi, WordPress.com, Seesmic and Google+ (although it will currently post only to your Google+ page, not to your profile). For Facebook, you can post to your profile, your Facebook pages and also to Facebook groups, which I find tremendously useful. For LinkedIn, you can post to your status update as well as to LinkedIn discussion groups.

Gremln supports Twitter, Facebook, LinkedIn and Seesmic. For Facebook, you can post to your profile and your Facebook pages but NOT to Facebook groups. For LinkedIn, you can post to your status update as well as to LinkedIn discussion groups.

SIDEBAR NOTE: *I would use the option to post to LinkedIn groups with discretion, as many group moderators view this as spamming.*

Like Social Oomph, HootSuite and Gremln have both free and 'pro' versions. The free version of either of these applications is sufficient for most new users. Both HootSuite and Gremln basic (free) versions will allow you to schedule Tweets/updates manually for up to five of any of the supported social media accounts. They let you import RSS feeds and have a virtually identical graphic interface for monitoring your social media streams.

Both programmes are excellent for scheduling Tweets/updates and allow you to save drafts of your Tweets/updates for future use. HootSuite has an 'auto-schedule' feature where it will choose an 'optimum' time to send your update for you. Gremln also allows you to set up 'recurring' updates so they will be sent out again after a specified number of days (more on this in Tip 95)

For more rigorous social media users, here's an overview of HootSuite Pro vs. Gremln Plus.

Cost and Number of Networks

HootSuite Pro currently costs $9.99 a month and supports *unlimited* social media accounts. Gremln Plus is slightly cheaper at

$6.00 a month, or a discounted price of $69 if paid in advance for the year. However, Gremln Plus only supports up to 10 social media networks. To cover all your networks with Gremln Plus, you'd have to pay between $25 and $99 per month. If you don't have more than 10 networks, and you don't care about scheduling posts to your Facebook groups, Gremln Plus might be fine for you.

Bulk Scheduling

Both HootSuite Pro and Gremln Plus now have a bulk uploader that allows you to schedule many updates at once, via a CSV file. I talk about this feature more in Tip 95.

Calendar/Publisher View

Both HootSuite Pro and Gremln Plus have a calendar view that is an excellent visual aid in seeing when your updates are scheduled. The primary difference I see between them is that HootSuite Pro's 'Publisher' view allows you to drag and drop your updates (which is super cool), whereas Gremln Plus requires you to right-click and edit the update if you want to make changes, which I find less convenient.

Trial of Paid Versions

HootSuite Pro has a 30-day free trial. Gremln Plus has a 14-day free trial. You can always opt out and stick with the free version of either if you don't feel the paid version is of value to you. There is no annual contract with either, but if you are using PayPal for recurring payment, be SURE to cancel the payment agreement in your PayPal account.

Summary

While these programmes are very similar, I prefer HootSuite Pro, mainly because of the unlimited networks, the inclusion of Facebook groups and the drag and drop feature in their Publisher. Admittedly, Gremln Plus is slightly cheaper. If you don't care about the above features, try out Gremln, especially if you want to explore the recurring Tweet option, which is kind of neat if you can stay on top of it and not get entangled in your own Tweets. Also, in a Tweet sent out by Gremln on 14 October 2012, they said they give a 50% discount to non-profit organisations.[22] So if you're a non-profit, drop them a line to arrange this, as $36 a year is a real bargain for this service.

TIP 98: TWEETDECK – PROS AND CONS

I'm going to give a bit of history here, because many people may have used TweetDeck in the past and then left it because it was unreliable. But recent changes to TweetDeck have made it a much 'sexier' application than it used to be, so I think it deserves attention, in case some of you have overlooked it.

TweetDeck is a free open-source application created by Londoner Iain Dodsworth in 2008, which was eventually bought by Twitter for £25 million in 2011. TweetDeck was never meant to be an automation tool, but rather a tool to make Twitter communications and interactions better. I started using TweetDeck almost as soon as it came onto the scene and, when I did, my entire Twitterverse changed. Suddenly I was able to communicate with other tweeple in a way that was impossible using the Twitter interface. I loved TweetDeck and raved about it to everyone.

But soon after, there came a time when it felt like the original developers at TweetDeck were trying so hard to 'keep up' with the requests of their fans that the product became unwieldy. They integrated other social networks besides Twitter, just as HootSuite had done. They added the capability to schedule Tweets. They let you set up multiple streams. In fact, it did a heck of a lot of the same things as HootSuite...but it 'looked' a lot slicker and felt more high-tech.

But TweetDeck had a problem. At that time, the only way to use TweetDeck was to download it and run it on your computer. The trouble was, the more bells and whistles the developers added, the more taxing TweetDeck became to the end user's CPU. This caused the programme to freeze up and crash quite a lot. I also found the scheduling really unpredictable. Sometimes it worked. Sometimes it didn't. In frustration, many of us former enthusiasts stopped using TweetDeck. That's when I switched over to HootSuite.

Then the rights to TweetDeck were purchased by Twitter. They stripped down some of the bells and whistles and made the desktop version more stable. They also developed it to work within your browser (as of this writing, it works within both Firefox and Google Chrome). Now TweetDeck is beautifully stable, and I personally haven't experienced a TweetDeck crash in either the desktop or browser version in at least the past six months. The scheduling also seems to work now. And, brilliantly, they have recently upgraded their software so you can now post not only to your Facebook wall, but also to Facebook pages AND groups. Twitter make no mention of a limit to the number of accounts or columns you can set up in TweetDeck[23] but I have a total of 29 Twitter and Facebook destinations on my TweetDeck profile (although, as of this writing, you cannot use TweetDeck to post to LinkedIn or Google+.)

But the best thing about TweetDeck is that it is completely free. Sweet.

Although there are a few minor advantages of one programme over another, when it comes to free programmes, TweetDeck, HootSuite Basic and Gremln Basic are pretty similar from a functional point of view. They are all web-based (although TweetDeck still provides a desktop version), you can schedule Tweets and you can set up streams to filter your information (we'll be looking at why this is useful later when we talk about *Personal Sustainability*).

While TweetDeck doesn't have *all* the other perks of the other programmes, there is still a character about it that 'feels' kind of slick and makes communication with other tweeple fast and easy. I still enjoy using it and feel it is part of any Twitter user's 'essential toolkit', especially as it's free.

TIP 99: PRE-SCHEDULE YOUR TWEETS WHEN YOU NEED PRECISION

As discussed earlier in *Part 7: Frequency and Repetition*, if you do not Tweet regularly, you are unlikely to be noticed on Twitter. Therefore, having a system where you can pre-schedule your Tweets is imperative if you are to ensure your great content is delivered to your audience without going crazy from having to be online all the time. Many of the applications we've been looking at so far allow you to pre-schedule your Tweets so you don't have to post them in 'real time'. Social Oomph, TweetDeck, HootSuite and Gremln all let you schedule Tweets manually (one at a time) for free. All include inbuilt link-shorteners. All except TweetDeck also give you the facility to save your Tweets as drafts.

Scheduling manually is fine when you're just getting started, but once you've developed a lot of content and you're finding that scheduling Tweets one at a time is a big chore, it's time to look at either HootSuite Pro or Gremln Plus. Both applications have additional scheduling capabilities, such as the 'bulk uploader' wherein you can schedule many Tweets at a time by uploading a CSV (comma separated value) file. For those of you who aren't familiar with CSV files, they can be made with Microsoft Excel and look very similar to spreadsheets, except they do not retain any special formatting (much in the same way a plain text file would work, versus a Word document). HootSuite Pro lets you upload up to 200 *different* Tweets per upload (i.e. you can schedule 100 Tweets to two networks at a time, 66 Tweets to three networks at a time, etc.). If any of your Tweets are duplicates (or if they are over the maximum character count), HootSuite will let you know and require you to make a change before uploading. I haven't yet found any documentation that says these same kinds of restrictions apply in Gremln Plus. Preparing your Tweets for upload the first time is a bit of a hassle, as you have to put the time/date in one column, the Tweet in a second column and the link in a third column. But once you've done it, you can reuse the same CSV file in the future simply by changing the dates and times, so in the long-term, it's a big time saver.

As mentioned earlier, Gremln (basic or plus) has the added capability of setting up 'recurring' Tweets, where you set up your content to repeat after a specified number of days. Unfortunately (so far) there is no way to programme an entire list of Tweets to do this, and you have to set these parameters for each individual Tweet. Back when the product was still called 'Twaitter' (and before I discovered Tweet Adder, which we'll look at next), I used this feature all the time. Then it started to drive me crazy. When you have a lot of recurring Tweets, they can sometimes accidentally get posted right on top of one another and it can be a nightmare to sort out.

Regardless of which application you use, pre-scheduling your Tweets is recommended when you have SPECIFIC Tweets that must go out at SPECIFIC dates and times, such as before a live broadcast or during a launch campaign for a book or other product. If you are not so concerned with precision, HootSuite also has an 'auto schedule' feature that can save you the hassle of having to decide when you should send out your Tweets. To use 'auto schedule' you still have to load up your Tweets one at a time, but you just click 'auto schedule' and HootSuite chooses an 'optimal time' to send out your Tweet. I tried it out and, while it works fine, the software's idea of 'optimal time' was quite different from what I would have selected myself. I wrote to HootSuite, suggesting they develop a way to incorporate this feature into their bulk uploader, and also that they allow the end user to define the frequency of what they consider to be 'optimal time', but as of this writing it does not yet have these capabilities.

If you're just looking for a way to make your Tweets recur without needing the precision offered in these two programmes, I advise looking at Tweet Adder, which we'll explore next.

TIP 100: AUTOMATE THE DELIVERY OF YOUR TWEETS WITH TWEET ADDER

Tweet Adder has many fabulous features, one of which is the ability to send out a specified number of Tweets in either a set or random order, at specific intervals throughout the day. If you purchase a Tweet Adder license for multiple accounts, each one of your accounts will have completely customised settings that you can tailor for their particular needs. Right now, let's just look at the Tweet automation features.

Tweet Adder enables you to do the following with your Tweets:

- You can write Tweets directly into the programme and save them.

- Alternatively, you can write a batch of Tweets, save them as a plain text file, and upload them directly to Tweet Adder. Unlike the bulk upload feature in either Gremln Plus or HootSuite, no special formatting is required. All you need to do is put one Tweet per line. There is also no limit on the number of Tweets you can upload in one go. You can upload hundreds if you happen to have them. This makes it much easier to use than either of the other two programmes.

- You can shorten your links directly within the Tweet editor, using your Bit.ly API key.

- It also has a link library in the Tweet editor, which means if you want to create a new Tweet containing a page link you've shortened in the past, you can find and insert the URL quickly and easily.

- Another nifty feature is that you can *export* your library of Tweets as a text file. That's really handy if you are building up your library of Tweets gradually (as most of us do) and you want to save them into a single file, edit them, get rid of old Tweets, etc.

Once your Tweets are in Tweet Adder, there is a selection of parameters you can set so your automation fits your specific communication needs and style. You can precisely specify:

- The maximum number of Tweets to go out within a 24-hour period.

- The frequency of your Tweets (example: every 30-45 minutes).

- Whether your Tweets are to be delivered in order or randomised.

- Whether your Tweets should be sent out once and then deleted, or saved and automatically sent out again later.

I have found that using Tweet Adder in combination with HootSuite Pro covers just about every possible automation need I might encounter. Tweet Adder keeps a steady flow of Tweets going out to my Twitter accounts, while HootSuite Pro takes care of Tweets that MUST go out at specific times, or updates I wish to send to Facebook, LinkedIn, etc. Automating my Tweets this way to *deliver my content* allows me to use my 'live' time on Twitter for *interaction*. If I know my content is set up to be delivered automatically, it means I can forget about me and focus all my attention on my followers. I look for new people to meet, opportunities to strengthen my Twitter relationships, and for good content to read and share with my followers.

TIP 101: THE PROS AND CONS OF AUTOMATED 'THANK YOU' MESSAGES

Earlier, we talked about the importance of thanking people who mention or RT you on Twitter. Tweet Adder has a feature that allows you to automate your 'thank you' messages.

Twitter's official policy on automated @ replies and mentions is again ambiguous. In their 'Automation Rules and Best Practices' they say, 'Automating these processes in order to reach many users is considered an abuse of the feature. If you are automatically sending @ reply messages or Mentions to many users, the recipients must request or approve this action in advance. For example, sending automated @ replies based on keyword searches [typically used by spammers] is not permitted.'[24] While Twitter's policy about using this kind of automation for spamming is clear in this statement, it doesn't specifically address occasional automated @ replies used solely for the purpose of saying 'thank you'.

It might sound impersonal to use an automated 'thank you' message, but I admit I have used this feature on occasion. I have tens of thousands of followers, and dozens of them will mention or RT me every day. Sometimes I miss the opportunity to thank them personally in a timely fashion, so a few nice automated 'thank you' Tweets have come in handy, and have made some of my followers smile. But whenever I'm online, if I see that someone has mentioned me, I will always be sure to thank them personally rather than allow automation to do it for me.

That said, automating your 'thank you' messages can look robotic and disingenuous (defeating the purpose of saying "thank you"). Also, Tweet Adder cannot distinguish between a legitimate @ message and a spammer, which can mean that sometimes your automated message will thank a spammer for mentioning you when all they were doing was spamming you. That can make you look pretty silly. Also, sometimes the automated 'thank you' in Tweet Adder will thank the *wrong* person for mentioning you. This can happen when someone sends a 'shout out' to you PLUS other people in their Tweet (such as on #FF). In such cases, Tweet Adder will sometimes thank one of the people on the list of recommendations rather than the person who sent the message. I've had a few occasions where Tweet Adder thanked someone who had no idea who I was, which made me look like a bit of a dingbat.

So, between the ambiguity of Twitter policy on automated @ replies and the less than reliable results you will get, using automated @ replies it is not a practice I wholeheartedly recommend. If, nonetheless, you do choose to use this feature, it's important to make sure you have a diverse selection of 'thank you' Tweets, and that you only send one or two per day, lest you defeat the purpose and impact of your 'thank you' messages.

TIP 102: THE PROS AND CONS OF USING AUTOMATED RTs

Tweet Adder lets you set up automated RTs. This means you can select specific people whose Tweets you would like to ReTweet to your followers. For instance, if you have a colleague whose promotion you'd like to support, or someone from your VIP list who regularly delivers good content, you might set up Tweet Adder to RT their Tweets. You can specify the maximum number of RTs you wish to send per day, so it doesn't get too predicable or boring for your followers.

This may sound like a handy tool to have, but in their 'Automation Rules and Best Practices' Twitter say, 'We discourage the automatic ReTweeting of other users based on a particular keyword and may suspend accounts that engage in this behavior, particularly if they are being frequently blocked and reported as spam.'[25] Again, this is a grey area; Twitter say they 'discourage' (not 'prohibit') this behaviour, for the very legitimate reason that they are trying to limit spammers who use bulk accounts. But if you want to use automation to support a few close colleagues or friends once or twice a day, is it a violation of policy? I cannot answer this question.

Policy aside, using automated RTs in Tweet Adder comes with a technical caveat: Tweet Adder cannot distinguish between what is a good Tweet and a not-so-good Tweet to RT. If you set your account to RT any old Tweet from your friend @MaryQSmith, for example, it might decide to RT something irrelevant, or even one of Mary's @ messages to someone else (effectively ReTweeting a conversation between two people). For this reason, Tweet Adder has a filter feature to narrow the parameters for which Tweets it can choose to RT. For example, if you are supporting a friend's marketing campaign, you might use the designated hashtag for that campaign as a filter, so it will only RT a Tweet with that hashtag. Another way to ensure you are sending RTs of content and not conversations is to specify the keyword 'http://'. That way, only Tweets with links will be ReTweeted. But even with these filters, you can still get pretty random results, often making automated RTs somewhat meaningless for both your followers and those whom you have ReTweeted.

Given the unreliability of automated RTs and the current Twitter policy, my personal view is that it's best to stick to sending RTs manually. Later, when we look at mobile options, you'll see how easy it is to do this is using the Twitter mobile app.

TIP 103: WHEN AUTOMATING, KNOW THE BEST TIMES TO TWEET

If you are pre-scheduling your Tweets, it is important to know *when* your Tweets should go out for optimum effect. If you've been on Twitter for some time, you are probably familiar with the activity patterns of your followers. For instance, I live in England, but about 75% of my network is in North America. If I am Tweeting about a local UK event, my Tweets need to be scheduled at times when I know my UK network is online. I know from experience that many of them are online during the day, but *most* of them come online in the evenings between 8-11pm UK Time.

However, if I'm Tweeting about my blog or things that are more web-based and appeal to a worldwide audience, I need to be mindful of when the bulk of my audience is online. As so many of my followers are on the West Coast of the United States, they tend to come onto Twitter during what is the middle of the night for me. If I were only to Tweet during UK 'business hours', I would not reach the majority of my audience.

If you use automation to address this issue, you need to be mindful of when you are scheduling your Tweets. If you use HootSuite, for example, you MUST specify a range of times that are optimum for your specific audience. If you are using Tweet Adder, however, your Tweets can be spread out evenly over a 24-hour period or you can specify the 'working' hours for your Tweets. Remember that Tweet Adder will only operate while the programme is switched on, whereas HootSuite runs around the clock, as it is based online. When we get to *PART 14: Expansion, Mobility and Influence,* we'll look at how to make Tweet Adder run around the clock using a virtual private server.

If you use BufferApp, you can specify the exact times your updates will go out through your 'buffer' on any given day. It's best to stagger these times across your networks, so they don't appear all at once. Also, it's best to post less frequently to your Facebook profile/pages than to your Twitter streams.

If you are not too familiar with the activity patterns of your audience, there are a number of tools you can use to analyse this. One is a programme called Tweriod, which has both a free and a paid service that allows you to run reports of your Twitter followers' activity patterns. It seems to be pretty consistent with what I have noticed after being on Twitter for several years. Try out the free service and see if it helps you understand the optimal times for you to schedule specific Tweets.

Tɪᴘ 104: Dᴏɴ'ᴛ Usᴇ Aᴜᴛᴏᴍᴀᴛᴇᴅ 'Nᴀᴍᴇ Aɴᴅ Sʜᴀᴍᴇ' Aᴘᴘʟɪᴄᴀᴛɪᴏɴs

7 Graces Checklist:
Invitation

Some people on Twitter use these really annoying Twitter automation apps that 'name and shame' you if you un-follow them. The irony is that I NEVER un-follow people unless: a) they're spammers; b) they are inactive for more than six weeks; c) they don't follow me; d) they never Tweet in a language I can understand; or e) they're downright crude or offensive. So when I receive these kinds of Tweets that say something like '@LynnSerafinn un-followed me today' it really annoys me, as it makes me look like the 'bad guy'. Grrr....

Please do not EVER use one of those programmes that 'name and shame' your un-followers. You will never 'get them back' that way and it makes you look like a sore loser. People are not 'obligated' to follow you on Twitter. Nobody 'owes' you their loyalty; you have to earn it.

And always remember there are hundreds of millions of people on Twitter. Be gracious! Find new people and move on.

TIP 105: NOT ALL 'TIME-SAVERS' WILL SAVE YOU TIME

I briefly need to mention that there are a lot of other automation technologies available that I'm choosing NOT to mention. The main reason I'm omitting them is that I don't want to waste your time talking about programmes I've already tried and tested and decided just aren't worth it.

Instead of going through all that, let me just say this: when you see Twitter or Facebook adverts about automation programmes, instead of spending hours looking them over and taking a test drive, the very first thing you should do is ASK on Twitter whether anyone else you know and respect has used them. It is true that you might have stumbled upon a brand new gem but, on the other hand, you might be looking at yet another half-baked beta product from the slush pile of 'here today, gone tomorrow' technologies aimed at exposing you to as many banner ads as possible in the hope of making passive sales commissions.

Any of the technologies I have been talking about in this book are ones I actively *use and recommend* (unless I say otherwise) and that have stood the test of 'time'...for the moment, anyway.

TIP 106: PRACTISE THE ART OF NON-ATTACHMENT

Ah yes...'for the moment'. It's important to keep those words in mind. At the end of the day, the wisest thing is to be a bit 'Zen' about all this technology. Every day, someone out there is trying to convince us they've built a better, faster, slicker 'toy', and even the best of us can get mesmerised by new products that come out (*'Warning, warning: geek alert!'*). In the Twitter application arena, it seems like new ones are released all the time. If we get swept away by all the bells and whistles, we can end up spending way too much time (or money) experimenting with new technologies, or becoming too attached or dependent upon them. This will end up making us crazy whenever a particular technology suddenly mutates or disappears altogether. There are thousands of people on Facebook who are STILL screaming about how much they hate the timeline feature that was introduced in 2011. Let's get real: it's not going to change back AND it's not worth losing sleep over.

The world of social media is a true lesson in 'non-attachment': if you cannot find peace amidst the constant change, you will find yourself stressed, overwhelmed and frustrated. Those who cannot let go and move on when things change are only creating more stress for themselves.

With regard to automation, here's my advice: automation tools are wonderful. They are useful and good fun. However, all of these technologies are subject to change; some will even disappear overnight. Twitter policy is also subject to change, and some things that are widely used today may fall out of favour with the Twitter gods tomorrow.

So use these automation tools while they're here, but be ready to change direction when needed. Be like the reed in the stream that bends with the current. When they disappear, laugh about it. Go out for coffee. Take a nap. Plant some petunias.

PART 10:
INTEGRATION

'Integration' refers to connecting Twitter to different online systems so they all work together automatically. It differs from automation in that once you set it up, you don't need to do anything more to it, unless you want to change the set-up, or the connectivity within the system gets broken (or altered) somewhere along the line. As a former recording engineer, I think of integration as similar to setting up a patch-bay in a recording studio, where all different kinds of equipment are ready to receive, process and send out an audio signal whenever you send the command. Whenever I begin working with a new client, one of the first things I do is integrate their online systems. Again, it's probably a very geeky thing to say, but I find it tremendously satisfying to see all their technological systems up and running and 'talking' to each other.

You got an idea of the concept of integration way back in Tip 13 when we looked at connecting your Twitter account to your Facebook page. Now we'll look at other ways to integrate Twitter to other systems, to maximise your reach across the World-Wide Web.

TIP 107: USE FEEDBURNER TO AUTO-BROADCAST NEW BLOG POSTS TO TWITTER

The wonderful thing about blogs is that they use something called 'RSS' or 'really simple syndication'. RSS capability means you can 'syndicate' the 'feed' from your blog to and from any service set up for RSS. The only thing you really need to know about how this works is that you need a 'feed' to make RSS work its magic. If you have a blog, you have a feed, even if you don't know it. Typically, the web address of your feed is the URL to your blog with the word 'feed', 'rss' or 'xml' appended to it. For example, the feed from my 7 Graces of Marketing blog is http://the7gracesofmarketing.com/feed/rss/. Go to that page and see what comes up.

You can also set up feeds from a specific category on your blog. For example, on my Spirit Authors site, I didn't want the feed to come from my root directory because many of my posts were 'protected' content for members only. The feed I wanted to share with the public was from a category I called 'news'. Thus, my feed was this: http://spiritauthors.com/category/news/feed/

These feeds are intrinsic to the way blogs are set up, but they do have limitations in that there is no way for people to 'subscribe' to them except in their browser. Also, even if you have set up your site to 'ping' your updates to many update services (which you should), very few people are going to know you've published a new blog post.

To get around these limitations, I usually suggest that my clients use a programme called Feedburner. Now owned by Google, Feedburner is a free application that allows you to 'burn a feed' from your blog, which you can then use in a number of ways. One cool thing it will do is send the feed from your blog directly to Twitter. This means every time you write a new post, it will be announced (once) on Twitter automatically. If you want, you can customise your Twitter announcements by saying something like 'New Blog Post' before the title. You can even append hashtags if you wish. If you also have your Twitter account set up to send your Tweets to Facebook, it means your blog will be announced to all your social media followers within minutes of it being published online.

While this takes the pressure off you to remember to Tweet every time you publish a new blog, do remember that Feedburner does this only *once*. It is not a replacement for the strategies discussed earlier where you create multiple Tweets for each blog post that are sent out (and recycled) over time.

In addition to Twitter/blog integration, one of the main things I use Feedburner for is their email subscription form. If you enable this feature, you can grab a bit of html code and paste it into a plain text widget on your blog, which becomes a web form so people can subscribe to receive your blog posts via email. Most subscribers on my sites have come to me (either directly or indirectly) via Twitter.

> **SIDEBAR NOTE:** *There is also a WordPress plug-in called Jetpack that comes pre-installed with WordPress 3.2 or above. It has a few features that are similar to Feedburner, including a blog post announcer (to Twitter, Facebook, LinkedIn and others) as well as email subscription capability. While widely in use, the plug-in has received a substantial number of bad reviews on the WordPress site, which means it might not be compatible with your particular WordPress set-up. If you try it and experience difficulty with it, use Feedburner instead.*

TIP 108: SET UP BLOG FEEDS IN HOOTSUITE, TWEET ADDER OR GREMLN

Now that you know something about feeds, you'll be delighted to know that Tweet Adder, HootSuite and Gremln also enable you to import your RSS feeds. Setting up your RSS feeds in one (or both) of these programmes ensures all your new blog posts will appear in your Twitter stream shortly after they are published. You can then direct these feeds to any of the social networks you have set up in these accounts.

You might ask why you would want to set up these feeds when you've already set them up in Feedburner. Isn't one feed enough? Won't using more than one be overkill? Well, here are several reasons why setting up feeds in a variety of programmes makes sense:

- Feedburner is a single feed going to a single Twitter account. You can customise the Tweet with words before and/or after the Tweet. In my experience, the update tends to go out within 10 minutes of publication. That's fine for your primary Twitter account, but nothing else.

- Tweet Adder can have unlimited feeds going to any of your Twitter accounts (depending upon how many licenses you have). You can also fully customise the Tweet and specify the maximum number of updates that can go out within a 24-hour period. The feed will be updated according to the settings you specify. It allows you to set it to 'between X and Y minutes', which can be anything from a few minutes to many hours, as you wish. This means you can set it so your feeds are likely to go out a long time after the feed from Feedburner.

- HootSuite can have multiple feeds going to multiple social networks (not just Twitter). You can customise the update, and you can specify how many updates can go out at a time and how frequently the feed should be checked (it gives you the options of every 1, 2, 3, 6, 12 or 24 hours). This means you can set it up to go out as much as a day after the post was published.

- Gremln can also send feeds to multiple social networks. You can customise the update, and specify how many updates can go out at a time and the distance between each update (up to 50 minutes). You can set it to recur (refresh) hourly, daily, weekly, month or yearly. You can also filter keywords to appear/not appear.

Because of the variables, I tend to set up my feeds in all of these programmes, but have them set to go out at different times and in slightly different formats so they don't look the same. This way, I get at least four unique updates within a 24-hour period for each new blog post I publish, even before I've created any recurring Tweets for it. They are also delivered to my other social networks, as per my settings in HootSuite and/or Gremln. All of this is achieved simply by publishing the article.

TIP 109: THINK BEYOND YOUR BLOG FOR RSS POSSIBILITIES

RSS feeds aren't limited to blogs. You might have a number of other content sources that have an RSS you can send to Twitter using the techniques I have described. For example:

- Most online radio shows have RSS. The RSS for my Blog Talk Radio show is http://www.blogtalkradio.com/lynn-serafinn.rss.

- If you have an account with EzineArticles, your articles have an RSS. Mine is
  http://feeds.ezinearticles.com/expert/Lynn_Serafinn.xml

- Podcasts on iTunes or other podcasting syndicators also use RSS. I use Audio Acrobat to set up my podcast, which then syndicates to various podcasting services. My feed URL is http://teknochik.audioacrobat.com/rss/lynn-serafinn-garden-of-the-soul-talk-radio.xml

If you're not sure whether you have an RSS (or what the URL to your RSS is), look for this icon (the image is usually bright orange when it appears online):

If you see this icon, you have an RSS. To find the link to the RSS, hover your mouse over the icon and you should see the link appear at the bottom of your browser OR right-click the link and select 'copy link location' (that's what it says in Firefox). Then paste the link into a text file or other place for safe keeping.

Think beyond just your blog when setting up your RSS feeds for Twitter. Then set them up in Tweet Adder, HootSuite and/or Gremln to make the most out of syndicating your content.

TIP 110: THE RECIPROCAL RELATIONSHIP BETWEEN TWITTER AND YOUTUBE

There is a seamless, *reciprocal* relationship between Twitter and YouTube, which makes their integration a truly powerful force:

- YouTube allows you to link your Twitter account so your YouTube activity is automatically Tweeted to your followers (you can also link it to your Facebook account). This means your followers will know whenever you upload a new video. If you wish, you can also set up your preferences so a Tweet is sent when you like or comment on a video, or subscribe to someone else's YouTube channel.

- Conversely, you can automate a nice selection of Tweets that take people either to your YouTube videos or blog posts in which your videos appear.

Why is this relationship between YouTube and Twitter important? Because YouTube is not just a video repository; it's the *second largest search engine* after Google. It's also (as of this writing) the *third highest ranking website* (after Facebook and Google, respectively) of ALL the millions and millions of websites in the world. This makes it a better choice for your videos than Vimeo, for example, which has a global rank of 126.

It has been my personal experience that if you make a video for YouTube and really 'land' the title, keywords and description, and Tweet about your video (or video blog), you can find your video on the first page of Google using your keywords *within a single day*. Why does this happen? Because of YouTube's page rank. Trying to get your *blog* onto the first page of Google is a lot harder because it's highly unlikely any of us (unless our business is a search engine or social media site) will ever attain anywhere near the page ranking YouTube has. Thus, the fastest and easiest way to increase traffic to your site is not so much to worry about your own SEO and page rank (which can be a slow process), but to 'piggy-back' your rank via YouTube.

Here's the strategy I use for my own videos, as well as what I advise my clients:

- Create a YouTube channel that is all about your topic of interest for your audience.

- Connect your YouTube account to Twitter and Facebook so YouTube alerts your followers of your activity.

- Just as you have been creating relevant blog posts for your audience, create relevant (short) videos for them.

- Upload your video to YouTube and your network will hear about it.

- After your video is uploaded, you can then embed it into a blog post on your site.

- SEO tip 1: Think carefully about keyword phrases people might use to search for a video on your topic. Choose the most important keywords and make them the *first words in the title* of your video on YouTube.

- SEO tip 2: On YouTube, make the *first* word in your video description *a link back to your blog* (or blog post, if the video appears in a specific post). In the body of the description, be sure to include the rest of your chosen keywords.

- At the end of your video description, put links back to your Twitter profile page, and other social media accounts. Be sure you ask people to follow you and tell them that you follow back.

- Use Twitter (and other social media) to drive traffic EITHER directly to the videos OR to your blog posts containing the videos. Of course, the success of this is dependent upon you creating compelling Tweets that are relevant and interesting to your followers.

- To highlight the fact that your Tweet links to a video (which is often of greater interest to people than a written article) you might start the Tweet with the word 'VIDEO'. Alternatively, put either 'via @YouTube' or '#YouTube' at the end of the Tweet.

- Even if people play the videos on your own site, it will increase the 'hits' or plays of your video on your YouTube channel. The more hits your video receives, the higher your Google ranking (for your chosen keywords),

- For videos of more importance, such as a book or film trailer, I also submit the link to the video to web directories, such as those you can find on Social Maximizer or Directory Maximizer.

- Authors: Be sure to embed your YouTube book trailer video on your profile at Amazon Author Central (more on this in the next tip).

If you don't yet have a YouTube channel, MAKE ONE. YouTube is a *vital* part of your social media infrastructure. Start to include short videos in your blogs and learn to 'work' this wonderful reciprocal relationship between YouTube and Twitter.

TIP 111: IMPORT YOUR TWEETS INTO AMAZON

If you are an author, you probably have your book(s) for sale on Amazon. But equally important is to have your author profile set up on Amazon via their 'Author Central' service. On this page, you can have links to all your published books, upload your book trailer (via YouTube) AND import your Twitter stream. Importing your stream means Twitter will automatically send your Tweets to your Amazon author profile. This helps your Amazon readers get to know more about you, and it encourages them to follow you on Twitter

Incidentally, the Amazon dot com page rank is number 10, with only a Chinese search engine separating it from Twitter. Leveraging your presence on Amazon is again more than we can delve into here; but let it be said that you should put some care into your 'Author Central' profile and be sure Twitter is connected to it.

PART 11:
BUILDING RELATIONSHIPS

7 Graces Checklist:
Connection; Invitation

T he majority of us form our relationships in life according to what sociologists call 'strong ties'. But success in Twitter (and social media in general) is dependent upon our learning the importance of having semi-strong and even *weak ties* to other people, as well as our more 'comfortable' strong ties.

In his book *The Tipping Point*, Malcolm Gladwell talks about how people he calls 'Connectors' tend to be very good at making 'weak ties'.[26] He explains how 'Connectors' are more comfortable with having loose connections to large numbers of people, while other personality types tend to worry that having too many loose connections will in some way make them 'obligated' to all those people.

Gladwell's *The Tipping Point* was first published in 2000, before the advent of either Twitter or Facebook. Social media has since made our potential for forming loose connections or 'weak ties' with others virtually unlimited. But just because we have the technical means to *do* something doesn't mean we have the natural desire or inclination for it. It's my suspicion that natural 'Connectors' probably constituted a high percentage of the early adopters of Twitter. Now that it's become a huge part of the mainstream, others who are not so naturally inclined have to consider a different way of looking at relationships, and understand the value of 'weak ties'.

Many people new to Twitter find this shift in thinking the *steepest* learning curve of all, even steeper than the formidable challenges of learning new technical skills. They can easily feel overwhelmed at the very thought of having to 'relate' to what feels like an unmanageable number of people who wish to connect with them on Twitter. So let's start small and introduce the idea of 'weak ties' in a few bite-sized chunks:

- Having a weak tie with someone is NOT the same as having 'no' tie with them.

- A weak tie is *still* a relationship.

- A weak tie is a valid form of Connection.

- Having weak ties can help build your brand in ways you may not even realise at first.

- A weak tie does not 'have' to be elevated to a 'strong tie' for it to be valuable; it is important to 'allow' weak ties to be weak ties, and to value them for what they are.

- Some weak ties *will* become stronger over time; this can happen organically and naturally with 'care and feeding'.

Think of your business as a biological system, requiring energy. Your weak ties are your 'potential energy' and your strong ties are your 'kinetic energy'. Your potential energy is your storehouse and should *always* be greater than your kinetic energy. If you have only kinetic energy and little potential energy, it means you have no backup system and no potential for growth. You will eventually find yourself *feeding upon* your energy supply rather than it feeding you. If all the demands of the system are taken from the kinetic energy supply, and there is nothing building a storehouse of potential energy to convert into new kinetic energy, the entire system will collapse as it is not *sustainable*.

In the case of your business, if you depend entirely upon your kinetic energy supply (your 'close ties'), you will soon lose customers and money. I've seen this happen to many online entrepreneurs who do not actively work to build their 'weak ties'. Their close followers get sick to death of them and feel like they are being 'sold to' all the time (usually for things that come at a higher and higher price tag).

Your 'weak ties' are your potential energy. You need to 'care for' and 'feed' that potential energy for it to be accessible at a later date. In the case of Twitter, the best way to 'feed' your weak ties is to give them lots of enriching content that can help them grow. The best way to 'care' for them is to reply to mentions and Tweets, and ReTweet content of theirs that looks interesting. Engage with *others* even if you are not engaging with *everyone*, and NEVER 'feed upon' them by trying to sell to them. Your aim is to build them up and make them 'healthy'.

Believe it or not, too much personal contact with 'weak ties' can *drain* them of energy. Remember these are people and they may also feel overwhelmed by the environment. Engage with weak ties if and when it feels natural, but if you try too hard, you are more likely to end up cutting the tie altogether. Focus on *giving* content, not on talking to every person you meet. Those who become 'fired up' with the energy you give them through your content will be become more and more likely to 'convert' into the kinetic energy of close or 'semi-close' ties. This is the point at which they may choose to buy your books, products, courses, consulting, and so on.

If you do not understand this sustainable 'life cycle' of relationships, you are apt to be disappointed. You will put too much focus on 'strong ties' and overlook the weak ones. You will try to push weak ties too quickly, rather than understanding the need to have a great storehouse of potential energy that will grow organically at its own pace, proportionate to the amount of care and feeding you give it. Worst of all, you are apt to burn *yourself* out by trying too hard, looking too desperate or spending way too much time engaging when you don't really need to.

Later on, in *PART 12: Personal Sustainability*, we'll look much more deeply at the dynamics of 'weak' and 'strong' ties, and explore a few strategies you can use to avoid the traps of draining your own energy and becoming overwhelmed.

TIP 113: DON'T PLAY THE CELEBRITY CARD...UNLESS YOU ACTUALLY ARE ONE

7 Graces Checklist:
Connection; Invitation

One of my biggest Twitter turn-offs is when people play the 'celebrity' card'. In a nutshell, this means making yourself inaccessible to your followers and showing little interest in engaging with them. Too many people new to Twitter do this, and they send an unconscious message to their followers that they think they are 'above' them. I've already talked about some of the ways you can alienate your followers, but let's look at them again in the context of the 'celebrity card' issue:

- Using True Twit: In *PART 3: Twitter Culture and Courtesy* I talked about True Twit and recommended that you NOT use it. True Twit is a service where everyone who requests to follow you is required to fill in a 'captcha' form to 'prove they're human'. There is both a practical and an ethical problem in asking your followers to do this. The practical problem is that if someone has tens of thousands of followers, there is no way on the face of the earth they will have time to address all the requests they receive via True Twit. The ethical problem is that many times people are following you *back* automatically, and asking them to prove they're human after you've followed them is absurd and unnecessary. It also sends an unspoken message of lack of trust, which is not the best way to start a new relationship. The Grace of Invitation means to be a model for a world filled with trust and respect. Trust people first; get rid of people who betray that trust later if you need to.

- 'Protecting' your Tweets: In *PART 2: Basics, Profile and Setting* I recommended that you NOT 'protect' your Tweets. Protecting your Tweets means people have to request to follow you and you have to approve them first. While approving contact requests is appropriate for Facebook, it's unnecessary and counter-productive on Twitter. Again, it sends an 'I don't trust you' message to potential followers, and it will limit the number of people who choose to follow you. Besides, do you really want to spend all that time trawling through those requests to decide whether or not to approve them?

- <u>Not following back:</u> Making a habit of not following people back sends a message of 'I'm better than you'. Set up your automated follow-back, as described earlier, and follow people back when they follow you.

- <u>Having a radically disproportionate ratio of followers to following:</u> Having a reasonably greater number of followers than people you follow can make you look 'desirable'. But having WAY more followers than people you follow sends the message to other tweeple that you think you're hot stuff. It's easy to tell the real celebrities from the 'wannabes' on Twitter. Genuine celebrities and big companies or media distributors (like newspapers, publishers, magazines, TV networks, etc.) will often have huge followings and almost no followers. For instance, today on Twitter, Oprah Winfrey has over 15 million followers and follows only 88 people.[27] The New York Times have almost 7 million followers and follow just over 700 people, the vast majority of whom are their own journalists.[28] This kind of disproportion makes sense in their case because they have a global reputation. But if, for example, you have something like 500 followers and you only follow 25, you're really sending the wrong message to your followers. It makes you look like you think you are more important than they are, or that you are not interested in who they are. Unless you *are* an international celebrity, please don't act like one. It will not help build either your relationships or your business.

- <u>Only ever talking about yourself:</u> If you never mention other people on Twitter, it shows you are only interested in yourself.

After a while, even your current followers are bound to switch off.

- <u>Never replying when people talk to you:</u> If you never reply to people who speak to you, you are sending the message that you don't have time for them and don't care what they think.

- <u>Never ReTweeting:</u> Something I find amazing is how some people on Twitter just love it when people RT their Tweets, but they never bother to RT anyone else. If someone RTs you, be grateful and look for ways to return the favour.

- <u>Never lightening up!:</u> If all you ever do is talk about serious stuff and business, people will get bored with you. Even actor George Takei (Mr Sulu from *Star Trek*) Tweets amusing comments that his followers seem to love. Share the HUMAN (and humorous) side of who you are on Twitter, not just your business side. Following someone who thinks they are an icon is dull. Following a human is interesting.

TIP 114: YOUR SO-CALLED 'COMPETITORS' ARE YOUR BEST ASSETS

7 Graces Checklist:
Connection; Collaboration

When I start with a new client who is unfamiliar with Twitter, I often manage their Twitter account for them for a few months. That way, I can help them grow their following while they are still on the learning curve. Recently, one of my new clients, who had just finished writing a book, complained that the handful of people who were following him were all other writers in the same genre. He told me he couldn't understand what he could possibly gain from connecting with them. After all, weren't they the 'competition'? Weren't they all out there trying to sell their books just like he was?

I told him he was missing a vital point. These authors had plenty to *teach* him, and to *give* to him:

- If they are established and successfully communicating with their readers on Twitter, just watching them is a great opportunity to learn. How do they behave? What do their readers like to comment on or ReTweet? *Everything* I ever learned when I was new to social media was from watching others.

- Checking out who follows authors in your genre is a really simple and effective way to find followers who might be interested in your books too.

- There is something about 'being in the company of' others that sends a subtle message to your potential audience. Author Martha Beck likes to call her 'group' of like-minded associates 'her team'. I often call mine 'my tribe' (a word that has become very popular over the past few years). When potential customers see you are a member of a particular 'team' or 'tribe' they tend to associate you with a shared ethos. If they identify with that ethos themselves, they are likely to identify with *you*, even if they don't know you that well yet. 'Hanging out' in the right company on Twitter is very important if you want to develop this kind of 'sphere of influence'. And please don't *ever* think you (or your book) are so unique and charismatic that you don't need a tribe. I've watched several authors get a really rude awakening after mistakenly believing they had the power to attract all the customers they needed to become a #1 bestseller on their own. No man (or woman) is an island. None of us is so important or powerful we cannot benefit from a circle of loyal supporters.

- Your so-called 'competitors' are your best possible *partners* for your book launch or other campaigns. Because you are both marketing to the same audience, it can only help to bring more customers to each other through the practice of the Grace of Collaboration. Of course, for you to become an effective collaborator you'll need to build your audience first or you will have nothing to *give* to the people in your collaborative network.

- If your 'competitors' become your true collaborators, they often will become your greatest *referrers*, too. In my collaborative network we are always connecting each other to new people, doing random 'shout outs' about each other, and sometimes even sending clients and/or business opportunities to one another.

Tip 115: Ask For Help!

7 Graces Checklist:
Connection; Transparency

It might surprise you to know that one of the fastest ways to build relationships with people is to ask for help when you need it. Asking for help shows humility, authenticity and transparency. It also shows respect for other people and their expertise. AND, of course, you get answers to your questions!

When might you ask for help? You might want help figuring something out on Twitter or other social media. You might want help getting more followers. Whenever my clients are nearing the 2000 mark (or some other 'milestone') I reach out to my network on their behalf to help get them over the 'hump'. It really works if you do it sincerely and honestly. You might put out an appeal for partners on a marketing campaign, for endorsers for your book, for bloggers to be on your blog tour or for people to leave a comment on your blog. One time I asked for help when I was looking for someone who did handbag repairs in my home town (actually that request was made on Facebook, but it's the same idea).

Struggling on your own with unanswered questions is the fastest way to fail in life, business and social media. Ask for help and see how it makes your shoulders feel lighter, frees up your creative energy and grows your network of loyal followers.

Tip 116: GIVE Help To Those Who Ask

7 Graces Checklist:
Connection; Inspiration

The obvious flipside of asking for help is GIVING help and answers to people who seek guidance. If other people have helped you, you should always look for ways to 'pay it forward' by passing on the information you have learned. Twitter is like a massive tribe with many, many sub-tribes. If you see someone out there who is lost and needs assistance, send them an @ message with a suggestion or comment. Don't act like a know-it-all and do NOT try to sell them something. Remember this is all about building relationships. When you give help without expectation of anything in return, you become a force for the Grace of Inspiration.

> *SIDEBAR NOTE: Asking for help and giving answers is also a great way to connect with people on LinkedIn using their 'Q&A' feature. You can read an article I wrote about this some time ago entitled 'How and Why to Establish Yourself as an Expert on LinkedIn'.[29]*

TIP 117: TALK TO PEOPLE!

7 Graces Checklist:
Connection

In the previous section, I talked about the pros and cons of automating 'thank you' messages when people mention you. While that can be very helpful to keep up with mentions, it is very important not to let this be a substitute for genuine interaction. Be sure to reply to people whenever they ask you a question or make a comment about one of your Tweets. And don't forget that it takes two to tango; in other words, you should be the one who *starts* discussions as well. If you see a Tweet and it interests, intrigues or amuses you, SAY something to the person who wrote it and get the ball rolling for an open discussion.

Amazingly, people on Twitter WILL remember conversing with you, even though it's all done in 140 characters and if you may not talk often. This helps build a personal connection between you. It also lays the foundation for future business connections. Later, when you have a book or product launch coming up, these people are much more likely to check out (and 'shout out' about) your new work as soon as it comes out than those you have not already engaged with.

TIP 118: RECOMMEND TWEEPS TO YOUR OTHER FOLLOWERS

7 Graces Checklist:
Connection; Abundance; Collaboration

Whenever you meet someone new on Twitter who seems particularly interesting, use it as an excuse to send a random 'shout out' about them. You don't have to wait for #FollowFriday or #WriterWednesday to do this. If you have read a good article by them, share it with your network with a comment about it. If you think they would be great connections for others of like mind, send out a 'follow my new friend so-and-so for great information on such-and-such' message. Give a 'shout out' if someone is reaching a new threshold for followers or a fundraising activity, encouraging your followers to support them. You can even use @ communication to refer one follower to another in your circle, saying why you think they should connect.

TIP 119: SPEAK OUT IN THE OPEN, NOT BEHIND CLOSED DOORS

7 Graces Checklist:
Connection; Transparency

Unless you are sharing private information such as an email address, Skype ID or phone number (or are talking about something genuinely private), it's usually best to make your recommendations and conversations 'in public' on Twitter (using @ instead of DM). Having a public discussion helps both your referrals AND you. It helps your referrals because more people will see your messages than if you send them privately to just one person. It helps *you* because it sends the unspoken message that you are a supportive, collaborative tweep who is not just there to 'get' but also to 'give' by recommending and connecting other people on Twitter. This type of open communication can be one of the greatest mind shifts for those who are new to Twitter, but it can make all the difference between Twitter success and failure.

TIP 120: SCAN AND REPLY TO YOUR DMS AT LEAST ONCE A WEEK

7 Graces Checklist:
Connection

These days, about 98% of all DMs I receive are automated 'thank you' messages from new people I have followed. Because of this, for a while I got into the habit of not bothering to check my DMs regularly, as I didn't think they would warrant a personal reply. I discovered this was a BIG mistake in judgment on my part because that 2% sometimes contained extremely important personal messages that were at risk of getting overlooked. Within my DMs, I have found offers to be on radio shows and to be a guest contributor to a book. I have also received client consultation requests (one of them from one of my most successful long-term clients) and I was contacted by a major corporation who wanted to use material from my book in their team. Not an everyday occurrence, such gems are easy to miss amidst the more common 'thank you' messages. For this reason, I strongly suggest you check your DM 'inbox' at least once a week, if not more frequently, to see who may be reaching out to you.

SIDEBAR NOTE: Because people tend to check their @ messages more regularly than DMs, if you want to connect with someone you know from Twitter, I recommend letting them know via an @ message that you will be sending them a DM. This will hopefully ensure they don't miss your important message. Alternatively, of course, send them an @ message to let them know you will be sending them an email (you can usually find their address or contact form on the website they have provided in their Twitter profile). In your email, be sure to remind them

> *that you know them from Twitter, and include your Twitter ID (especially if it is different from your personal name).*

TIP 121: SET UP GOOGLE ALERTS TO HELP FIND NEW TWITTER FRIENDS

I've been using Google Alerts for the past few years. I have two primary keyword strategies. First I have a keyword alert set up for my personal name. This way, any time someone posts something about me on their blog, YouTube channel or other website, I hear about it. Then I visit that blog and connect with the blogger in some way. Either I leave a comment or I connect with them on Twitter (or both). I've met a lot of new people this way, who are already predisposed towards my work.

The other alerts I set up are for specific keywords. This is to help me find more people in my 'tribe' who are blogging on similar topics of interest. Again, I connect with them by leaving a comment on their blog or sending them a Tweet (usually both). In the Tweet, I strike up a conversation by mentioning the article I read on their blog. Doing this shows you are interested in the other person's professional work; if they are truly of like mind, they will hopefully engage with you and become part of your active network.

TIP 122: SEND A MESSAGE TO POSSIBLE COLLABORATORS

7 Graces Checklist:
Connection; Invitation; Collaboration

Sometimes you come across someone really special on Twitter and you just have to reach out. For instance, say it's someone whose book inspired you and you'd like to ask them for an interview for your blog. Perhaps you'd like to collaborate with them in some capacity. Or you'd like to ask this person to do a guest blog, be part of a book you're writing, or be an endorser for your book. Maybe you'd like them to be a guest on a telesummit or radio show you are hosting. Or perhaps you'd just like to say 'hi' in a more personal way than you can on Twitter.

If you feel really 'drawn' to someone special on Twitter in this way, but you don't know them personally, it is quite acceptable to get in touch via a contact form on their website. I think using a contact form is more polite than writing via email, unless they only have their email address on their site.

When you contact them, be SURE to:

- Say you follow them on Twitter and give them your Twitter ID.

- Say something *specific about their work* that has led you to contact them.

- Tell them a *little* bit about yourself professionally (a couple of sentences) and why you feel there may be a possible connection between your work.

- Tell them precisely and succinctly what you are proposing (as per some of the suggestions I have given above).

- Invite them to speak further with you if they wish, and provide them with your contact details (including Skype) and times of availability.

- Allow them an 'out' by saying something like, 'If now is not a good time for you, I hope we can connect some time in the not-too-distant future.'

- Be polite!

Under NO circumstances should you ever, ever, ever:

- Try to sell them something

- Write your whole life story, quote reviews of your book or make the email all about you

- Or, conversely, say nothing at all about yourself and tell them 'Google me' or 'see my website to find out about me'

- Act like you are God's gift to the human race

- Tell them you have an 'opportunity' for them

- Criticise their website or business, claiming you can make it better

- Give them a 'deadline' to 'act now before you lose out'

- Put them on your mailing list (never, ever!)

Tip 123: Suggest Setting Up A Skype Call When The Time Is Right

7 Graces Checklist:
Connection; Invitation; Collaboration

After you've established true connection and a point of convergence and relevance with one of your Twitter followers, you may feel the time is right to reach out and connect in 'real time'. If so, perhaps you could suggest a short 'get to know each other' Skype call. Don't do this as soon as you meet someone who seems interesting; if it seems to come out of the blue, it will feel like an 'invasion' to the other person. They may even think you are out to sell them something (please don't have that be your motivation!). You should always have exchanged some quality dialogue before making the suggestion to speak in real time.

If you use the guidelines in the previous tip about sending an email communication as a rough guide for how to approach the Skype chat, you should be fine. If you are the person who made the suggestion to meet, it means the ball is in your court to set the tone for your meeting. Make the first meeting no more than 30 minutes, and completely friendly and non-committal. Make it your sole mission to get to know this person and see if there is any potential for future collaboration. If you both feel there is, you can always set up another Skype chat a few weeks later.

I cannot count the number of people I originally met on Twitter with whom I have spoken on Skype. It's probably in the hundreds by now. Many of them I went on to meet in person later. The key to advancing to this stage in your relationship with your tweeps is to understand and put into practice ALL the information discussed in this chapter. And finally, always allow plenty of time and space to cultivate the Graces of Connection and Invitation before you attempt to bring about the Grace of Collaboration.

PART 12:
PERSONAL SUSTAINABILITY

This section is all about preserving your sanity when using Twitter, which is one of the most common concerns of new Twitter users, yet oddly the least strategically addressed. Preserving your sanity is all about knowing how to avoid 'overwhelm'. Overwhelm sets in when there is too much 'information' coming at us at one time. This can take many forms: too many people, too many facts, or too many new skills to learn. Because overwhelm is a really big issue when it comes to Twitter, all the tips in this section will address how to avoid the various kinds of overwhelm that can arise, so you can find a point of personal sustainability as you progress.

TIP 124: AVOID OVERWHELM BY FILTERING WHO YOU PAY ATTENTION TO

In *The Tipping Point*, Malcolm Gladwell talks about how our human brain has a limited capacity to digest and make sense of data.[30] We struggle with sequences of numbers longer than seven, for example, which is why telephone numbers (not including area codes) tend to be seven digits long. But we also struggle to make sense of, or perform well within, large groups of people. Gladwell talks about 'the rule of 150', which basically states that human beings do not connect or perform well when we are put into groups larger than 150 people at a time. For this reason, throughout history we see many examples of social, religious and military organisations that (sometimes purposefully, sometimes unconsciously) limit their communities or factions to 150 people.

It's important to bear in mind this valuable information about ourselves as human beings as we venture out to build our little 'empires' on Twitter. On the one hand, we want to gain thousands and thousands of followers; on the other hand, we must also follow thousands and thousands of people to get to that point. But if our brains will 'fry out' if we try to connect too closely with more than 150 people at a time, how will we ever reach our goals?

Clearly, the only way we have a fighting chance of reaching them is when:

- We know the difference between (and importance of) 'weak ties' and 'strong ties'.

- We know our human limitations, and we honour the 'rule of 150' to filter the information we receive through social media.

To avoid the overwhelm of 'too many people', it's important to adopt a mindset that your aim should be to follow the activity of no more than about 150 key people in your stream at any given time. Following them is much easier if they are broken into categories. We've already discussed various ways to 'filter' your followers by creating lists. We talked about setting up a **private** 'VIP' list (making it 'private' rather than 'public' is very important). This list could be made up of perhaps 100 (or so) people you want to watch more closely on Twitter. You do this most easily by setting up a stream for that list in HootSuite or TweetDeck. The objective of following their Tweets with more attention should be to find ways to connect, share, discuss, ReTweet, etc. Over time, some of the people on your VIP list might prove to be not as relevant or engaging as you hoped. When that happens, it's time to remove them from your VIP list and return them to your main Twitter stream. Because it's a 'private' list, no one will be offended you have taken them off. Remember that when you take them off the list, they're not 'gone' from your radar; it just means you're not watching them as closely.

However, over time a few of the people on your VIP list will gradually move from being a 'weak tie' to a 'strong tie'. You might keep them on your VIP list, or you might move them to your 'tribe' list (which I would call a 'very strong tie'). This is generally a smaller and more niche-specific list of people who are much closer to you in your field of interest and/or primary audience. Alternatively, they may be linked to you via a specific project or marketing campaign. Again, you can set up a stream for them using either HootSuite or TweetDeck to watch their activity and engage with them more easily.

Another way to filter your followers (or even people you don't yet follow) is to set up a stream with specific hashtags or keywords. What is different about filtering information by using hashtags or keywords is that the results are *not limited to people you follow.* You might find a whole new world of people out there who are interested in the same subject matter. Please note that if your keywords are multiple words, you MUST enclose them between double quotation marks, e.g. "social entrepreneur", "law of attraction", etc.

In filtering your Twitter data through such streams, you are regulating the flow of information, which helps keep you from falling into the 'too many people' overwhelm state. Filtering tweeps in this way means you can give 90% of your attention to what matters most to you, rather than what other people want you to look at. Using these filters, I look for good Tweets to share with my own followers and ways to comment on other people's Tweets. I 'favourite' a few good Tweets or links to articles. I read a few good blog posts and leave comments. I tell people I liked their article and ask them how their week is going.

After you've gone through your filtered tweeps, you can direct that remaining 10% of your attention to peruse your 'home' stream, to see if any nice surprises appear there. I will often find hidden pearls of wisdom, inspiration or humour in that 10%, and sometimes I'll even add new people to my other 'watch these people' lists.

TIP 125: AVOID OVERWHELM BY ALLOWING FOLLOWERS TO COME AND GO

7 Graces Checklist:
Invitation

Filtering your content allows you to focus on cultivating stronger ties *gradually with a small minority*, while allowing the majority of your connections to remain valuable 'weak ties'. While a few will ascend into the 'inner circle' of very close connections, many more will come and go into and *out of* the 'strong tie' category over time.

Don't get upset about the fact that people will go back into the 'weak tie' category even after they have been a 'strong tie'. This is part of the natural ebb and flow of online (or any) relationships. Many of your online followers will get close for a period of time and then become less available or aloof. But unless you (or they) have done something to sever your connection, chances are this is just part of the cyclical nature of your relationship with them. And really, it's something we *all* do at an unconscious level to ensure personal sustainability. Always bear in mind that when someone moves from being a 'strong tie' to a 'weak tie', they are *not* disconnected from you, but have simply moved from your 'kinetic energy bank' into your 'potential energy reserve'.

Knowing how to treat this 'potential energy reserve' is vital in our long-term relationships. What we need to remember is that, for many people, a little bit of distance can *strengthen* relationships. When you give people space to come closer and move away from you without cutting them off and having them 'lose' you entirely, you demonstrate that you respect their personal choices and boundaries. When you show this kind of respect, most people will respect you (and feel grateful to you) in return. The more you work with social media, the more you will observe that the vast majority of people prefer to watch the action at a distance and step in only when the time is right for *them*.

SIDEBAR NOTE: *Of course, if you see a LOT of followers leaving you within a short time span, you'd better take a good look at whether you are 'feeding' them or 'feeding upon' them. Are you invading them with too much content? Irrelevant content? Are you trying to bring them 'in' too quickly? Are you trying to take more than you are giving? Or maybe you are simply going after the wrong audience for your content. While individual followers will come and go, a mass exodus is reason to examine your own 'game plan' (more on making your 'game plan' later in this section).*

TIP 126: AVOID OVERWHELM BY SETTING TIME LIMITS

I believe setting time limits for your activity is extremely important in avoiding overwhelm. When people first meet me and find out how strong my social network is, they tend to assume I spend all day and all night online. Perhaps in reading this book, you might also have made the same assumption. If that's the case, you might be shocked at how *little* time I spend on social media every day. Here's my typical Twitter routine:

- On workdays (which for me are Monday through Thursday) I spend about 40 minutes first thing in the morning checking over the Twitter accounts I manage (my own, my staff's and my clients) to make sure their automation systems are all working and addressing any issues that might need addressing. However, if I only had one Twitter account (which I imagine is the case for many of you), I'd probably spend a maximum of 5 minutes per workday on this (20 minutes per week).

- Around lunchtime, or whenever I take a break from work, I'll spend about 5 minutes per account replying to my 'mentions' and another 5 minutes skimming through Tweets of my filtered streams on HootSuite. I'll RT a few people, make a few comments. Then, if I feel like it, I'll look at the main Twitter stream to see what's new. In total, this is about 10 minutes a day per workday (40 minutes per week).

- If I'm waiting for dinner to finish cooking, I'm out travelling on a train or bus, or I'm generally in a place where I have nothing else to do, I'll take out my Blackberry and reply to mentions, make a few comments or send a few RTs using the Twitter mobile app. I might even send a random Tweet about something I just attended, something I just read or a place I just visited. I kind of don't 'count' this as work, as I'm doing it without any true business 'aim'. It's done for socialising.

- Twice a month, I'll spend about 5 minutes per account clearing out stale tweeps.

- Twice a month, I'll spend about 20 minutes finding new lists to follow and start following them.

- Once a month, I'll spend about an hour composing and uploading new Tweets, and getting rid of old ones that are no longer useful.

If I add all this up, the average time I actively spend prepping or engaging on Twitter (apart from entertainment and socialising) **for a single account is less than 6 hours *per month***. To make progress on Twitter it *is* important that you make a time commitment to it—but this time commitment must feel 'doable' and manageable for you.

SIDEBAR NOTE: Having two (or more) Twitter accounts doesn't necessarily mean your time commitment is twice as great, as a lot of what you do for one account can be done for another within the same time period.

TIP 127: AVOID OVERWHELM BY HIRING SOMEONE TO HELP

For some of the more 'routine' tasks on Twitter, such as clearing out the dead wood, researching new lists to follow and checking automation systems, you might consider hiring a Virtual Assistant (VA). This can help free you up to work on creating great content and building relationships. A word of caution, however: please don't let your VA *replace* you by managing all your interpersonal communications. This might be OK if you run a very large business and your VA is your 'face' online. But if YOU are your 'brand' (if you are an author, a speaker, etc.), allowing someone else to speak on your behalf can backfire on you, big time (I've seen it happen). I don't personally think it's too much to ask the 'front person' of a company to commit to spending 10-15 minutes of each work day on Twitter for the purpose of personal engagement.

TIP 128: AVOID OVERWHELM BY CREATING A ROUTINE

As you can see, I've established my own personal routine for my Twitter activity. Finding a personal Twitter 'rhythm' that works with your lifestyle helps spare you from Twitter overwhelm. In the beginning, when you are learning the ropes, it's easy to spend more time on it, as you are naturally curious and worried you might be 'missing' something. But with time, you will find your pace.

To experiment with how that pace works best for you, my suggestion is that you set aside specific times that you will go on Twitter each day, as well as specific days of the week/month you will devote to the longer, more complex tasks (like creating new content). For instance, I spend the first few minutes of my day checking in on Twitter, before I open any emails or do anything else. Then I don't go back to it until after lunch. If I feel like looking at Twitter in the evening after dinner, I will, but this is more for personal interest and I don't count it as part of my 'routine'. Similarly, when I know I need to create new content, I pencil a morning in my diary when I know I won't be seeing clients (I'll even block it out in my online diary, so no one can book with me). I make sure I do it first thing in the morning and aim to get it all done within an hour. Once it's done, my content is usually sorted and out of the way for another month, except for random Tweets I'll make up along the way throughout the month, or if I've been inspired to write a blog post I didn't plan in advance.

Making Twitter part of your 'weekly business routine' will help you avoid overwhelm by getting much more done than if you were to dip in and out of it randomly. Without this, you are unlikely to know where you have come from and where you are going. But with a weekly routine, you will be much more likely to know what you are 'supposed' to be doing and when. You'll be more aware of how your platform is taking shape, the types of followers you are attracting and what kind of content they prefer. You also won't miss out on the little gems that come along your way in the form of mentions, RTs and DMs.

TIP 129: AVOID OVERWHELM BY HAVING A GAME PLAN

In my experience, most overwhelm comes from getting caught in 'the great unknown'. If you don't know where you're going or how to get there, it's really easy to spin into a state of overwhelm. While a routine gives you a day-to-day structure for *what* you want to do, it's equally important to have a MAP that shows you *where* you want to go. This map is your 'game plan'. Your game plan should include things like:

- Defining your ideal audience

- Clearly knowing what you want to say to that audience

- Developing content that communicates this message in a compelling way

- Identifying specific keywords that can help you find this audience

- Creating a 'pace' for how you wish to grow your following

- Defining when you would like to reach different 'milestones' in your following

Once established, you can continue to expand this same market while you begin to diversify. You can look at other audiences who would be a good match for your ever-evolving message, and repeat the whole process you did with your primary audience. If you do not approach Twitter with some sort of strategy in mind, you are likely to end up in a scenario where you have no real identity and the majority of your followers are opportunistic people only following you to build their own numbers.

PART 13:
MARKETING FOR MONETISATION

I f you happen to have read the title of this chapter and jumped right to it before reading the earlier chapters of this book, please trust me when I say you are setting yourself up for disappointment. Over the past few years, many clients have come to me after having tried on their own to emulate what they *thought* they saw me do on my marketing campaigns, only to find they couldn't make it work the way they had hoped. This is because what they saw on the surface was just a tiny fraction of what makes a marketing campaign successful. Those who had been partners on former campaigns had a bit more insight into what goes on behind the scenes, but still they didn't see the whole picture.

No marketing campaign can come out of a bubble, and this is especially so for the strategies I will discuss in this chapter. All of these strategies are collaborative in design, which is to say their success is at least 40% dependent upon you *already* having developed a strong, relevant, inspired fan base/following for your brand, and another 40% dependent upon you *already* having cultivated a strong, motivated and switched-on network of collaborative partners. The remaining 20% relies on careful planning, clear communication, great marketing copy, competent technical support for both customers and partners, and a great team of workers to make sure the campaign runs smoothly. It is this 40+40+20 that makes a whole campaign.

If you feel you have already achieved that 40+40 on Twitter and have the means to pull together the final 20, you may be ready to engage in one of these marketing ideas. If you haven't reached this point yet, by all means read this chapter to give you inspiration for what is possible. But I do recommend you wait until you have laid the requisite groundwork as shown in detail in the earlier chapters of this book before attempting to launch a campaign.

A final thought before we proceed. While I might cite specific Graces for some of these 'tips', every one of these marketing campaigns is the culmination of all of the 7 Graces: Connection, Inspiration, Invitation, Directness, Transparency, Abundance and Collaboration. When all 7 are employed and woven together, your Twitter marketing campaign will dance in a way that is simply impossible through 'old school' advertising.

TIP 130: USE TWITTER TO DRIVE A JOINT VENTURE PARTNER (JVP) CAMPAIGN

7 Graces Checklist:
Connection; Directness; Collaboration

One of the things I am most 'known' for online is creating Amazon bestseller launches for authors. When I manage such a campaign, Twitter figures prominently in the mechanics of its delivery. The key to a successful online campaign is the *quantity, quality and relevance of your JVPs* (or 'Joint Venture Partners'), who help to promote the launch.

To create the Twitter component for your JVP campaign, someone will need to:

- Gather the Twitter IDs of all your partners.

- Collate these partners onto a special Twitter list just for that campaign.

- Ensure that all the partners are told about the list, and are 'educated' on how to follow the list in either HootSuite or TweetDeck.

- Create a few hundred Tweets (yes, I said a few hundred) that will be used to promote the various components of the launch campaign. These Tweets should take people to your launch (or pre-launch) page, or other 'events' you might be running in support of your launch.

- Focus some of your Tweets on the various partners themselves. For example: *FREE eBook from @MaryQSmith when you buy @JoeAuthor 's new book ABC [link]*. Note: the space between the Twitter ID and the apostrophe is intentional, to ensure the hyperlink is retained.

- Create a *bespoke* hashtag for the campaign and add it to every one of your Tweets.

- Make sure your partners receive the Tweets WELL in advance, with very clear instructions for when and how to use them.

- Be careful not to 'overwhelm' your partners with too much information all at once. For example, if you are using some Tweets for weeks 1-2 and others for weeks 3-4, don't send them all at once. Make each communication focused, with clear dates and instructions, letting your partners know that a different set of Tweets will follow for such-and-such dates.

- Monitor the action on your campaign by tracking your hashtag either in HootSuite or TweetDeck. This helps you see which partners are most active, which ones are dead-weights, and who else (besides your JVPs) may be ReTweeting your campaign Tweets.

- Shower those partners who have been active with praise in a group email, taking good care NOT to 'name and shame' those who haven't been Tweeting. Usually, these less helpful partners will 'crave' a bit of the praise the others are receiving and start to pick up the pace.

- When in doubt, before judging a partner's lack of activity, drop them an email to ask if they're OK or if they need any help with Twitter. Sometimes they've had a personal tragedy. Sometimes they're confused. Good customer care for your partners is essential.

The Importance of Diversity:

You need a *large* quantity of Tweets to ensure diversity. This is important from a marketing quality standpoint, but also in adhering to Twitter's official rules. Twitter seriously frown upon duplicate Tweets appearing within a short period of time, whether from a single account or across multiple accounts. When you're doing a major campaign, it's vital that you create truly diverse and imaginative Tweets that are not merely a slight variation of one another. It's also a good idea (if possible) for the Tweets to take people to different landing pages for different campaign events, so your Tweets don't all use the same links. It's also important that your *partners* are established well enough on Twitter that they have diverse Tweets *in addition* to the ones for your campaign. If the Twitter gods think someone is getting too repetitive and has little (if any) content other than this single campaign, their Tweets are likely to get filtered out from search results, resulting in potential new followers (including other partners on the campaign) not being able to find them via your hashtag. This happened to one or two of my new partners. We were baffled at first as to why they didn't appear in the stream, but I finally figured out it was due to lack of diversity in their own Tweets. In the worst-case scenario, lack of diversity can even cause an account to get suspended, but this generally only happens if the account is actively spamming its followers or promoting a scam. Be sure to advise your less experienced partners that they should take care to 'mix it up' as best they can.

MONETISING:

If your Tweets are well-constructed, and they send people to a page that is engaging and relevant to their interests (very important), and hopefully contains a free offer of some kind, Twitter can be one of the greatest leads generators for your launch campaign. These leads then become the best prospects for customers for your book, course, product or whatever it is you are promoting.

SIDEBAR NOTE: It's not within the scope of this book to go into how to coordinate a team of good JVPs, how you should write the Tweets for your campaign, or the many reasons why someone would want to be a JVP. I occasionally deliver courses on creating and managing Amazon book launches, which cover this in detail. If you would like notification of any upcoming courses, I recommend subscribing to the Spirit Authors blog.[31] You can also read an article I wrote entitled '7 Reasons to Partner on Someone Else's Book Launch NOW'.[32] If you are interested in being a partner, please drop us a line on the Spirit Authors contact form[33] and we'll keep you on the partner list for future launches.

TIP 131: USE TWITTER TO PROMOTE A VIRTUAL BLOG TOUR (VBT)

7 Graces Checklist:
Connection; Directness; Collaboration

A Virtual Blog Tour (or VBT) is another great vehicle to promote a book or product launch, or simply raise awareness around a particular speaker or issue. A VBT is when you run a series of articles or interviews (typically about a specific book or author) on different blogs over a set period of time. Most of my VBTs run for two weeks, but some have been as long as a month. Each blog will be assigned a different day on the tour to post the interview. Every article is unique, although they will all focus on a topic having to do with the particular book, author or product. It's important that both the blogger and the article appeal to the reading audience of that blog, so choosing the right bloggers for this is very important. Again, it's not within the scope of this book to go through all the details of how to set up a VBT, but I do have an introductory article on my Spirit Authors website called 'What is a Virtual Blog Tour? How Do You Set One Up?' that you may find useful.[34]

In all the VBTs I set up for my clients, Twitter is THE essential ingredient. You will need to create a specific Tweet for each 'stop' on the tour, with an @ mention of both the author and the host. Each Tweet should include a bespoke hashtag for the campaign or tour, so you can find them all in one place. And finally, the Tweets should be written simply and clearly and in such a way as to arouse the curiosity of relevant readers. If they are too generic (like 'read this blog article') they're unlikely to get any attention. I already gave some examples of VBT Tweets earlier in the book, but here's a reminder of what they might look like:

> *Why is Collaboration better than Competition? Top business ethics author @LynnSerafinn on @gallagherPOC 's blog http://bit.ly/NYMQgl #7GoM*

> *Can a new paradigm help biz owners who hate marketing? Author & marketer @LynnSerafinn on @charlyjl 's blog http://bit.ly/Mk76Gm #7GoM*

> *7 Marketing Principles for Your Coaching Business. Author @LynnSerafinn on @parent_coach 's blog http://bit.ly/um4hd7 #7GoM*

> *Do we have a 'relationship' with marketing? @PaulaTarrant interviews bestselling author @LynnSerafinn http://bit.ly/rsb8Z1 #7GoM*

> *How can we avoid the '7 Deadly Sins' in marketing? Author @LynnSerafinn on @MemoirGuru 's blog http://bit.ly/vUzQYS #7GoM*

MONETISING:

Each blog post should include information about some sort of special free offer that ultimately leads people to the book or product you are promoting. I often have a free telesummit planned near the end of the VBT and use the VBT to direct people to attend this event. It is during the telesummit that people become increasingly interested in the book, as we showcase the author throughout the event. In this way, the VBT becomes a powerful tool for monetisation. You can also 'repurpose' the content from the VBT to create eBooks that you can either sell or use as a leads-generating product.

TIP 132: RUN A TWITTER CONTEST

> ***7 Graces Checklist:***
> ***Directness; Transparency; Abundance***

Twitter contests were all the rage in 2009, but then dropped in popularity. This is possibly because so many of them ended up being 'annoying' to other people on Twitter, and ultimately to the Twitter gods themselves. Twitter's primary complaint about early Twitter contests was that they encouraged people to create multiple accounts solely for the purpose of entering the contest, and they often resulted in the same Tweets going out over and over to the same audience. But recently, I've seen a resurgence of interest in contests on Twitter, possibly because there are now some interesting apps out there that help make them easier and more fun to run.

Contests can be a great way to increase both your Twitter following and your brand identity, and increase engagement between you and your followers. They can also be used as a leads generator and even help increase sales of a certain product. If all that sounds good to you, you might consider setting up a Twitter contest for a particular promotion or launch. But before you start planning your contest, it's important you read the official Guidelines for Contests on Twitter[35], which clearly state the following:

- As a contest organiser, you MUST actively discourage the creation of multiple accounts. Sometimes people will do this thinking it will give them an advantage in the contest. Twitter require that the contest organiser include a rule clearly stating that anyone found using multiple accounts to enter will be ineligible for the prize. Violation of this policy could result in them (or you) having their account suspended.

- You must also discourage followers from posting the same Tweet repeatedly by saying something like 'whoever ReTweets the most wins'. Twitter suggest you set a clear contest rule stating multiple entries in a single day will not be accepted.

- Twitter also request that you ask users to include an @ reply to you in their update so you can see all the entries. Depending upon a hashtag for **tracking entries and choosing a winner** is not reliable enough for contest integrity, because certain users might be getting filtered out of search results (as mentioned earlier). Using your Twitter handle in the required Tweet is the only way to ensure the entries will be seen and thus ensure the winner is chosen fairly.

- Be sure your hashtag is 'current and relevant' to the contest itself, such as #ContestName or #CompanyName. If you use a 'trending' hashtag, thinking this is a clever way to get seen on trending topics pages, you are likely to get your account suspended, as this is no different from spam.

- And finally, Twitter ask that you abide by the Twitter Rules[36] and consult their search best practices[37] before starting a contest, as well as make sure your contest upholds any applicable laws and regulations in your country or region.

There are several different types of contests you can run, but the one I'll discuss here is what the folks at Binkd (who offer a free Twitter contest application) call a 'sweepstakes'. A sweepstakes is simple: people enter for a chance to win and a winner (or winners) is chosen at random. It is the easiest type of contest to create and run, and also the easiest for people to enter. Because of this, you tend to get more entrants than other types of contests that involve some effort on the part of the contestants. In their article 'Running Profitable and Successful Contests', Binkd recommend a sweepstakes be limited to only 1-2 days and be timed carefully to match your promotional campaign.[38]

The four basic components of a sweepstakes-style Twitter contest are 1) a contest entry page, 2) a prize, 3) some contest rules, and 4) a 'Tweet'. Here's an overview of how they fit together:

The Page:

Through Twitter or other communication, you send people to a designated landing page for your contest. You can either make this page within your own website or through a third-party app, such as Binkd or BeeLiked. On this landing page, people can read about the contest and the prize, and are given the chance to enter the contest free of charge. NOTE: sending people to a sales page before they hit the entry page is a violation of Twitter rules (and is apt to make your followers really angry!), but you can certainly include information about the brand or product the contest is promoting.

The Prize:

The prize can be anything, really. But the most compelling prizes are going to be something of real value and *relevance* to the people entering the contest AND (I believe) to the nature of the contest and brand itself. For example, if I were to run a contest to promote this book, the most logical prize would be something that helps people become more effective at ethical online marketing, because that is congruent with the subject of the book. You might think you will get more entrants if you offer a 'glossy' prize like an iPad, but then it will become a contest about the iPad and not about the brand. Your contest is likely to attract every Tom-Dick-and-Harriet who might be looking for an iPad but have absolutely no interest in your brand. If you remember our discussion about 'knowing your audience' earlier in the book, you'll certainly know by now that 2,000 relevant and interested followers are worth a heck of a lot more than 20,000 random followers.

In their guidance on selecting a prize, Binkd offer the opinion that 'unless you are VERY well recognized in the industry, [you shouldn't] offer your services as a prize.'[39] I've seen a lot of coaches, for instance, offer coaching as their prize, and it doesn't always pan out the way they hoped. However, if you do want to offer professional services, make it something specific to the brand or product, rather than generic. Think outside the box. You can create a *package* of prizes that might include some quality time with you plus physical or digital products. You can also include prizes from *partners* to sweeten the deal. As this is a 'prize' and not a 'free gift' try to make it something they cannot get otherwise without paying a decent price. I don't advise making your prize a free ticket to a live event, as then you are restricting your audience to those who live close enough to attend (unless you intend to pay airfare!).

As part of the prize (and a way to help raise the profile of your contest), you might include a profile of the winner (or winners) on your blog, newsletter, radio show or other platform. This is especially attractive to people who own businesses and might welcome the free publicity.

The Rules:

Your contest rules should be spelled out VERY clearly on your landing page. These rules should show the criteria for entering, the method for entering and the specific rules that will disqualify entries. Here's an example of what this might look like:

You can enter this contest in 3 easy steps:

- *First, make sure you are following @LynnSerafinn on Twitter.*

- *Next, enter your name and email in the form below [insert a web form to collect names and emails here]. Your privacy is very important to us! We promise your details will never be sold or shared with any third party. In registering, you agree to receive an email from us about the contest results on or around [insert date], as well as additional information on how to attend the free webinar on [insert date].*

- *After you complete your entry form, send the following Tweet to your followers on Twitter: [insert the Tweet you want them to send here]. So we can track all entries accurately, please do not make any changes to the Tweet.*

Contest rules:

- *One winner will be drawn at random from those who have completed all three steps above.*

- *You must still be following @LynnSerafinn at the time of the prize draw on [insert date] to qualify for the prize.*

- *Because every Tweet sent out is counted as an entry, you are welcome to Tweet this message more than once during the contest, BUT you may not Tweet it more than once per day. Anyone Tweeting more than once per day or using multiple accounts to increase their chances of winning is in violation of official Twitter contest policy and will immediately be disqualified from winning the prize.*

- *The winner will be announced on Twitter on [date] and will also be announced to all entrants via email.*

The Tweet(s):

While you may have many objectives for your contest, one of the main ones should be to increase brand identity. For this to happen, you want your contest Tweets to go 'viral' on Twitter. That's why the final criterion for entry should be that people send out a Tweet about the contest. Here's an example of what such a Tweet might look like:

Just entered to WIN $800 marketing package from
@LynnSerafinn to celebrate new Twitter book #Tweepelicious.
Enter at [link]

It's important that your Tweet state the prize clearly, including the value of the prize (if not apparent). In accordance with Twitter rules, the Tweet must have a hashtag that is specific and relevant to the contest and brand. The Tweet above also has my Twitter handle, which is another Twitter contest requirement. As explained before, this is because hashtags alone will not always show up in search results, whereas 'mentions' always will. Including your handle is not only important for tracking, but it also can drive new people to your Twitter profile and help increase your following indirectly.

Your hashtag can serve another purpose, too. While your contest entrants are sending out this Tweet, you should also be Tweeting about your product or brand using this same hashtag. These Tweets should take people to articles (not sales pages) that have useful or interesting information for your readers. At the end of the articles, you can lead your readers to your product and/or the Twitter contest. In this case, when using the #Tweepelicious tag, I would be Tweeting lots of different Twitter tips with a link to the book sales page. Then, on the sales page I would mention the contest. In this way, the contest reinforces the launch and vice-versa.

Promotion:

People often have the mistaken impression that contests will go 'viral' on their own steam. They don't. Back when I did my first Twitter contest in 2009, I really didn't know what I was doing and I didn't get very good results. Promoting your contest properly is vital or it will fall flat on its face. If you rely solely on your fan base, you won't increase your following, which is the main reason for running the contest. Like any other online campaign, utilising the aid of JVPs is extremely important (and you might even have a special prize for your partners). Being organised and announcing the contest in advance so people know it's coming will also get them 'primed' for it. When the contest starts, both you and your partners should announce it in your newsletters, blogs and social media.

MONETISING:

Monetising from a contest is a 'slow burn'. Most people coming in will be new to you. This means they are at 'pre-entry level' and are not necessarily ready to buy from you. For this reason, it's a good idea to follow up the contest with some sort of freebie, like a free webinar on a topic of interest to them. You might even use this webinar as the place where you announce the winner of the contest (a clever angle to encourage everyone to attend). If your webinar is informative and relevant to your audience, some of these new contacts might become 'warm' enough to purchase an entry-level product, such as a book or something else that only involves nominal investment and personal commitment. Over time, if these people stay on your list and get to know you better, they might take an interest in other products as well. Don't judge your return on investment by the level of sales you make, but by the number of relevant new *leads* you gain. Remember the weak tie rule and be patient in respecting and cultivating these relationships.

TIP 133: USE TWITTER TO PUBLICISE THE CONTENT OF YOUR ONLINE SHOP

7 Graces Checklist:
Inspiration; Invitation;
Abundance; Collaboration

Back in *PART 6: Creating Effective Content*, I said it was best policy to 'hardly ever' use Tweets that lead your Twitter followers to a sales page. Instead, we've been focussing on creating a body of diverse, content-rich material that your followers will find relevant, useful and valuable. When your followers see that at least 95% of your Tweets are content-driven, the occasional Tweet about a sale item is not received as being 'invasive', especially if the items you are Tweeting about are *genuinely* of use to your specific audience. For instance, I have a book shop on my Spirit Authors website that showcases books that are either useful to authors, or books of interest to people who like self-help books. Thus, it is very selective and targeted for my followers. The shop also has many books written by my clients and network partners.

If you don't have your own products or a way to fulfil and deliver goods, you could set up an Amazon shop using the 'a-store' feature on Amazon Associates.[40] An Associates account is the same as an affiliate account. In other words, if people buy a product using your Associates link, you make a commission on the sale. The commissions are NOT huge, but they do add up over time and can become a steady passive income. I'm always delighted when I receive an unexpected payment from this source.

In Tweeting about your shop, you again have to remember the 'Yeah...So What?' Test. Write your Tweets in such a way that your readers know exactly why they would want to check out the item you are recommending. Here are some examples of what your Tweets might look like:

How to Publish & Sell Your Article on Kindle by
@KateHarperCards. Great tips for authors at @SpiritAuthors
http://bit.ly/JrlV7T

#AUTHORS: Class Act: Sell More Books at School & Library
Author Appearances by Barbara Techel @joyfulpaws
http://bit.ly/OwleD7

#WRITING tips: 30 Ways to Liberate Soulful Creative Energy
by @AudaciousEditor Stephanie Gunning
http://bit.ly/OwlGBd

New Relationship #Marketing: Build Large, Loyal, Profitable
Network by social media expert @MariSmith
http://bit.ly/Plx5k5

#AUTHORS: If you're wondering how to get #RADIO interviews, I recommend this book from Fran Silverman http://bit.ly/JrlAll

Take note of these details:

- If the author is on Twitter, I include their Twitter handle, with hopes that they will RT the Tweet. If they aren't on Twitter (or I can't find them) I just write their name.

- To save characters, you can delete some of the words in titles like 'the', 'a', etc.

- You can include the Twitter handle of the account that represents your shop (in my case it would be @SpiritAuthors) if you intend to send the Tweet from one of your other accounts.

- The link should take people to the *specific* book in your shop, not to the book on Amazon. The logic behind this choice is to drive visitors to your website, so even if they don't buy anything, maybe they'll check out your blog.

Something you might not be aware of is that you will make a commission not only when someone buys the promoted book through your link, but also if they buy *anything else* from Amazon before they check out. They don't even have to have seen the product on your website. Because of this, I've made commissions on some really strange things over the years, including toys and electronic goods I've never heard of. Also, by checking what people are buying through my Associates links, I often find other books that make good additions to my shop.

As an aside, whenever you are promoting your own book, if you want people to buy it on Amazon, be sure to use your Amazon Associates link on all your sales pages.

SIDEBAR NOTE: *This tip embraces the Grace of Abundance in many subtle ways. Some people are afraid to promote other people's products because they believe it will take the spotlight away from them. But it is Scarcity mentality to believe that if someone buys someone else's book they will not buy yours. If you wish to embrace Abundance fully, it is* *much in your favour to show your readers that you are a source of good content, even if that content is not your own. When you open up the restrictions in this way, your readers feel free and empowered. You'll not only see the money start flowing more easily, but your readers will see you as someone who is confident enough to be generous without needing to hog the spotlight or manipulate their loyalties.*

TIP 134: TWEET ABOUT THIRD-PARTY PRODUCTS USING YOUR AFFILIATE LINKS

7 Graces Checklist:
Directness; Transparency

In much the same way that you can Tweet about your shop or Amazon store, you can also Tweet about selected third-party products you endorse using your affiliate links. However, I want to drive home the need for caution, ethics and (once again) relevance when using affiliate links.

Caution:

There is a breed of people on Twitter who use it *only* for affiliate marketing. Typically, they sell 'get followers fast' scams or other questionable products. As mentioned earlier, most of these tweeps do NOT have many followers. That's because Twitter has their eagle-eye on them and their accounts are continually getting suspended. Undaunted, these persistent spammers will set up another account, often using 'proxies' (more on this in *PART 14: Expansion, Mobility and Influence*). I actually saw an outrageously transparent (in a bad way) advert on one of those 'find a techie' sites where someone was looking for people to set up multiple accounts and work with proxies because 'their accounts would almost certainly get suspended quickly'. Aggressive, single-minded, predatory affiliate marketing put off any potential followers you might have and it will get you banned from Twitter. If you are interested in developing a reputation, brand and long-term relationships, promote affiliate campaigns *sparingly* without diluting the quality of your overall content.

Ethics:

In my opinion, you should only use your affiliate links to promote products whose features you have at least previewed, and whose company customer service and return policy are ethical. Selling products you know nothing about leaves you 'responsible' in some way if someone doesn't like the product or they get ripped off. Don't sell products from people you don't know just because the price tag of the commission looks good. To me, the most ethical way to promote using an affiliate link is by writing an article or making a video review of the product, where you comment on its use and tell people why you are recommending it. If you use this method, the link in your Tweets should take people to the review on your website, rather than directly to the product sales page. In the body of your review, you would then give readers your affiliate link to purchase the product. It is also important to disclose that you are using your affiliate link.

Regardless of which method you use, if you do not feel confident about backing both the product AND the company who makes the product, don't promote it. Otherwise, your attempts to make a little extra income on the side will only result in damaging your own reputation, which is worth far more than any commission you might have made.

Relevance:

I've mentioned relevance so many times in this book, but it simply cannot be stressed enough. If you are Tweeting affiliate links for a product, make sure they are relevant to YOUR audience. Make sure the product is something your specific followers would find useful. If you give them great resources, you are building stronger bonds of connection. Tweeting about 'any old thing' is an 'old school' marketing strategy wherein you hope to catch random fish by casting a wide net. That is a lot of work for little results, and it doesn't do anything to develop who YOU are on Twitter. Stay focussed on *your* brand even when you may be Tweeting about third-party products. How does this product reinforce *your* reputation in your field? How does it provide your followers with something you know they want that is consistent with *your* own image? For example:

AUTHORS: Have a look at the WordPress PDF Stamper Plugin.
Protects your eBooks from being pirated. VERY clever!
http://ow.ly/dcvRM

AUTHORS: Interesting WordPress plug-in to stop your eBook
from getting shared with people who haven't PAID for it:
http://bit.ly/YjweH6

The followers of my @SpiritAuthors account on Twitter are predominantly authors. I also work with authors as a consultant under that brand name. Thus, anything that might be a valuable product for authors is relevant to both my audience and my brand. I wanted to test whether this product would be of interest to my followers, so I posted one of these Tweets earlier today. Within the first 30 minutes, the link received over 100 hits. While this is good, I'm likely to get an even better result if I were to write a review or make a demo video of this product and post it on YouTube and my blog. I would then use Twitter to link to the product review, and within the review would be my affiliate link. Demonstrating that you use a product yourself speaks much more authentically to your audience than sending them to the sales page.

Here are some Tweets for a different product:

COACHES: Your clients can get 30 days free on
@AllisonMaslan's Interactive Live Coach. Fun way to get
organised http://bit.ly/IItVEz

What the heck is an 'Interactive Life Coach'? Take a 30-day
free test drive and find out at http://bit.ly/IItVEz

These Tweets are useful because, while I'm primarily a marketing consultant, I'm also a certified coach and have a lot of followers who are also coaches. Because of this connection, one of the most successful affiliate products I have promoted on Twitter has been the goals-setting software programme called 'Interactive Life Coach' designed by one of my author clients, Allison Maslan.[41]

When using affiliate links, bear in mind that you might not see immediate sales on a particular product, because people often bookmark a page so they can look at it later. The 'cookies' from the e people clicked your link will stay in the system a specified of days (according to how the webmaster has set up the affiliate programme), which means if they come back to purchase the product within that timeframe, you still make the commission.

SIDEBAR NOTE: *If you send emails, newsletters or blog posts about one of your affiliated products, you should always alert your readers to the fact that you are using an affiliate link, telling them you will make a commission if they happen to purchase the product. Of course, it is not very practical to do this in a Tweet.*

TIP 135: USE TWITTER TO SUPPORT YOUR OWN AFFILIATE PROGRAMME

7 Graces Checklist:
Connection; Directness; Collaboration

The flipside of monetising through third-party affiliate programmes would be to promote one of your own products or services by coordinating a JVP campaign using your own affiliate programme. Running an affiliate campaign can be a highly effective way to create a motivated sales force for you, if you choose *relevant* partners (i.e. their audience is interested in what you do) who already have a good connection to you.

There are many affiliate platforms on the market available at various costs. Some of the most popular are 1ShoppingCart, iDevAffiliate and WP Affiliate. I've used all three of these, both as an affiliate coordinator and as an end user, and the one I like best is WP Affiliate. While there's always going to be a bit of a learning curve for all these products, I've found WP Affiliate much easier to set up and far easier for affiliates to find their way around within their affiliate area. It's also the least expensive option of the three, and it integrates easily with its companion shopping cart system WP eStore and other products from the same company. Of course, using it is contingent upon you having a paid WordPress site for your sales (rather than a regular website or a free site on WordPress.com), so it may not be the right choice for everyone.

If you don't have a paid WordPress site, iDevAffiliate is a good second choice. It is reasonably priced and has a lot of great features, but is not as visually accessible for the end user. The most expensive (albeit often considered the 'industry standard') is 1ShoppingCart. The main reason it's so pricey is that it is not only an affiliate programme, but (as the name implies) a complete Shopping Cart system. If you visit their websites via the links provided at the end of this book, you can compare the three systems to see which is the best option for your specific needs.

Using Twitter to support your affiliate programme is not dissimilar to using it to support your book or product launch, as discussed earlier. The difference is that your affiliate partners will need to get Tweets that contain their unique affiliate link. You do this by writing your Tweets in a single document and uploading them into the affiliate tools area of your website. Then, when your affiliates log in and download your Tweets, their unique tracking links will already be embedded in them. These tracking links tend to be very long, usually resulting in making your Tweets more than 140 characters, so you'll need to tell your affiliates to shorten their links using Bit.ly or another programme before they post them on Twitter. Here are some examples of Tweets we used for the 7 Graces Global Conference 2012:

What's the REAL cause of our economic problems? Change the paradigm June 22-24. [Affiliate link] #7GGC #CSR

Competition makes us weaker, not stronger. Let's CHANGE the paradigm! [Affiliate link] #7GGC #CSR

Typically, I create a few dozen of such Tweets for every campaign, so there is variety and diversity of content. Using this strategy, our partners generated about 1000 hits per day on Twitter in April through June 2012.

While creating great Tweets for your campaign is certainly important, in my experience, adequate customer care for your *affiliates* is even more important for the success of your Twitter affiliate campaign. JVP affiliates need to know how and where to get the Tweets, how and when to use them, and how to track their clicks and sales. I've created and run many affiliate campaigns using Twitter and let me tell you, such care is well beyond the scope of most business owners or Virtual Assistants, as it requires the ability to provide strategic marketing advice as well as technical support and troubleshooting. If you do not know how to support your affiliates in this way, I recommend you hire someone (like me!) who has had experience in creating, managing and supporting affiliate campaigns.

TIP 136: ATTRACT CLIENTS THROUGH TWITTER

7 Graces Checklist:
Connection; Inspiration; Invitation

Believe it or not, you CAN attract clients through Twitter (I hate to say 'get' clients). I guess you might call this the 'grand prize' as it's neither something that happens overnight nor does it tend to happen *directly* as the result of a Tweet. In the introduction to this book, I told the story of how my very first book launch client, Allison Maslan, came to me as a result of a single Tweet sent out by *someone else*, and how this subsequently changed both Allison's and my own career completely.

If you would like to attract clients through Twitter, the key is to follow (with a passion!) all the tips I've been giving you, especially those regarding the quality and quantity of your content, the relationship between you and your audience on Twitter, and the relevance of your content to that audience. Let your Tweets take your followers to GREAT original content that is useful to their specific interests and needs. Be sure you have a good bio and headshot at the end of every one of your blog posts, and make it super simple for people to reach you to ask for a consultation (a contact form is best). And finally, understand the psychology and importance of weak ties and provide several different ways on your blog for your readers to stay connected to you, without them feeling too committed.

Before you start wondering how you might attract clients through Twitter, it's important to understand the process of how your followers 'move' from different levels of engagement with you on Twitter:

- <u>No commitment, no tie:</u> Someone sees a link to your article on Twitter and clicks it to see what it's all about. This is NO commitment because people don't have to be following you on Twitter to see your links.

- <u>No commitment, weak tie:</u> When people read your post, the object is to inspire them enough to come back to the blog or find you elsewhere. Following you on Twitter is often the least 'threatening' option because it does not require any exchange of energy on the part of the reader. For this reason, it's really important to ensure it is easy for people to find links to all your social networks when they read your blog.

- <u>Weak commitment, weak tie:</u> The next level of commitment is when people sign up to receive your blog posts. This is less of a commitment than signing up for a newsletter because they are not being 'sold to', just receiving useful articles. Be sure to use Feedburner or another programme to create a sign-up form that lets people subscribe to your updates.

- <u>Medium commitment, weak tie:</u> Often people try to push their mailing list on their readers right away without giving them any other means of 'no commitment' or 'weak commitment' connection to test the waters. I think this is a mistake and you should create an environment on your site where people can get to know you organically, until they feel ready to deepen the 'commitment' by voluntarily signing up to your mailing list (without the use of annoying pop-up windows that try to 'force' to do this!). Be sure signing up for your newsletter is easy and obvious, but don't make it pushy. These days, most newsletters fail the 'Yeah...So What?' Test, so it's a good idea to combine it with some sort of free download offer that is valuable to them and in alignment with their interests and your brand. The 'medium commitment, weak tie' is also the place where people are likely to consider buying your book.

- <u>Strong commitment, medium tie:</u> Very few people are likely to contact you after reading a single article, as Allison did with me (she's an Aries; maybe that explains it). Perhaps they will if they've read a book you've written, but a single article is not usually enough to prompt the vast majority of people into jumping from anonymity into a strong tie connection with you. Most will have had their eye on you for some time before making their move. Make that move easy for them by providing a contact form on your site, telling them they may ask for a consultation with you through the form, for instance. Providing an email address is not always as helpful as you might think. It leaves you open to spammers, for a start, but it also means your reader has to click away from your site and open their email software. Using an online form eliminates both of these issues. I receive no fewer than twenty contact requests a week via my online forms, and if I trace back to how they first found me, most of them either knew me through Twitter or were referred to me by someone else who knew me on Twitter (with Facebook a close second).

- <u>Strong commitment, strong tie:</u> The 'Big Kahuna' is, of course, getting a new client (or long-term customer). From this point forward, you can create a strong, long-lasting relationship.

Always remember: just because 99% of your audience is silent 99% of the time, this does NOT mean they aren't paying attention to what you do 100% of the time. For example, back in 2007 I ran a group coaching workshop that a young woman named Vanessa attended. I had never heard from Vanessa until September 2010 when she called me up out of the blue, telling me she was working for an author with a major publisher and she wanted to hire me to do a large-scale book launch and several other small projects. She had been watching me silently for three years, reading all my newsletters and Tweets, when suddenly our distant relationship landed me a chunky contract that lasted nearly a year. Never underestimate the potential of your 'silent' audience. Always create multiple pathways for them to connect and stay in touch with you, and remember that for many people, Twitter is the path of least resistance.

TIP 137: GET GIGS AND MEDIA INTERVIEWS THROUGH TWITTER

7 Graces Checklist:
Connection; Invitation; Directness

Getting speaking and media gigs (radio, TV, magazine interviews) through Twitter is also possible, bearing in mind the same advice I've given regarding attracting clients. You can actively track down radio and media people on Twitter if you wish, although what is *more* likely to happen is someone who is actively seeking a speaker for an event or broadcast (either in person on online) or a source for a journalist's article might seek *you* out on Twitter. It's happened to me many times. Such head-hunters will locate you the same way YOU would try to find them—through a bit of research using keywords and hashtags.

There are some simple keys to increasing the likelihood of being asked to be a speaker, source or media guest through Twitter:

- Focus on establishing yourself (or your company) as an expert in a clearly definable field. Make your brand easy to understand. I find it fascinating how so many speakers have an image that is utterly ambiguous on their websites. If you remember the old film *Gypsy* about Gypsy Rose Lee, they sang a song called 'You Gotta Have a Gimmick'. Similarly, in the music industry popular songs need a 'hook'. If you're trying to promote yourself as a speaker, be sure your Tweets take people to a page where they can *really* get an idea of who you are as a speaker and how you stand out from the thousands of other speakers on Twitter. When I start working with a client, the first thing we do is get to the core of their brand, and make it as clear and direct as possible on their website. This doesn't always happen in a single session, as it can sometimes involve a lot of deep soul-searching and letting go of past ideas about yourself. You'll know you've really 'landed' your brand if it brings tears to your eyes, puts a lump in your throat or just makes you want to jump up and down. If you're still 'trying to decide' what it is, you haven't got it yet.

- Make your Tweets and blog posts consistent with that field of expertise, ensuring there are relevant keywords and hashtags that are likely to be picked up by anyone looking for a particular topic.

- Make sure your blog is media-friendly by having a dedicated media page with an up-to-date, downloadable media kit (in PDF format) that readers can print and read at their leisure. Remember, if someone is hunting for media sources on Twitter, they may be on a mission to research lots of different people, so make it quick and easy for them to download things they may wish to look at later when they have more time.

- Your media page should also include some high-res professional headshots and a *few* of your most impressive past media appearances (audio and/or video). Don't put every single interview you've ever done. Not only is it boring, but it can backfire on you. If people see you have been on many, many media outlets, they may get the impression that you're 'old news' and the media is saturated with you. OR, if you include every rinky-dink gig you've ever done, they might think, 'Is this the best he/she can get?' Just choose two or three samples of your very best work.

- And finally, make sure you have a contact form that clearly SAYS you welcome media requests. It might sound like a dumb thing to have to say, but it's best to plant the seed in their minds that you openly welcome working with the media.

SIDEBAR NOTE: *There is a website called Klout that claims to measure your social 'influence'. If you are looking to use social media as a means of establishing yourself as a speaker, it might be wise to look at your ranking, and consider ways you can improve it. We'll look at Klout in* PART 14: Expansion, Mobility and Influence.

TIP 138: RUN CROWD FUNDING CAMPAIGNS THROUGH TWITTER

7 Graces Checklist:

Connection; Inspiration; Invitation; Directness;

Transparency; Abundance; Collaboration

Typically running between 30 and 90 days in length, a crowd funding campaign is a way to raise money for something specific, such as acquiring start-up funds for a new independent enterprise, money for a special project or expansion within an existing small company or community group, or funding to produce an artistic project such as a book, film, art exhibition, festival or theatre production. The popularity of crowd funding has steadily risen in the past few years, as the currently repressed economic climate has made it increasingly difficult for independent business owners to acquire bank funding or find investors. A quintessential 21st Century invention, it would not be possible to organise and deliver a crowd funding campaign without Web 2.0 technology that enables us to integrate online payment management, social media, multimedia and many other components. I see crowd funding as part of a burgeoning new business paradigm, destined to impact the world of commerce in a big way over the next generation.

Parallel to the rise of crowd funding, and perhaps in response to the wide-spread economic, social and environmental crises we currently see on our planet, is also the rise of a new breed of entrepreneur—the 'social entrepreneur'. I have heard some people use this term erroneously to refer to someone who uses social media to promote their business online. But while many social entrepreneurs may use social media, using social media does not make you a social entrepreneur; *using your business to serve society does.* Although social entrepreneurs are certainly business people with business mindsets, what makes them different is that they are more driven by the desire to create a stronger society and a more ethical world than by the desire to make unlimited profits. The true social entrepreneur does not ask, 'How can I find a few rich people who will invest money in my business?' but rather, *'How can I build a community who will invest fully in my vision?'*

For many of these new-paradigm entrepreneurs, crowd funding seems to be the answer to this question. It addresses our current economic challenges by bypassing the 'old school' investment model. It helps turn 'crowds' into communities, through the power of a shared vision, which is based upon shared values. For these reasons, the idea of running a crowd funding campaign can be very attractive to aspiring social entrepreneurs. But unfortunately, many of them hop onto the crowd funding bandwagon before they fully understand what they're getting into. While some crowd funding campaigns have raised anywhere from tens of thousands to millions in contributions, statistics show that a whopping 90% of crowd funding projects FAIL.[42] I've watched several campaigns end up with next to nothing because they made some major errors in their approach.

Crowd funding is a massive subject, and one which I'll be exploring more deeply in a future publication. But for the purposes of this book, let's briefly take a look at how crowd funding works with Twitter, and how you can avoid the top 5 major Twitter *faux pas* many people make:

1. Not taking time to build your Twitter tribe first

2. Not realising this is a marketing campaign

3. Tweeting your 'inner circle' for money

4. Not having enough diversity in your promotional Tweets

5. Not understanding the different motivations of your funders

MISTAKE 1: Not taking time to build your Twitter tribe first

Here in the UK, BBC Radio 4 recently interviewed Andrew Denham, who ran a highly successful crowd funding campaign that raised £40,000 in six days for his project, The Bicycle Academy.[43] The purpose of their project was to teach people how to build their own bicycles; the first batch of these hand-made bikes would then be donated to underprivileged people in Africa, who had no means of transportation.

Denham said that one of the most 'invaluable' results of their crowd funding campaign was that it 'created 183 evangelists' who helped support *and promote* their project. In other words, he had a committed 'tribe'. What mobilised this tribe was the fact that several clearly definable values were intrinsically woven into their project— green energy, green transport and philanthropy, with a secondary value-focus around physical fitness and healthy living. Those who supported the project knew *exactly* why they were supporting it. By coming together to support the project, they were collectively making a statement about the importance of these values.

One way to describe a 'tribe' is a group of people connected by a desire to express their shared values. While a crowd funding campaign can surely help to expand a tribe, it is my observation that many fail at crowd funding because they believed the campaign would *create* their tribe. This is a big mistake. Before people will back you, they need to know who you are, what you stand for and what you bring the world. They also need to know that you are not some fly-by-night phantom who has no longevity. For these reasons, unless you already have a tribe via other means, you need to spend *at least* several months (hopefully a year) building your tribe before you launch your campaign.

Twitter is the perfect place to build a tribe, and we've already looked at many strategies for how to do this. By creating an effective profile, knowing your audience, delivering compelling content, utilising lists to find your tribe members, and building relationships through engagement, you will gain a reputation as a leader in your field. Only when you have achieved this kind of presence should you start planning a crowd funding campaign. If you jump into it without this foundation, you are likely to be amongst the unfortunate 90% who fail.

MISTAKE 2: Not realising this is a marketing campaign

Many people embark on a crowd funding campaign with the naïve notion that the crowd funding site alone will give them the visibility they need for the campaign to succeed. While a few stray people might come directly to your campaign via the crowd funding site, to succeed you need to understand that crowd funding is ultimately a *marketing campaign.* And just like any other marketing campaign, you need to give it ample care and planning.

If you intend to use Twitter for your campaign (and you should), remember that successful marketing on Twitter is always a *collaborative* effort, as we've discussed earlier in 'Tip 130: Use Twitter to Drive a Joint Venture Partner (JVP) Campaign'. Take care to organise your marketing team and coordinate your marketing partners **at least four months** in advance of the launch of your campaign.

MISTAKE 3: Tweeting your 'inner circle' for money

Once of the biggest mistakes I see crowd funding organisers make is asking their closest Twitter (or other social media) connections to contribute money to their campaign, when they should be asking them to be their *marketing partners.* Your inner circle (typically 30-50 people who are your closest Twitter friends and colleagues) are different from 'the masses'. They are already committed to you and your cause, so treat them like gold dust (because they *are*). Don't ask them for money. Ask them for *help.* If you contact them through Twitter, say something like:

> *@LynnSerafinn Hi Lynn. I'm planning a new project. Would love to have you as a partner. Can we chat sometime soon?*

Because your inner circle people love you, they will probably donate to your cause anyway, but that should never be your reason for contacting them. Always treat them with utmost respect as your friends, peers and colleagues.

MISTAKE 4: Not having enough diversity in your promotional Tweets

Earlier when I spoke about JVP campaigns, I said I typically compose *hundreds* of Tweets for a single book launch. Putting this kind of care into composing Tweets for your crowd funding campaign is equally important, for these reasons:

- It increases the diversity of keywords, making them appear in more Twitter searches.

- Too much repetition can cause your Tweets to be filtered from Twitter search results.

- The diversity will appeal to different target audiences.

- Having a wide selection of diverse Tweets encourages your marketing partners to Tweet more frequently.

- It keeps your readers from getting bored or irritable due to being bombarded with the same thing over and over.

Frustratingly, many crowd funding organisers overlook these factors. They don't bother to create Tweets for their partners, and I typically see *one Tweet* being sent out over and over. Making compelling and diverse Tweets is a vital part of your promotions. You wouldn't skimp on writing a magazine article, so don't skimp on Tweets. Go back to *PART 6: Creating Effective Content* for ideas and guidelines.

MISTAKE 5: Not understanding the different motivations of your funders

The creators of the crowd funding site Rocket Hub have undertaken a terrific analysis of the different kinds of people who join a crowd funding campaign: the 'committed', the 'inspired' and the 'shoppers'.[44] People in your inner circle are what they would call 'the committed'. The 'inspired' are those who read your Tweets or blog and already 'get' who you are. To stir and motivate the potential energy of your 'inspired' audience, your Tweets must establish a connection between their values and those of your crowd funding campaign. Here's an example of a Tweet that is NOT likely to get much response from your 'inspired' group:

Please support our IndieGoGo campaign to raise funds for our
@OurProject project [link]

I see this kind of Tweet a LOT on Twitter. It's unlikely to generate much response for several reasons:

- It is written with the mistaken assumption that your followers already know what '@OurProject' (whatever that may be) and 'IndieGoGo' are.

- It fails the 'Yeah...So What?' Test. Your followers want to know WHY they should bother to help you raise funds for this project. What's the mission? What's the bigger purpose? Why does the world need this project? Why now? Why you?

- But most of all, it asks for money before establishing either connection or relevance between you and the reader.

Here are examples of Tweets that are more likely to attract the 'inspired' audience:

We want to start a WAVE of #Peace throughout the world. Won't you be a part of it? [link]

We want to give away our book on #green energy & #eco solutions FREE to communities. You can make it happen. [link]

You should also compose Tweets that speak from your partners' voice to their own 'inspired' audience, showing the relationship they have with the project:

I'm helping my friend @OurProject start a WAVE of Peace in the world through this excellent documentary [link]

#TRANSITION: Help @StirToAction print new book on social reform to be distributed FREE to community groups. http://ow.ly/deemt

You can also build momentum by telling people where you're at in your campaign. This next Tweet received a lot of RTs when I posted on the last day of a crowd funding campaign I was supporting. They reached their target within 15 minutes of my posting it, finally raising 102% of their target:

#TRANSITION: @StirToAction project needs only £21 to hit £5k target. Plz help print this free book on #sustainability http://ow.ly/deemt

Rocket Hub calls the last group 'the shoppers'. This is a large group of people who many not be as intrinsically motivated as the 'inspired' group. To them, the deal-breaker (or maker) is often the 'perks' you are offering in exchange for supporting your cause. If the perks don't titillate them, they won't bother to support your campaign, even if they like what you are doing. As the majority of your followers on Twitter are likely to fall into this category, it is important you write a good portion of your Tweets with them in mind. Here are some examples:

THRILLED to get invite to launch party for helping
@StirToAction print new book on creating better world. More
perks at http://ow.ly/deemt

NICE! I helped @StirToAction print new book on social reform
& got a FREE book & invitation to launch party.
http://ow.ly/deemt

Notice how while the focus is on the 'perk' I still include important keywords that confirm relevance, such as 'creating a better world' and 'social reform'.

Closing thoughts

A crowd funding campaign should not be considered a 'get funds quick' scheme. The key to success is in the name: *crowd* funding. It is vitally important you keep 'the crowd' at the forefront of all your promotional work. If you give proper care to building your tribe, identifying your partners on Twitter, planning your promotions and creating your Tweets carefully so they appeal to the different types of people in your audience, you have a far greater chance of success. Properly executed, a good crowd funding campaign can be one of the finest examples of all 7 Graces of Marketing in action.

For further information, you can find a list of crowd funding resources at the end of this book in *Resources And Useful Links*.

PART 14:
EXPANSION, MOBILITY AND INFLUENCE

TIP 139: KNOW WHEN IT'S OK TO SET UP MULTIPLE TWITTER ACCOUNTS

According to official Twitter policy, it is against their rules to create 'serial accounts for disruptive or abusive purposes, or with overlapping use cases'. They go on to say, 'Mass account creation may result in suspension of all related accounts. Please note that any violation of the Twitter Rules is cause for permanent suspension of all accounts.'[45]

Twitter policy in mind, you might wonder why I am even suggesting you might wish to set up multiple Twitter accounts. You might also be surprised to know that a great many ethical Twitter users have more than one account. It is my observation that there is a degree of freedom for people to expand on Twitter as long as they are careful that they are compliant with these two very important conditions: 1) they are not set up for disruptive or abusive purposes; and 2) they are not set up for overlapping use.

Twitter does not give any further details of how they define their criteria for what constitutes a 'disruptive or abusive purpose'. I believe their reason for being intentionally vague is because of the nature of technology, i.e. if they become too specific about what is and is not allowed, someone will find a technical loophole. But I feel we can safely assume that any kind of 'spam' or 'scam' would clearly constitute a 'disruptive or abusive purpose'. Basically, if you annoy, harass or cheat people, you're being disruptive and abusive.

Of course, professional spammers and scammers will sometimes orchestrate very elaborate schemes whereby they hire people to set up multiple Twitter accounts for them for the sole purpose of trying to sell some too-good-to-be-true product, such as one of those 'pay such-and-such amount of money to get 10,000 followers fast' rip-offs, or any number of (ridiculous) porn accounts. Others might set up different accounts with the aim of re-selling affiliate products, with no intention of providing any real value to, or establishing any two-way communication with, their followers. What makes these 'scam' accounts even worse is when they start 'spamming' by sending @ messages to people trying to direct them to the scam. Such users are not only in violation of Twitter policy, but their actions are also futile, as their accounts will inevitably get suspended and honest Twitter users get really annoyed with them. I've said this before, but please DO report these accounts to Twitter. I believe the only way to get rid of them entirely is for Twitter users to be vigilant about having zero tolerance for them.

Many of the above examples also give an indication of what constitutes 'overlapping purposes'. If you have multiple accounts that are all saying the same thing and nothing else, this is clearly not only 'overlapping' purposes but *identical* purposes. However, if you have two different brands, and you have two different kinds of messages for two different audiences, then you have a legitimate reason to create two different accounts. For instance, my account @GardenOfTheSoul is nearly 100% dedicated to sending out Tweets about my radio show. My @SpiritAuthors account is reserved for links to articles relevant to authors, and my @7GracesOfMarketng account is reserved for links to articles about business ethics, sustainability, social change, etc. My main account @LynnSerafinn might mention some of the things on these other accounts, but the main purpose of my @LynnSerafinn account is to be 'me' both personally and professionally. It's the account I use to joke around and share humour. I might even start talking about music or current events. Yes, as people get to know me, they become aware of my various brands, but when they talk to @LynnSerafinn, they're talking to me, not my 'brand'.

If your business has two or more distinctly different avenues, this would be a legitimate reason to consider more than one Twitter account (if you can give adequate time and attention to them). If you Tweet in different languages, that would also be an obvious reason to have two accounts. One of my clients spoke four languages and had a large customer base in Italy, Germany, Holland and England. Naturally, he had to have different accounts not only to speak to these respective audiences in their native tongue, but also to speak on topics relevant to each respective audience.

You might also wish to have different accounts if you feel the need to separate business from pleasure, politics or other personal views. For example, I had a client who had a Twitter account for their property services company, but they also wanted to promote a somewhat 'political' message to their community in northern California about saving a local oyster farm. My advice to them was to create a second account because promoting a political message through their official business page might confuse (or put off) current and prospective customers. They also made a separate WordPress blog solely for the purpose of posting information and updates about the lawsuit surrounding the issue. My client did a LOT of research and put a lot of work into collating all the data for that second website, and created no fewer than 500 Tweets on different aspects of the case. Their efforts were highly effective is influencing public opinion, which, in turn, helped influence local officials. While my client made no secret of their stance on the issue, it really was best not to drag political views into their business platform.

I am not categorically recommending that everyone should set up more than one account, even if they have two different audiences or purposes. For instance, if you have written a book that speaks to the same target audience as that of your main account, there is no need to create a second account (in fact, it might dilute your audience). Besides, having multiple accounts can be a lot of work. You need to monitor both accounts and create fresh content for them regularly. In fact, if you don't have a lot of *unique* content for the proposed account (or you're not prepared to make some), you don't need a second account.

In addition to content, you need to have a 'game plan' for both accounts. What is the unique purpose for each? How do you distinguish your audiences and how will you find them? How will you measure success? How will you tangibly justify the time and energy you will put into them? Without considering these questions first, many people set up a second account and then lose steam for it a short time later.

Please bear in mind that, being a free service, Twitter does not 'owe' its users anything. They are perfectly within their legal and ethical rights to suspend any account they deem in violation of policy. But based upon my observation and experience, I also believe the Twitter gods have no real objection to honest users expanding and diversifying their influence, as long as they preserve the integrity Twitter wish to maintain in their environment. So my advice is this: if you have reached a point in your Twitter development where you feel you need to define and differentiate your audiences and you are prepared to create the content for both of them, you might consider creating a second account. If you cannot meet both these criteria, just focus on developing your single account and strengthening that brand.

TIP 140: USING PROXIES TO MANAGE MULTIPLE ACCOUNTS

This tip is for people who either own or manage multiple Twitter accounts (as you might if you are a Virtual Assistant). If you use or manage only one Twitter account, you can skip this tip for now and come back to it at a later date if your situation changes.

As part of my work as a consultant, I will typically manage many of my clients' accounts, especially to lessen the learning curves as they are still finding their way around Twitter. In managing other people's accounts, I take on the responsibility to ensure they operate within Twitter policy so their account stays in good standing. The thing is: if you manage more than one account from the same IP address, at a technical level they are all being *transmitted by* the same user, even if technically they are *not owned* by a single user. This can be tricky if you are managing several accounts and one of the accounts happens to be compromised by hackers and consequently gets suspended. It is feasible *all* the accounts coming from that IP address may get suspended if the violation really ruffles Twitter's feathers. While Twitter is pretty good about reinstating accounts that have been hacked, you still don't want to run the risk of compromising the other accounts that may simply be the 'collateral damage' of an attack on another client's account.

This is where private proxies come in handy. Private proxies are unique IP addresses belonging only to you. If you purchase a unique proxy for each of your Twitter accounts and assign a different proxy to each one of them, it means the actions of one will no longer affect the others. It also means they are likely to respond more quickly when uploading or downloading data because no one else is sharing the bandwidth on that account with you. I use proxies in conjunction with Tweet Adder to protect the integrity of my clients' accounts by ensuring they are not affected by something that might accidentally go wrong with my PC or one of the other accounts.

There are such things as free proxies, but they are not 'private' and defeat the object of getting a proxy in the first place. If you do want to use proxies to protect multiple accounts, it is important to use a reputable company with a strong service track record and good customer support. The one I use is 'My Private Proxy'. The cost starts at $2.49 per month for a single proxy and goes down depending upon how many proxies you purchase. I have found their proxies to be good and they have responded quickly to any customer service issues I have had. I'm sure there are others on the market, but do check very carefully before purchasing. When in doubt, ask in forums or on LinkedIn amongst people whose opinions you trust. I've tried to access a few sites that triggered my McAfee Site Advisor; that's always a good indication you don't want to go there!

SIDEBAR NOTE: Many honest people have used proxies for years to browse the Internet anonymously. But sadly, just as using a proxy can help you protect your clients' accounts, hiding behind a proxy can equally enable unscrupulous spammers to run serial accounts (sometimes more than 100,000) for 'disruptive and abusive purposes' on Twitter. This kind of behaviour is precisely what Twitter have been targeting in their recent lawsuit. Use proxies to protect yourself from hackers, not from Twitter. You won't win.

TIP 141: USING A VIRTUAL PRIVATE SERVER WITH TWEET ADDER

If you do not intend to run Tweet Adder, you can probably skip this step, unless you're curious about what a virtual server is, or you happen to have another local programme you'd like to run 24 hours a day, 7 days a week.

Because Tweet Adder is a desktop application rather than web-based, it only runs when your local computer is turned on and running the programme. Very few of us want to run our computer all day and all night, or leave it on while we're away for the weekend or on holiday. This is where a 'virtual private server' or VPS (sometimes called 'cloud hosting') can come in handy.

Purchased from an Internet hosting service, having a VPS is just like having an additional computer, except that it is 'virtual' rather than physical. You access your VPS from *any* computer through a 'remote desktop' controller (do a Google search for 'remote desktop' plus your operating system and you'll find out how to set this up on your system). When you log into your VPS, you'll see a desktop just as you would if you were to log into your own computer. And just like your own computer, you can *run software programmes* on your VPS. Because your VPS is hosted remotely by your hosting provider, it is always turned on, unlike your personal computer, which you may switch off at night or when you go out. This means you can set up a VPS to run Tweet Adder around the clock, 365 days a year, even when you are away from work.

The VPS service that Tweet Adder recommends is from '3 Essentials'. I have been using them since early 2012 and I can confirm they are a reliable company. There are different packages for Tweet Adder cloud support, the only real difference between them being the amount of RAM they have. Regarding choosing a package, 3 Essentials advise, 'To determine which Tweet Adder cloud plan best suits your needs depends on how many twitter accounts you will be using simultaneously, how many followers you have, how much following you do per account and the number of Tweets you perform.' If you only have one or two accounts, you can probably get away with the cheapest package.

When you purchase the Tweet Adder cloud plan from 3 Essentials, your VPS will come with the Tweet Adder software already installed.

To run the programme, you will of course need to have purchased a registration key(s) from Tweet Adder.

3 Essentials boast a 99.9% 'up time' (meaning your service will hardly ever be disrupted)' and offer 24/7 technical support. In the time I have used their services so far, they have never once gone down. I have also utilised their live chat tech support on more than one occasion and found them very helpful and quick to rectify any issues I had.

Getting a VPS is, admittedly, another monthly business expense, and many of you reading this will probably not feel it justifiable. However, for others it is invaluable. And remember that all of the packages give you 10 gigabytes of storage, which means you can also use this area as a remote backup for your PC files. Furthermore, if you support many client accounts, remember that not all your clients are in your time zone and the optimum time for posting Tweets to their audience might be while you are asleep, in which case a VPS could be a viable solution.

SIDEBAR NOTE: *I mentioned earlier that Tweet Adder is prone to crashing. I've been told this is due to a 'memory leak' in the coding of the programme, which means it doesn't always clear out old, useless memory. This makes Tweet Adder a big strain on the CPU of your PC. I've personally found that while Tweet Adder still occasionally crashes on the 3 Essentials server, it seems to crash far LESS frequently than it did on my own PC. Perhaps this is because I am not running any other programme on 3 Essentials, so Tweet Adder has more space to 'play'. If you are using a VPS and don't see your Tweets posting, it probably means Tweet Adder has crashed. If that's the case, log onto your virtual desktop and turn Tweet Adder back on, the same way you would if it were on your local PC. Another 'trick' I learned in the Tweet Adder forum is simply to move the crash screen out of the way if it pops up. Oddly, if you do this, the programme will still run for some time (sometimes for days) before it finally crashes. It's certainly an annoying glitch, but the programme still does great things, so I just report the bugs to their support team as they appear.*

TIP 142: TWEET BY TEXT

If you haven't discovered it already, Twitter allows you to send and receive Tweets via your mobile phone. Text Tweeting is particularly useful if you do not have a smartphone and have no access to the Twitter mobile app. You can set this up via the 'settings' in your Twitter account. Please note that you *cannot use the same mobile number for more than one Twitter account* (the same way you cannot use the same email address for more than one account).

When setting up your mobile preferences on Twitter, you can specify which types of notifications you receive, as well as which hours of the day you would like to receive them. I don't advise receiving notifications when people follow you or when you receive a DM, as you will very quickly become inundated with text messages. Setting up your preferences enables you to stay on top of when people are talking about you on Twitter, or when they show they like your content through RTs and 'favourites'. It also gives you the opportunity to thank them for reading and sharing your content.

TIP 143: GET A MOBILE APP FOR YOUR SMARTPHONE AND USE IT EVERY DAY

As of this writing, Twitter also offers free mobile apps for iPhone, Android, iPad, BlackBerry, Windows Phone 7 and Nokia s40 (if you don't see your model listed, check their mobile app download page[46] to see if this list has been updated). If you happen to have one of these phones, I strongly recommend using the Twitter app, as it is far easier to use than text Tweeting and enables you to move around within the Twitter environment in ways simple text Tweeting cannot. With the app, you are not only able to send Tweets, but you can also read your stream, perform searches, and send mentions and RTs with two taps on your touch-screen. You can also follow, un-follow and block other people, and check out their profiles and Twitter stream before deciding whether you wish to follow them. You can also add people to lists. It's even faster than using your PC to find out more about people you already follow. You can also switch accounts easily if you happen to have more than one.

I use my Twitter app more frequently than any other means to access Twitter, and I can only assume many millions of people out there might say the same thing. What is important about this is that because so many regular Twitter users are NOT accessing Twitter via Twitter's official site, but via mobile applications, it means the page ranking for Twitter is grossly underestimated and it is probably much closer to Facebook than its page rank would indicate.

TIP 144: ENCOURAGE PEOPLE TO TWEET DURING A LIVE OR ONLINE EVENT

Many of you reading this might regularly host online or in-person events. After what can be months of preparation, it's easy to get caught up in the moment during your event and overlook the fact that the event itself is also an excellent marketing opportunity to help spread your message and your brand. If your event is in an online environment (such as a live stream, webinar or telesummit), be sure you have links on the event page that allow them to share on Twitter and Facebook. If you are hosting an in-person event (such as a workshop, lecture, seminar or conference), ask your participants to *leave their mobiles switched on* but put on 'silent'.

In either case, invite your audience to send out Tweets (and Facebook updates, of course) whenever one of the speakers at the event says something particularly interesting, informative or inspiring. Encourage them to share any quotes they hear, whether serious or humorous, and to share their own thoughts about what is going on. Tell them you would like to create a massive, global chat on the topic.

In addition to the invitation and spreading word about the event, there are two key technical ingredients to making this kind of viral campaign work: 1) always provide your audience with a hashtag *specifically for the event* and ask them to include the hashtag at the end of every Tweet; and 2) provide them with the presenters' Twitter handles and ask them to include the relevant handle(s) in their Tweets. Here are some screenshots of just a few of the Tweets sent out during the 7 Graces Global Conference in 2012:

femininelst Femme 1st
Amazing day at **#7GGC**, beautiful connections & such powerful energy, very blessed to have been a part of it @lynnserafinn @RachelElnaugh
06/24/2012   Reply   Retweet   Favorite

ethicalvalue ethicalvalue
@RachelElnaugh I didnt know why I came the the **#7GGC** event today but you were one person i was meant to meet, thankyou for sharing+inspiring
06/22/2012   Reply   Retweet   Favorite

rachelelnaugh Rachel Elnaugh
What an amazing day first experiencing @mybizadventures then on to **#7GGC** this evening - both brilliant events doing fab work in the world
06/22/2012   Reply   Retweet   Favorite

wholeself Kate Griffiths
Just had fab 1st day @ **#7ggc** w/ @Moonpoppy @LynnSerafinn @katierosewindow @ecosuperman @SpiritusShelagh & others. Yeehah!
06/22/2012   Reply   Retweet   Favorite

lorlorsyol Lorena Loriato
Abundance vs. Scarcity with beautiful Shelagh Jones **#7GGC** @7GracesMarketng @LynnSerafinn
06/24/2012   Reply   Retweet   Favorite

moonpoppy Callie Carling
"It's time for the new-age movement to grow some feet" ~ @LynnSerafinn at the **#7GGC** http://t.co /teEUlkVY
06/24/2012   Reply   Retweet   Favorite

To make this work effectively, you should remind attendees to Tweet at regular intervals throughout the event. You might also wish to send them the hashtag and Twitter handles of the presenters in advance via email after they have signed up for the event. You may even include this information on the confirmation page after they have registered for the event (perhaps with some suggested Tweets).

You'll notice that only one of the examples above has a link to the registration page for the event. You might wonder what value these Tweets have without a link. Remember, if people are intrigued enough by the topic, they may click the hashtag to see what it's all about. When they see the Twitter search stream for that tag, they'll not only see the 'buzz' from participants, but they will also see whatever promotional Tweets you have sent out. These promotional Tweets, of course, contain a link to the registration page. In the example above, @MoonPoppy has included a link because she was in attendance at the conference, but also because she was an affiliate helping promote the event. During the event, you (as the event organiser) should be sending out Tweets that contain both the hashtag and the link to your registration page. You can either pre-programme them or have someone do them for you live during the event, to make it more organic.

People love their mobile phones, and to engage them during a live event in this way is not only a great way to publicise your event, but also to create an immediate sense of community amongst the participants, who should be encouraged to follow and connect with each other on Twitter. You can even create a special Twitter list for them.

TIP 145: TWEET TO MENTION YOUR OTHER ACCOUNTS

If you have a second Twitter account, you might want to 'recommend' it to your current Twitter followers. Let's say you just started a new Twitter account specifically for a new book, radio show, blog or other project. You can send out an RT or @ mention, quoting something you said or telling people specifically *why* they might want to follow that account. You can even include your second account in your #FF or #WW mentions. It's important not to do this too frequently as it may be seen as a violation of policy (having two accounts for overlapping purposes) and also because it's pointless to have two accounts with all the same followers anyway! An occasional 'shout out' is fine, as long as you make sure it is likely to be relevant and of interest to your current audience.

TIP 146: INSTALL A TWITTER PROFILE WIDGET ON YOUR BLOG

Twitter has a number of nifty little tools you can use to promote your Twitter account on your website. The one I like to use is their profile widget,[47] which displays your most recent Tweets. It can be customised to match the colour scheme of your website and you can set it to the precise width you require. Once you have it configured the way you want it, grab the html code and paste it into your website, typically in a text widget either in a sidebar or footer, depending upon the design of your blog site:

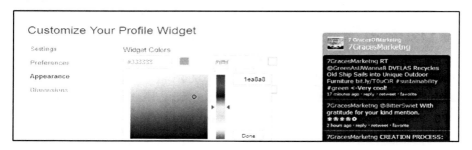

Putting a Twitter profile widget on your site allows people to see what you talk about on Twitter. If they like what they see and want to connect, they can click your Twitter handle at the top of the widget and be taken directly to your Twitter page, where they can follow you.

TIP 147: USE TWITTER BUTTONS ON YOUR BLOG POSTS

Another handy resource is the Twitter button.[48] The code for these buttons can be put anywhere that accepts html code, including your blog posts and newsletters. You can select a button that enables people to follow you with a single click, Tweet about your post, mention you or your event, or send out a Tweet using a specified hashtag, which can be very handy if you are running a particular campaign. You can even set it up to link to a specific page and include a custom message.

Using a variety of customised buttons on your site can increase your following, as well as encourage people to spread the word about a particular topic on your blog or website.

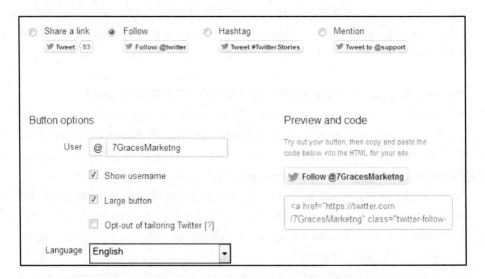

TIP 148: INSTALL A GOOD 'FOLLOW ME' PLUG-IN ON YOUR BLOG

In addition to the options in the previous two tips, there are also many decent free 'follow me on Twitter' (or other social media) plug-ins available for WordPress. Try to find something that will appear either as a 'floating' widget or sidebar widget on your site, so links to all your social media accounts are available at all times. Here's a screenshot of the widgets on my 7 Graces site (you may need to view it online):[49]

On the **right-hand side,** you can see a floating widget from a now-defunct plug-in called 'Share and Follow' (which does not seem to be compatible with all of the most recent WordPress updates). Each of the icons in the widget is linked to one of my social media accounts: Facebook, LinkedIn, Twitter and YouTube. There's also a link to the RSS feed of the blog. The advantage to 'Floating' widgets is that they are visible even if people scroll down the page, meaning they never have to search for a way to connect with you on social media.

I'm showing you a picture of the plug-in to give you an idea of what you might look for, but I'm not inclined to recommend a specific one here, because it seems as soon as I find a favourite, WordPress will invariably put out an update and suddenly a whole bunch of plug-ins no longer work the way they used to. Also, plug-ins will sometimes conflict with specific WordPress themes, and not knowing which theme you are using, I cannot know which plug-ins will work for you. The best thing to do is to go into the plug-ins area on your WordPress dashboard and do a search for either 'follow' or 'Twitter' or 'social media'. Have a good look at the ratings and check out the compatibility and any comments on WordPress.org. Then, install it and test out the features and appearance. Note that plug-ins are the most common cause of conflicts on WordPress sites, so if a particular plug-in doesn't work for you, just deactivate it (or delete it) and try something else.

TIP 149: SET UP A GOOD SHARING PLUG-IN ON YOUR BLOG

Just as it's essential to have a good 'following' widget or plug-in on your blog, you also need good 'sharing' capability. The Twitter button shown in Tip 147 can be used as a 'share this' button on your blog. However, if you wanted the button to appear on all your posts, you would have to add the code for your button on every post you publish. Assuming you use WordPress, using a good 'sharing' plug-in is a much easier and more efficient way for your button to appear across your site.

Look at the left-hand side of the screenshot of the 7 Graces site we just looked at and you will see a floating widget for *sharing*. This makes it easy for people to share the blog post or page on Twitter, Facebook, Google+ and other networks. This particular sharing widget is part of a WordPress plug-in called 'Facebook Like Box Widget'.[50] I've installed it on many client sites and it *usually* works nicely. Again, I am reluctant to recommend a specific plug-in for the reasons I have given previously, but you will find many possibilities by doing a bit of research on the plug-ins section of WordPress.org.

---

*SIDEBAR NOTE: There is a plugin-called **Jetpack** that comes pre-installed with WordPress 3.2 or above. It offers a range of features including email subscriptions, automated blog announcements to Twitter, Facebook, etc., 'share' features and much more. Unfortunately, it has received a substantial number of very bad reviews on the WordPress community, so I wouldn't say this plug-in has proved to be the 'one stop' answer to WordPress functionality. Tread carefully and always read the reviews.*

TIP 150: PUBLISH YOUR TWITTER HANDLE EVERYWHERE

Your Twitter handle should be everywhere anyone sees your name. Include it in the signature of all emails and newsletters. Make sure it is visible whenever people read your blog posts. Include it in your other social media profiles, such as Facebook, LinkedIn and Amazon Author Central. Put it on any print media or marketing you might have. And don't forget to put it on your business card!

TIP 151: LEAD YOUR TWEEPS TO YOUR OTHER SOCIAL MEDIA ACCOUNTS

So far in this book, we've focused primarily on encouraging people on Twitter to come to your website, blog or newsletter. Well, Twitter is also the perfect vehicle to invite people to engage with you on your other social media accounts, such as Facebook and LinkedIn. For example, if you have a Facebook group or business page that is an expansion of the topic you are Tweeting about, it makes sense to invite people to continue and expand upon the dialogue. When inviting people, be sure you don't just say, 'Come find us on Facebook.' Give people a *reason* to find you. Remember 'relevance' is always the key. Here are some Tweets that tend to result in a few new (and relevant) people coming to our 7 Graces Facebook page:

CREATE A BETTER WORLD: Be part of the dialogue in the 7
Graces Project on Facebook:
http://www.facebook.com/groups/7GracesGlobalGarden/
#CSR

Want to change the world? Be part of the 7 Graces Project.
Join us on Facebook
http://www.facebook.com/groups/7GracesGlobalGarden
#CSR

TIP 152: TO KLOUT OR NOT TO KLOUT?

Earlier when I talked about getting speaking gigs, I briefly mentioned a web-based programme called Klout.[51] Bragging that they are 'the standard for influence' on the web, Klout is quite controversial amongst social media users. Some love it; some think it's a lot of hogwash. I'm a bit in between.

When you sign up to Klout, it gives you a 'score' for how 'influential' you supposedly are on social media, specifically Twitter, Facebook, Google+, LinkedIn, YouTube, as well as many other social networks that are somewhat less 'influential'. Some people seem to love it and flaunt their 'Klout' on Twitter. Others seem distressed by their low scores, while many others retain a degree of cynicism towards it.

Now here's the thing you might find interesting, if not unnerving: you have a Klout score even if you have not registered on Klout. It's sort of like a page rank. Someone (or some 'thing') out there is making 'judgements' about your influence whether you are aware of it or not.

I find Klout interesting, but definitely NOT reflective of the whole picture. For example, Klout only lets you link a single Twitter account to your profile. In my case, however, I have four accounts, each with a different audience, with a total Twitter following of over 90,000 as of this writing. Because Klout only counts one of my accounts (which has about 38,000 followers), it is missing about two-thirds of my so-called 'influence' on Twitter.

Klout is also limited in how it measures your 'influence' on Facebook in that it lets your choose EITHER your Facebook profile OR one of your Facebook pages to be included in your stats. It also does not let you include Facebook groups you might manage, which traditionally can be extremely powerful places of 'influence'. But rather than address these issues, the people behind Klout have been focussing on adding more 'smaller' social networks, which, in my opinion, do not count much in your total 'influence'. Rather than increasing the number of 'lesser' social media networks, I think Klout would do better to increase the depth of reporting on the 'big two' social networks: Facebook and Twitter. If they allowed their users to include multiple Twitter accounts, Facebook pages and groups, their ratings would be much more useful and accurate measurements of true influence. I have written to them a number of times suggesting these changes, as I feel they would increase their subscriptions massively.

In spite of these current limitations, there is some evidence that Klout is becoming a screening tool for employers. My Twitter friend and social media specialist @MsMir[52] recently told me about a case cited in *Wired* magazine[53] where a marketer with 15 years of experience in consulting for huge brands like AOL, Kraft and Ford was immediately turned down in the middle of the interview because his Klout score was only 34 (he lost out to someone who had a score of 67). In fact, the applicant didn't even know what Klout was (which already didn't go in his favour, as he was supposed to be a marketer).

Regardless of whether this was a one-off incident or a signal of the wave of the future, our presence and influence on social media is rapidly becoming part of the fabric of our personal and professional lives. And regardless of whether Klout fully fits the bill as 'the standard' of our social media influence at this time, it does at least lead the way to the inevitable.

So, if you find yourself saying, *'To Klout or not to Klout? That is the question,'* my suggestion is to check your Klout every now and then, but don't get bent out of shape if your score is lower than you thought it would be. Instead, just focus on creating great content, frequent interaction and strong relationships, and your Klout score will take care of itself with time.

PART 15:
AND FINALLY...

TIP 153: SHOW UP!

Much as I like and use automation, to get the most out of Twitter it's important to show up in person regularly. Like Facebook, Twitter is a *social* network and if you want to discover its true value, you have to make an appearance (hopefully) at least once a day.

TIP 154: DARE TO HAVE FUN!

Twitter is not just a place for headlines. It's a place to be silly, too. Don't be afraid to share humour or links to cheesy songs. Dare to say something absurd, bizarre or completely unexpected. Dare to RT someone's Tweet because it made you laugh. Start a crazy conversation. Talk about how you burnt dinner or keep losing your car keys. Be real. Be human. Go on Twitter to meet other real humans.

TIP 155: DON'T QUIT!

Please, you've made it this far and I'm going to get really cross if I hear you started a Twitter profile and then gave up before reaping the benefits. Building your fan base and influence on Twitter is a long-term process that demands a long-term investment. Think of how yucky a packaged microwave dinner tastes compared to a nice slow-cooked, homemade meal. If you quit, your efforts will be half-baked and you'll have wasted most of your time on Twitter. Make Twitter part of the fabric of your business, and don't quit.

TIP 156: USE THE 7 GRACES AS YOUR SELF-ASSESSMENT CHECKLIST

Paste the 7 Graces up on your wall and use them as a personal checklist for everything you do on Twitter and social media in general. They can help you make important strategic decisions in your marketing, and help you assess how well you are expressing your personal commitment to your ethics and values. If you need a reminder, here they are again (you can also print out the chart in the introduction to this book):

1. **Connection** – to aspire to unity with Self, people and planet.

2. **Inspiration** – to give value, express generosity and share wisdom freely.

3. **Invitation** – to practice openness, engagement, hospitality and respect.

4. **Directness** – to embrace simplicity and straightforwardness in our communication.

5. **Transparency** – to use our businesses to express who we really are and what we value most.

6. **Abundance** – to aim towards sustainable wealth through ecological and economic balance.

7. **Collaboration** – to continually seek ways to create truly innovative projects together.

TIP 157: SPREAD THE LOVE!

Now that you're an expert, help other people learn how to use Twitter so they come to love it, too. If you see someone struggling, help them out. Tell them about this book (wink).

TIP 158: FOLLOW ME ON TWITTER!

Here are my Twitter accounts. If you follow me, I'll follow you back (provided you don't use True Twit!). I won't un-follow you unless you're a spammer, are rude to me or others, engage in unethical business practices, or you quit Twitter:

- @LynnSerafinn – my main Twitter account, where I not only Tweet about work but life in general.

- @7GracesMarketng – (that's not a typo, by the way) where I Tweet about business ethics, ethical marketing, social entrepreneurship and creating a better world.

- @SpiritAuthors – where I Tweet tips on writing, publishing and book marketing, and also news about new mind-body-spirit books.

- @GardenOfTheSoul – where I Tweet about my radio show, as well as events, books and articles on spirituality.

After you follow me, send out one of these Tweets (or something similar) and I'll do a 'shout out' about you to all my followers, recommending they check you out:

Now following @LynnSerafinn. Just read her book
#Tweepelicious. 158 ethical marketing tips for Twitter.
http://bit.ly/RDhD0t

Just read book #Tweepelicious by @7GracesMarketng. Ethical
Twitter marketing for writers, social entrepreneurs.
http://bit.ly/RDhD0t

But you're an expert now. I'll leave it to you to make up your own Tweets.

I'll see you in the Twitterverse!

~ @LynnSerafinn

P.S.: As a thank-you gift for buying (and reading!) this book, I'd like you to have a free 90-minute *Tweep-e-licious!* audio class AND a fully hyperlinked PDF with all the resources discussed in the book. Just go to **http://the7gracesofmarketing.com/tweep-resources** and enter the coupon code **TWITTERLOVE** when prompted.

ACKNOWLEDGEMENTS

I'd like to express my gratitude:

- To the members of our 7 Graces Global Community, who inspired me to write this book and encouraged me along the way.

- To my clients past and present, who complained about not understanding Twitter, thus giving me the incentive to create a guide for them.

- To my followers on Twitter, who helped me learn what works and what doesn't work when communicating in 140 characters.

- To Shelagh Jones, for her help in my research.

- To Shelagh (again), Rich Gallagher, Alison Perry and Allison Maslan for their invaluable feedback and comments during the creation process.

- To my daughter, Vrinda Pendred, for her excellent (if not sometimes merciless!) editing and proofreading work.

- To graphic designer Renee Duran, for another fabulous book cover.

- To Tony Eldridge for writing a single Tweet that changed my life, and to Allison Maslan for reading and replying to that Tweet.

- To everyone who buys, reads and uses this book to help make the Twitterverse a wonderful place to play, grow, connect and express ourselves.

- To writers, social entrepreneurs and changemakers everywhere who are using Twitter and the 7 Graces to make the world a better place.

I offer my most sincere and heartfelt thanks to all of you.

~ Lynn Serafinn,
3 December 2012

REFERENCES

For the sake of integrity, all citations from the text can be found in this section. These references refer primarily to books, articles and other printed matter, with the occasional reference to specific websites. Rather than cite software resources in this section, I've opted to organise them into categories in the *Resources and Useful Links* section that follows. I felt it was the best way to enable you to find the information you need easily.

1. Eldridge, Tony. 2009. 'Pre-Natal Care For Your Book'. Marketing Tips for Authors By Lynn Serafinn. Retrieved 2 September 2012 from http://blog.marketingtipsforauthors.com/2009/10/pre-natal-care-for-your-book-by-lynn.html

2. Serafinn, L. 2011. *The 7 Graces of Marketing: how to heal humanity and the planet by changing the way we sell.* London: Humanity1Press. Available at http://the7gracesofmarketing.com/book

3. Alexa Top 500 Global Sites. 'Top 10' page rank statistics cited in this book were retrieved 2 September 2012 from http://www.alexa.com/topsites.

4. Alexa Google.com Site Info. Retrieved 2 September 2012 from http://www.alexa.com/siteinfo/google.com.

5. Twitter Blog. 21 March 2012. 'Twitter Turns Six'. Retrieved 15 August 2012 from http://blog.twitter.com/2012/03/twitter-turns-six.html.

6. Twitter Blog. 12 August 2012. 'Olympic (and Twitter) Records.' Retrieved 15 August 2012 from http://blog.twitter.com/2012/08/olympic-and-twitter-records.html.

7. These statistics were Tweeted by @SecondSync, a UK-based social analytics company for television. Retrieved 7 October 2012 from https://twitter.com/SecondSync/status/255047908683051008.

8. Twitter. 6 April 2012. 'Shutting Down Spammers'. Retrieved 16 September 2012 from http://blog.twitter.com/2012/04/shutting-down-spammers.html.

9. Colt, D. and Wallerstein, T. E., LLP. 9 July 2012. 'Skootle and Kester's Reply to Twitter's Response to Order to Show Cause'. Retrieved 16 September 2012 from http://cdn.abovethelaw.com/uploads/2012/07/07-09-2012-Skootle-and-Kesters-Reply-to-Twitters-Response-to-Order-to-Show-Cause.pdf.

10. Danzig, C. 31 July 2012. 'What's in a Name? That Which We Call Spam...'. Retrieved 16 September 2012 from Above the Law at http://abovethelaw.com/2012/07/whats-in-a-name-that-which-we-call-spam/#more-179210.

11. Williams, D. 29 August 2012. 'Twitter Certified Products: Tools for Businesses'. Retrieved 16 September 2012 from http://blog.twitter.com/2012/08/twitter-certified-products-tools-for.html.

12. Holt, M. August 28, 2012. 'TweetAdder Responds to Lawsuit'. Retrieved 16 September 2012 from The Pro Twitter Forum at http://docmagi.com/forum/index.php/topic,686.0.html?PHPSESSID=224399cea995bcf82296e557dd921549.

13. Hussain, A. 2011. 'How to Create a Custom Twitter Background (With Video)'. Retrieved 2 September 2012 from http://blog.hubspot.com/blog/tabid/6307/bid/27216/How-to-Create-a-Custom-Twitter-Background-With-Video.aspx. *NOTE: This article/video is useful for those who have at least a basic understanding of how to use Photoshop.*

14. Freeman, K. 2012. 'Twitter Drops LinkedIn Partnership'. *Mashable Social Media* website. Retrieved 24 July 2012 from http://mashable.com/2012/06/29/twitter-drops-linkedin-partnership/.

15. LinkedIn Help Centre. 2012. 'Twitter Update Won't Post on LinkedIn.' Retrieved 24 July 2012 from http://help.linkedin.com/app/answers/detail/a_id/5457.

16. Spirit Authors. Book marketing tips and author promotion from Lynn Serafinn. http://spiritauthors.com.

17. BlogTalkRadio. Create an online radio show. http://www.kqzyfj.com/click-6066773-10866479.

18. Larson, D. 2012. 'All the easiest ways to search old Tweets'. Retrieved 31 August 2012 from *Tweet Smarter* blog at http://blog.Tweetsmarter.com/twitter-search/10-ways-and-20-features-for-searching-old-Tweets.

19. Topsy – Advanced Search. Free advanced Tweet or person search available. Be sure to specify 'Twitter' in the dropdown menu for 'type of results'. http://topsy.com/advanced-search.

20. Twitter, 2012. 'Automation Rules and Best Practices'. Retrieved 22 August 2012 from https://support.twitter.com/articles/76915-automation-rules-and-best-practices.

21. Twitter. 2012. 'About Twitter Limits (Update, API, DM and Following)'.Retrieved 22 August 2012 from https://support.twitter.com/articles/15364-about-twitter-limits-update-api-dm-and-following.

22. Tweeted by @Gremln. Retrieved 14 October 2012 from https://twitter.com/Gremln/status/257121540892655616.

23. Twitter Help Center. 2012. 'Getting Started with TweetDeck: Using TweetDeck Columns'. https://support.twitter.com/articles/20169620-getting-started-with-tweetdeck#columns

24. Twitter, 2012. 'Automation Rules and Best Practices'. Op. cit.

25. Ibid.

26. Gladwell, M. 2000. *The Tipping Point: how little things can make a big difference.* London: Abacus (an imprint of Little, Brown Book Group), pp38-46. On Amazon at http://bit.ly/LynnTippingPoint.

27. Oprah Winfrey (Oprah) on Twitter. Retrieved 20 December 2012. http://twitter.com/oprah.

28. The New York Times (nytimes) on Twitter. Retrieved 20 December 2012. http://twitter.com/nytimes.

29. Serafinn, L. 2010. 'How and Why to Establish Yourself as an Expert on LinkedIn'. Retrieved 31 August 2012 from http://spiritauthors.com/news/how-and-why-to-establish-yourself-as-an-expert-on-linkedin/.

30. Gladwell, M. Op. cit., pp179-192.

31. Spirit Authors blog. Op. cit.

32. Serafinn, L. 2010. '7 Reasons to Partner on Someone Else's Book Launch NOW'. Retrieved 31 August 2012 from http://spiritauthors.com/news/7-reasons-to-partner-on-someone-elses-book-launch-now/.

33. Spirit Authors contact form. http://spiritauthors.com/contact.

34. Serafinn, L. 2010. 'What is a Virtual Blog Tour? How Do You Set One Up?'. Retrieved 31 August 2012 from http://spiritauthors.com/news/what-is-a-virtual-blog-tour-how-do-you-set-one-up/.

35. Twitter. 2012. 'Guidelines for Contests on Twitter'. Retrieved 22 August 2012 from https://support.twitter.com/groups/31-twitter-basics/topics/114-guidelines-best-practices/articles/68877-guidelines-for-contests-on-twitter.

36. Twitter. 2012. 'The Twitter Rules'. Retrieved 22 August 2012 from https://support.twitter.com/groups/33-report-a-violation/topics/121-guidelines-best-practices/articles/18311-the-twitter-rules#.

37. Twitter. 2012. 'Twitter Search Best Practices'. Retrieved 22 August 2012 from https://support.twitter.com/articles/42646-twitter-search-best-practices#.

38. Binkd. 2012. 'Running Profitable and Successful Contests by Binkd'. Retrieved 22 August 2012 from http://guidance.binkd.com.

39. Binkd. 2012. 'Selecting Prizes'. Retrieved 22 August 2012 from http://guidance.binkd.com/Pre-Contest/Prizes.aspx.

40. Amazon Associates. Set up a shop or just use your Associate links to promote Amazon products. https://affiliate-program.amazon.com/.

41. Interactive Life Coach. Allison Maslan's Online Success System. http://bit.ly/IItVEz.

42. BBC Podcasts. *Peter Day's World of Business*. 'InBiz: Join the Crowd' Broadcast date 23 August 2012. http://downloads.bbc.co.uk/podcasts/radio/worldbiz/worldbiz_2012 0823-2030a.mp3

43. Ibid.

44. Cohen. J. 2010. 'Fuelers – Who Are They?'. Retrieved 20 October 2010 from http://rockethub.org/profiles/blogs/fuelers-who-are-they.

45. Twitter. 2012. 'The Twitter Rules'. Op. cit.

46. Twitter Mobile App Downloads. https://twitter.com/download.

47. Twitter Profile Widgets. http://twitter.com/about/resources/widgets.

48. Twitter Buttons. https://twitter.com/about/resources/buttons.

49. The 7 Graces of Marketing. http://the7gracesofmarketing.com.

50. Facebook Like Box Widget. http://wordpress.org/extend/plugins/facebook-like-box-widget/.

51. Klout. 'The Standard for Influence'. http://klout.com.

52. Slozberg, M. 2012. 'Do You Have Klout?' Retrieved 4 September 2012 from http://www.geminirisingltd.com/do-you-have-klout/586.

53. Stevenson, S. 2012. 'What Your Klout Score Really Means'. *Wired Business*. Retrieved 4 September 2012 from http://www.wired.com/business/2012/04/ff_klout/.

RESOURCES AND USEFUL LINKS

These resources are organised in roughly the same order in which they were presented in the book, organised into categories. The resources in each category are in alphabetical order EXCEPT when it is an official Twitter policy or guideline, in which case this will always appear first.

> **NOTE:** There are a LOT of links here. To make it easier, you can download a PDF file of these resources with clickable links PLUS a 90-minute audio class at
> http://the7gracesofmarketing.com/tweep-resources.
> When prompted, enter coupon code: **TWITTERLOVE**

TWITTER – GENERAL INFORMATION AND POLICIES

Twitter. 2012. 'About Twitter Limits (Update, API, DM and Following)'.Retrieved 22 August 2012 from
https://support.twitter.com/articles/15364-about-twitter-limits-update-api-dm-and-following.

Twitter. 2012. 'The Twitter Rules'. Retrieved 22 August 2012 from
https://support.twitter.com/groups/33-report-a-violation/topics/121-guidelines-best-practices/articles/18311-the-twitter-rules#.

Twitter. 2012. 'Twitter Basics' (Manual of Twitter functions, policies and resources). Retrieved 22 August 2012 from
https://support.twitter.com/groups/31-twitter-basics.

Twitter. 2012. 'Twitter Search Best Practices'. Retrieved 22 August 2012 from https://support.twitter.com/articles/42646-twitter-search-best-practices#.

TWITTER LAWSUIT

Twitter. 6 April 2012. 'Shutting Down Spammers'. Retrieved 16 September 2012 from http://blog.twitter.com/2012/04/shutting-down-spammers.html.

Balasubramani, V. 27 June 2012. 'Court Refuses to Dismiss Claims Against Alleged Twitter-Bot Spammer—Twitter v. Skootle'. In *Technology and Marketing Law Blog*. Retrieved 24 September 2012 from http://blog.ericgoldman.org/archives/2012/06/court_refuses_t.htm.

BBC Technology News. 2011. 'Man Sued for Keeping Company Twitter Followers'. Retrieved 16 September 2012 from http://www.bbc.co.uk/news/technology-16338040.

Colt, D. and Wallerstein, T. E., LLP. 9 July 2012. 'Skootle and Kester's Replay to Twitter's Response to Order to Show Cause'. Retrieved 16 September 2012 from http://cdn.abovethelaw.com/uploads/2012/07/07-09-2012-Skootle-and-Kesters-Reply-to-Twitters-Response-to-Order-to-Show-Cause.pdf.

Danzig, C. 31 July 2012. 'What's in a Name? That Which We Call Spam...'. Retrieved 16 September 2012 from *Above the Law* at http://abovethelaw.com/2012/07/whats-in-a-name-that-which-we-call-spam/#more-179210.

Doshi, N. 31 July 2012 (updated version). 'Twitter Goes After Spammers'. Retrieved 16 September 2012 from http://www.symantec.com/connect/blogs/twitter-goes-after-spammers.

Holt, M. August 28, 2012. 'TweetAdder Responds to Lawsuit'. Retrieved 16 September 2012 from *The Pro Twitter Forum* at http://docmagi.com/forum/index.php/topic,686.0.html?PHPSESSID=224399cea995bcf82296e557dd921549.

Illston, S. (US District Judge). 20 July 2012. 'Order Severing Defendant from Misjoinder'. Retrieved 16 September 2012 from http://cdn.abovethelaw.com/uploads/2012/07/Skootle_order.pdf

Isaac, M. 5 April 2012. 'At Long Last, Twitter Files Anti-Spam Lawsuits'. In *Wired*. Retrieved 16 September 2012 from http://www.wired.com/business/2012/04/twitter-spam-lawsuit/.

Justice, A. April 2012. 'Twitter Ethics: Lawsuits, Spam-Bots and You'. Retrieved 16 September 2012 from http://socialmediasun.com/twitter-ethics/.

Ribeiro, J. 6 April 2012. 'Twitter files lawsuit against alleged spammers and spam tool providers'. In *Computer World*. Retrieved 16 September 2012 from http://www.computerworld.com/s/article/9225916/Twitter_files_lawsuit _against_alleged_spammers_and_spam_tool_providers.

Site Reference. 16 April 2012. 'Twitter files lawsuit against alleged spammers and spam tool providers'. Retrieved 16 September 2012 from http://site-reference.com/articles/twitter-lawsuit-targets-spammers.

Williams, D. 29 August 2012. 'Twitter Certified Products: Tools for Businesses'. Retrieved 16 September 2012 from http://blog.twitter.com/2012/08/twitter-certified-products-tools-for.html.

TWITTER – BUTTONS, MOBILE APPS AND WIDGETS FROM TWITTER

Twitter Buttons. Where you can create and get html code for Twitter buttons to put on your website of blog. Encourages people to follow you on Twitter, share your blog post, etc.
https://twitter.com/about/resources/buttons.

Twitter Mobile App Download Page Twitter mobile apps are currently available for iPhone, Android, iPad, BlackBerry, Windows Phone 7 and Nokia s40. Check to see if others have been added since this writing.
https://twitter.com/download.

Twitter Profile Widget. Where you can create and get html code for a Twitter widget for your website or blog. http://twitter.com/about/resources/widgets.

Customising Your Twitter Profile Page
'Your Profile Page on Twitter'. September 2012. Official features and advice from Twitter. Retrieved 24 September 2012 from https://business.twitter.com/pdfs/ProfilePage_onesheet.pdf

Hussain, A. 2011. 'How to Create a Custom Twitter Background (With Video)'. Retrieved 2 September 2012 from http://blog.hubspot.com/blog/tabid/6307/bid/27216/How-to-Create-a-Custom-Twitter-Background-With-Video.aspx. *(This article/video is useful for those who have at least a basic understanding of how to use Photoshop.)*

Remick, J. 2010. '10 Sites to Get a Custom Twitter Design'. Retrieved 2 September 2012 from http://web.appstorm.net/roundups/self-publishing/10-sites-to-get-a-custom-twitter-design/. *(Please note: this article was written in 2010 before Twitter changed their current site design, and some of these products may no longer be available.)*

TwitBacks. Free, custom Twitter backgrounds. http://www.twitbacks.com.

Walker, L. September 2012. 'Twitter Header: Basic Tutorial. New Twitter Design Introduces Custom Header Images'. Retrieved 1 October 2012 from http://personalweb.about.com/od/twitter101/a/Twitter-Header-Basic-Tutorial.htm.

Twitter Lists – Policy and Information
Twitter. 2012. 'How to Use Twitter Lists'. Retrieved 22 August 2012 from https://support.twitter.com/articles/76460-how-to-use-twitter-lists.

Twitter. 2012. 'I'm having trouble with lists'. Retrieved 22 August 2012 from https://support.twitter.com/articles/20169276-i-m-having-trouble-with-lists.

Weitner, A. 28 February 2012. 'How many Twitter lists am I on? (One way of finding out)'. Retrieved 22 August 2012 from http://adamweitner.com/2012/02/28/how-many-twitter-lists-am-i-on-one-way-of-finding-out/.

TWITTER LISTS - SEARCH AND MANAGEMENT TOOLS

Hawkey, M. 2010. 'Populating a Twitter List via Google Spreadsheet ... Automatically!' Retrieved 31 August 2012 from http://mashe.hawksey.info/2010/11/auto-twitter-list/. *(Very techie, and probably not needed if you use a programme like ReFollow, but worth a read if you're up for a challenge.)*

Listorious. Search for over 2 million top Twitter users and lists using keywords. Website: http://listorious.com. Twitter: @Listorious.

Paper.li. Create an online daily 'newspaper' using any number of filter parameters, including your Twitter followers, Twitter lists, Facebook, RSS. Website: http://paper.li. Twitter: @SmallRivers

Refollow. 'Manage your friends and followers, establish new relationships, un-follow or block users, sort by importance, lock relationships, and much more.' While I don't use Refollow for following, etc., I've found this to be the very best tool for managing lists. Website: http://refollow.com Twitter: @refollow.

AUTOMATION – TWITTER POLICY

Twitter, 2012. 'Automation Rules and Best Practices'. Retrieved 22 August 2012 from https://support.twitter.com/articles/76915-automation-rules-and-best-practices.

AUTOMATION – TWEET SCHEDULING

Gremln. Free and several different Pro options that range from $6 to $99 per month. Web-based. Schedule Tweets; manage updates for multiple social media accounts (not just Twitter). Can also automate RSS feeds. Bulk upload up to 200 Tweets with pro version, and set up Tweets to recur at specific day intervals. http://gremln.com/UserPages/Plans.aspx

HootSuite. Free and Pro versions. Web-based. Schedule Tweets; manage updates for multiple social media accounts (not just Twitter); create custom streams to filter the data you most want to follow. Also great for interaction because you can reply, RT, DM, follow, un-follow, add to lists, etc., all from one dashboard. Can also automate RSS feeds. Bulk upload up to 200 Tweets with pro version. http://ow.ly/cHlDW.

Social Oomph. Free and Pro versions. Web-based. Free version allows you to schedule updates. Paid versions all you to send automated welcome DMs, schedule Tweets, set up recurring Tweets, auto follow back, auto un-follow those who un-follow you. Pro version is not limited to Twitter. Somewhat pricey, but has a lot of features. http://www.socialoomph.com/96430.html.

Tweet Adder. One-off fee for license, according to how many Twitter accounts you wish to manage. Desktop-based, but can be run via virtual server. Automate Tweets, queue up new people to follow automatically from keyword searches or Twitter lists, auto-follow back, auto-welcome DM, auto un-follow those who do not follow you, RSS feeds, keyword search, auto RTs and replies. Works only with Twitter. http://www.Tweetadder.com/idevaffiliate/idevaffiliate.php?id=11067.

TweetDeck. Free. Desktop- or web-based (works with Google Chrome and Mozilla Firefox). Schedule Tweets one at a time; manage updates for multiple social media accounts (not just Twitter); create custom streams to filter the data you most want to follow. Also great for interaction because you can also reply, RT, DM, follow, un-follow, add to lists, etc., all from one dashboard. Similar to HootSuite Basic. http://Tweetdeck.com.

AUTOMATION – FOLLOWER/FOLLOWING MANAGEMENT

CAVEAT: *Take caution not to use features that may violate Twitter policy.*

JustUnfollow. Free and paid version. Filter your followers and following, and follow or un-follow them. Less convenient and more limited than some of the other tools, but worth having a look at. http://justunfollow.com.

Manage Flitter. Handy analytics with different filters such as default image, lack of activity, non-English speaking, etc. http://manageflitter.com/pro/track.

Parry, D. 2012. '6 Tools to Manage Your Twitter Followers'. Retrieved 4 September 2012 from http://searchenginewatch.com/article/2175789/6-Tools-to-Manage-Your-Twitter-Followers.

Refollow. For following and un-following. This is similar to Manage Flitter, but easier to use. It is the best tool I've found for Twitter list management and the only one I've found that doesn't require you to click on the names one by one in order to add or remove them from lists. http://refollow.com.

Social Oomph. Free and Pro versions. Web-based. Send automated welcome DMs, schedule Tweets, auto follow back, set up friend finder using specified keywords. Pro version supports many other social networks besides Twitter. http://www.socialoomph.com/96430.html.

Tweet Adder. One-off fee for license, according to how many Twitter accounts you wish to manage. Desktop-based, but can be run via virtual server. Automate Tweets, queue up new people to follow automatically from keyword searches or Twitter lists, auto-follow back, auto-welcome DM, auto un-follow those who do not follow you, RSS feeds, keyword search, auto RTs and replies. Works only with Twitter. http://www.Tweetadder.com/idevaffiliate/idevaffiliate.php?id=11067.

UnTweeps. Free for three usages per month. Economical subscription fees if you wish to use it more frequently. Allows you to un-follow Tweeps who haven't Tweeted in X number of days (you specify the parameter). http://untweeps.com.

HASHTAGS AND SEARCHES
Larson, D. 2012. 'All the easiest ways to search old Tweets'. Retrieved 31 August 2012 from *Tweet Smarter* blog at http://blog.Tweetsmarter.com/twitter-search/10-ways-and-20-features-for-searching-old-Tweets.

Segar, A. 'Twitter: Is there a way to search Twitter by keywords in the user's bio?' Retrieved 31 August 2012 from http://www.quora.com/Twitter-1/Is-there-a-way-to-search-Twitter-by-keywords-in-the-users-bio.

Topsy – Advanced Search. Free advanced Tweet or person search available. Be sure to specify 'Twitter' in the dropdown menu for 'type of results'. http://topsy.com/advanced-search.

Twellow. The 'Yellow Pages' for Twitter. 31 million profiles indexed and categorised into 3000 categories. Helps you find Tweeple in local areas. http://twellow.com.

Tweriod. Free and paid service. Analyses when your followers are most active so you can choose the best times to Tweet. http://www.tweriod.com.

TWITTER CONTESTS – GUIDELINES AND RESOURCES

Twitter. 2012. 'Guidelines for Contests on Twitter'. Retrieved 22 August 2012 from https://support.twitter.com/groups/31-twitter-basics/topics/114-guidelines-best-practices/articles/68877-guidelines-for-contests-on-twitter.

Binkd - Free Twitter Contest App. http://www.binkd.com/free-twitter-contest-app.

Binkd. 2012. 'Running Profitable and Successful Contests by Binkd'. Retrieved 22 August 2012 from http://guidance.binkd.com.

Binkd. 2012. 'Selecting Prizes'. Retrieved 22 August 2012 from http://guidance.binkd.com/Pre-Contest/Prizes.aspx.

Dancy, J. 2012. 'Your Checklist for Running Facebook/Twitter Contests'. Retrieved 22 August 2012 from http://www.flowtown.com/blog/your-checklist-for-running-facebooktwitter-contests#ixzz24JbsG6Bn.

Eldridge, T. 2010. *Conducting Effective Twitter Contests: with videos [Kindle Edition].* http://amzn.to/WuPJg0

Lee, A. 2012. '4 Awesome Types of Successful Twitter Contests'. Retrieved 22 August 2012 from http://www.jeffbullas.com/2012/05/14/4-awesome-types-of-successful-twitter-contests/.

Miller, J. 14 August 2012. 'Twitter Competition Prize Ideas'. Retrieved 22 August 2012 from http://beeliked.com/social-media-buzz/twitter-competition-prize-ideas/.

CROWD FUNDING - INFORMATION

BBC Podcasts. *Peter Day's World of Business.* 'InBiz: Join the Crowd'
Broadcast date 23 August 2012.
http://downloads.bbc.co.uk/podcasts/radio/worldbiz/worldbiz_2012082
3-2030a.mp3

'EIS Tax Relief Overview: Enterprise Investment Scheme Overview'. (n.d.).
Retrieved 25 August 2012 from http://www.crowdcube.com/pg/eis-tax-
relief-overview-43.

O'Brien, J. 20 May 2012. 'US Firms Put Social Values before Big Profits'.
Retrieved 25 August 2012 from http://www.bbc.co.uk/news/business-
18089604.

HM Revenue and Customs. 2012. 'Seed Enterprise Investment Scheme
(SEIS).' Retrieved 25 August 2012 from
http://www.hmrc.gov.uk/seedeis/.

Rocket Hub. 2012. 'Crowd Funding Success School'. Great free resource
for planning and managing a crowd funding campaign. Retrieved 20
December 2012 from http://rockethub-
media.s3.amazonaws.com/rockethub-success-school.pdf

Wendling, M. 23 August 2012. 'BBC News: Crowdfunding Startups Show
How to Side-Step Bank Loans'. Retrieved 25 August 2012 from
http://www.bbc.co.uk/news/business-19286163.

Wikipedia. 'Crowd Funding'. 2012. Retrieved 24 August 2012 from
http://en.wikipedia.org/wiki/Crowd_funding.

CROWD FUNDING SITES – PERKS-/REWARDS-BASED

GoFundMe. Operating since May 2010. 'Raise money, accept donations,
collect gifts'. Not just aimed at entrepreneurs, GoFundMe encourages
people to use their website to raise funds for charities, weddings,
graduations and challenging circumstances like accidents and illnesses.
Website: http://www.gofundme.com. Twitter: @GoFundMe.

IndieGoGo. Operating since 2007. 'The world's funding platform. Go fund
yourself'. Primarily for creative projects and social enterprises. Website:
http://IndieGoGo.com. Twitter: @IndieGoGo.

Kickstarter. An 'all or nothing' funding platform for creative projects only. Based in New York City. Website: http://kickstarter.com. Twitter: @kickstarter.

Rocket Hub. Operating since 2010. 'Top International Funding Community. Launchpad and community for independent artists and entrepreneurs'. Website: http://rockethub.com. Twitter: @RocketHub @RocketHubWire.

Sponsume. Operating since August 2010. 'Your crowd funding platform for artistic and entrepreneurial projects'. Independent venture based in London. The first crowd funding platform dedicated to creativity and innovation launched in the UK (but serves projects around the world). Website: http://Sponsume.com. Twitter: @Sponsume.

Crowd Funding Sites – Equity Based

Crowdcube. Operating since 2010. 'Raising business finance through online investments. Helping start ups and growing businesses by providing business finance opportunities for online investments with our equity based crowd funding platform'. Based in the UK. Website: http://www.crowdcube.com. Twitter: @Crowdcube.

Growth Funders. Operating since 2012. Online investment platform bringing together entrepreneurs with business ideas and investors with available funds. Based in the UK. Website: http://www.growthfunders.com. Twitter: @growthfunders.

Seedrs. Online platform for finding and investing seed capital. Investors buy stocks in your start up business. There is a £150,000 maximum on the amount of capital you can raise. Based in the UK. Website: http://seedrs.com. Twitter: @Seedrs.

Affiliate Programme Software

1Shopping Cart. Full shopping cart solution that includes an affiliate software package. Very pricey, but widely used and reputable. http://1shoppingcart.com.

iDev Affiliate. Reasonably priced and dependable affiliate software programme. Purchase it for a one-off fee, or opt in to pay an additional

annually fee to get access to software upgrades.
http://www.idevdirect.com/14488.html.

WP Affiliate. Reasonably priced and very user-friendly affiliate plug-in for WordPress. Integrates nicely with WP eStore (shopping cart and product management plug-in). Highly recommended for WordPress users. http://ow.ly/dM8Lx.

CONTACT FORMS
Contact forms by Contact.Me for WordPress. The free version of this plug-in that is partially customisable and brandable.
http://wordpress.org/extend/plugins/contactme/

ContactMe Easy Contact forms Facebook Fan Page. This is a free app, exactly the same as the WordPress plug-in. In fact, if you have it installed on your blog, you can install the same form on your Facebook page just by activating the app and logging into your existing account.
http://www.facebook.com/contactforms

Gravity Forms. Highly customisable forms for WordPress. Not free, but varying prices depending upon your use requirements. Not necessary if you're just looking to create simple contact forms, but fabulous if you need to create a detailed intake form. http://www.gravityforms.com/

Jetpack byWordPress.com. Plug-in from WordPress that comes pre-installed with WordPress 3.2 or above. Offers a range of features including a contact form. Unfortunately, it seems to have received a substantial number of bad reviews on the WordPress community, so test it carefully before use. http://wordpress.org/extend/plugins/jetpack/.

EMAIL SUBSCRIPTION, NEWSLETTER DELIVERY AND AUTO-RESPONDER PROVIDERS
AWeber. Widely used email, newsletter and auto-responder service. Integrates nicely with social media. Fairly intuitive to use. Extremely reliable, but they have a strict policy of requiring a second opt-in if you wish to import a contact list from another source. Price varies according to the size of your list. http://www.aweber.com/?404800.

Feedburner. Email subscription management for blogs only. Enable the email option and readers can subscribe to receive your blog posts via email. Will also syndicate your blog posts to your Twitter account when you first publish them. Free to use. Owned by Google. http://feedburner.com.

GetResponse. Widely used email, newsletter and auto-responder service. Integrates nicely with social media. Fairly intuitive to use. Extremely reliable. They do not require a second opt-in if you wish to import a contact list from another source (which makes this my first choice in this category). Price varies according to the size of your list. http://www.getresponse.com/index/teknochik.

Jetpack byWordPress.com. Complex plug-in from WordPress that comes pre-installed with WordPress 3.2 or above. One of its many features is an email subscription capability for your blog (not for newsletters or auto-responder delivery). While widely available, the plug-in has received a substantial number of bad reviews which means it might not be compatible with your WordPress set-up. If you have difficulty with it, use Feedburner. http://wordpress.org/extend/plugins/jetpack/.

MailChimp. More recently established email, newsletter and auto-responder service. I have not used them yet, but I do know that the prices are a bit deceptive as they are calculated according to how many 'emails' you send per month, i.e. if you send one email to 500 contacts, it counts as 'sending 500 emails'. The wording on their site can sometimes lead new users to believe it is substantially cheaper than its competitors, but if you calculate it carefully you'll see otherwise. http://mailchimp.com.

WORDPRESS PLUG-INS

Facebook Like Box Widget. Free WordPress plug-in developed by Sunento Agustiar Wu. Although promoted as a Facebook widget, the coolest thing about this plug-in is that it has an optional component where you can set up a floating 'share' widget that supports most social networks. http://wordpress.org/extend/plugins/facebook-like-box-widget/.

Jetpack byWordPress.com. Complex plug-in from WordPress that comes pre-installed with WordPress 3.2 or above. Offers a range of features including email subscriptions, automated blog announcements to Twitter, Facebook, etc., 'share' features, contact form and more. Unfortunately, it seems to have received a substantial number of bad reviews on the

WordPress community, so I wouldn't say this plug-in has proved to be the 'one stop' answer to WordPress functionality. Tread carefully and always read the reviews. http://wordpress.org/extend/plugins/jetpack/.

WordPress Plug-ins. As they say on WordPress.org 'Plug-ins can extend WordPress to do almost anything you can imagine'. In this book, I mainly talked about sharing and following plug-ins, but plug-ins can do so much more. Browse the directory here: http://wordpress.org/extend/plugins/.

ADVANCED TOOLS
My Private Proxy. Private IP addresses.
http://www.myprivateproxy.net/billing/aff.php?aff=303.

3 Essentials Virtual Private Server. Run any software programme 24 hours a day or use for extra storage. Recommended for use with Tweet Adder. Access via remote desktop.
http://www.3essentials.com/Tweetadder-vps-desktop-hosting.asp?a_aid=85e71af8

STATISTICS AND ANALYSIS
Alexa - Top Sites. Top-ten page rank statistics cited in this book accessed 2 September 2012 from http://www.alexa.com/topsites.

Google Alerts. Set up free alerts via keywords to find material for blogging and Tweeting. Set up alerts for appearance of your own name on other people's blogs. http://www.google.com/alerts.

Klout. 'The Standard for Influence'. Free service that ranks your social influence based upon followers, activity and interaction on Twitter, Facebook, LinkedIn, Google+ and other social networks. http://klout.com.

Slozberg, M. 2012. 'Do You Have Klout?' Retrieved 4 September 2012 from http://www.geminirisingltd.com/do-you-have-klout/586.

Stevenson, S. 2012. 'What Your Klout Score Really Means'. *Wired Business*. Retrieved 4 September 2012 from http://www.wired.com/business/2012/04/ff_klout/.

Twenty Feet. Analysis tool for your Twitter activity. Free for one account. Automatically Tweets any positive changes to your account once a week. https://wiki.twentyfeet.com

RADIO AND PODCASTS

Audio Acrobat. Record, upload and syndicate your audio podcasts. http://teknochik.audioacrobat.com/

BlogTalkRadio. Create and broadcast an online radio show. Free and paid versions. http://bit.ly/LynnsBTR.

WEB DIRECTORY SUBMISSION SITES

Social Maximizer. Submit your site to hundreds of social bookmarking sites. http://bit.ly/LynnSocialMaximizer.

Directory Maximizer. Submit your site to SEO friendly web directories. http://bit.ly/LynnDirectoryMaximizer.

BOOKS

Gladwell, M. 2000. *The Tipping Point: how little things can make a big difference.* London: Abacus (an imprint of Little, Brown Book Group). http://bit.ly/LynnTippingPoint

Serafinn, L. 2011. *The 7 Graces of Marketing: how to heal humanity and the planet by changing the way we sell.* London: Humanity1Press. http://the7gracesofmarketing.com/book

ARTICLES – RELATED TOPICS

Albanesius, C. 27 September 2012. 'Pages See Drop in 'Likes' Amidst Facebook Purge'. *PC Magazine.* Retrieved 1 October 2012 from http://www.pcmag.com/article2/0,2817,2410281,00.asp.

Freeman, K. 2012. 'Twitter Drops LinkedIn Partnership'. *Mashable Social Media* website. Retrieved 24 July 2012 from http://mashable.com/2012/06/29/twitter-drops-linkedin-partnership/.

Huffman, K. 2012. '100 Top Marketing Book Authors on Twitter'. Retrieved 1 July 2012 from http://www.smmmagazine.com/exclusives/top-marketing-book-authors-on-twitter/.

LinkedIn Help Centre. 2012. 'Twitter Update Won't Post on LinkedIn.' Retrieved 24 July 2012 from http://help.linkedin.com/app/answers/detail/a_id/5457.

Rundle, M. 27 September 2012. 'Facebook Begins Deleting Thousands of Profiles in Massive Purge'. *Huffington Post.* Retrieved 1 October 2012 from http://www.huffingtonpost.co.uk/2012/09/27/facebook-begins-deleting-fake-accounts_n_1918305.html?utm_hp_ref=tw.

Serafinn, L. 2010. '7 Reasons to Partner on Someone Else's Book Launch NOW'. Retrieved 31 August 2012 from http://spiritauthors.com/news/7-reasons-to-partner-on-someone-elses-book-launch-now/.

Serafinn, L. 2010. 'How and Why to Establish Yourself as an Expert on LinkedIn'. Retrieved 31 August 2012 from http://spiritauthors.com/news/how-and-why-to-establish-yourself-as-an-expert-on-linkedin/.

Serafinn, L. 2010. 'What is a Virtual Blog Tour? How Do You Set One Up?'. Retrieved 31 August 2012 from http://spiritauthors.com/news/what-is-a-virtual-blog-tour-how-do-you-set-one-up/

Twitter Blog. 21 March 2012. 'Twitter Turns Six'. Retrieved 15 August 2012 from http://blog.twitter.com/2012/03/twitter-turns-six.html.

Twitter Blog. 12 August 2012. 'Olympic (and Twitter) Records.' Retrieved 15 August 2012 from http://blog.twitter.com/2012/08/olympic-and-twitter-records.html.

FOR AUTHORS

Amazon Associates. Set up a shop or just use your Associate links to promote Amazon products. https://affiliate-program.amazon.com/.

Author Central. Make your author profile; show all your titles; integrate your Tweets, videos, etc. https://authorcentral.amazon.com.

ROYALTY FREE IMAGES

123rf.com. Royalty free images. Pay as you go or subscribe. http://www.123rf.com/#teknochik.

iStockPhoto. Royalty free images. Pay as you go or subscribe. http://bit.ly/OM8rqW.

7 Graces Resources

The 7 Graces Project CIC. New social enterprise aiming to provide an educational alternative, business incubator and mentorship scheme for a new generation of ethical, community-focussed entrepreneurs. http://the7gracesofmarketing.com/the-7-graces-project-about-us

The Book. Serafinn, L. 2011. *The 7 Graces of Marketing: how to heal humanity and the planet by changing the way we sell.* London: Humanity1Press. http://the7gracesofmarketing.com/book

The 7 Graces blog site. Articles, news and audios from our latest community meetings. http://the7gracesofmarketing.com

7 Graces Facebook group. Called 'The 7 Graces Global Garden', this is where we come out to play, connect, share resources and offer support as we change the world together. http://www.facebook.com/groups/7GracesGlobalGarden

7 Graces MeetUp group. We meet monthly in London, but every meeting is simulcast on Skype, so all our members can connect with each other in real time. http://www.meetup.com/7-Graces-Global-Community-London

The 7 Graces Hour Radio. Airs Wednesdays at 6pm UK, 1pm Eastern, 10am Pacific. On the air since January 2009 (formerly called 'The Garden of the Soul'). Inspiring authors, social entrepreneurs and changemakers making the world a better place. http://www.blogtalkradio.com/lynn-serafinn *You can also find the show on iTunes.*

ABOUT THE AUTHOR

Lynn **Serafinn, MAED, CPCC** is a certified, award-winning coach, teacher, marketer, social media expert, radio host, speaker and author. Her book *The 7 Graces of Marketing — How to Heal Humanity and the Planet by Changing the Way We Sell* is an international #1 bestseller in marketing and business ethics, and was selected as a finalist for the prestigious Brit Writers Award in 2012. She is listed in the top-20 of the Top 100 marketing authors on Twitter by *Social Media Magazine.*

Lynn's eclectic approach to marketing incorporates her global vision, her vast professional experience in the music industry and the educational sector, with more than two decades of study and practice of the spirituality of India. In her work as a promotional manager she has produced a long list of bestselling mind-body-spirit authors, and her marketing campaigns and online broadcasts have reached millions around the planet.

Lynn is also the Founder of The 7 Graces Project CIC, a new social enterprise aiming to provide an educational alternative, business incubator and mentorship scheme for a new generation of ethical, community-focussed entrepreneurs. Her recently established publishing company, Humanity 1 Press, aims to provide a platform for independent authors of cutting-edge books about new paradigms for business and society in general.

Lynn is a dual citizen of the US and Great Britain, but (in the words of Captain Nemo) considers herself to be a 'Citizen of the World'. Her daughter, Vrinda Pendred, is an author and founder of Conditional Publications, a charitable publishing house for authors with neurological conditions.

Lynn is also grandmother to a wildly creative and precocious boy named Percy.

ALSO FROM LYNN SERAFINN

The 7 Graces of Marketing:
how to heal humanity and the planet by changing the way we sell

International #1 Bestseller –
Marketing & Business Ethics

2012 Brit Writers Award Finalist

'Is marketing making us ill?' That is the question posed in this eye-opening, informative and inspiring read. A bold, holistic and often spiritual take not merely of the world of advertising, but our entire world view, this book reveals how our relationships with Self, others, our businesses, our economy and the Earth impact every aspect of our lives. Addressing both the conscious and unconscious mechanics of marketing, Lynn shows the impact consumer culture has upon our physical and emotional health, our economy and the delicate ecological balance of our natural world. A book as much for the conscious consumer as the business owner, *The 7 Graces of Marketing* shows why traditional methods of selling are ultimately doomed to fail, and how both business owners and consumers can begin to heal the world by embracing an entirely new paradigm.

*'At last—**a brilliant reframe of marketing and selling**...where competition and scarcity give way to collaboration, abundance and greater connection among all humanity....**I love it!'***

~ **DR. JOE VITALE**
Author of bestsellers *The Attractor Factor* and *Buying Trances*

Buy the book and receive 10 hours of free audio downloads from over 20 of today's most dynamic thought leaders
the7gracesofmarketing.com/book

ALSO FROM LYNN SERAFINN

The Garden of the Soul:
lessons from four flowers that unearth the Self

Said to be 'as spiritual as Deepak Chopra and as magical as Paulo Coelho', The Garden of the Soul takes the reader on a daring and magical journey through birth, death, love, art, spirituality and transformation in an eloquently poetic and unforgettable way. While gritty enough to grab reality by the horns and present some of the most frequently avoided topics of human experience, Lynn also shows us a highly crafted writing style that pushes the creative envelope for what can be done within the context of a personal memoir, blending it with a magic and unique metaphoric language that speaks directly to the heart.

'...a magical adventure toward deeper understanding of the relationship between Self and the world.'
~ **ALAN SEALE,** author of *The Manifestation Wheel*

Find the book on Amazon: http://amzn.to/UOUFmT

**FREE 50-minute audio of LIVE performance of
a story from the book, read by the author:
http://bit.ly/VeryGoodKing**

SPIRIT AUTHORS

Spirit Authors is an online resource for new and aspiring authors, especially those in the mind-body-spirit genre. You'll find a collection of extremely helpful (free) articles on the Spirit Authors blog, packed with information about writing, self-publishing and marketing your book. There's also a Spirit Authors Shop, with recommended titles for both authors and readers.

Spirit Authors: http://spiritauthors.com
Be sure to subscribe to receive all Lynn's great info articles.

Receive 5 FREE podcasts on writing, publishing and marketing your book from 18 top industry professionals: http://bit.ly/SpiritAuthorsPodcasts

HUMANITY 1 PRESS

Founded by Lynn Serafinn in 2011 H1P is an independent niche publishing company for authors of cutting-edge non-fiction books discussing new paradigms for business, marketing, society, the environment, the economy and social entrepreneurship.

Our company operates differently from mainstream publishers in that we want to help cultivate bright new minds and help bring their ideas to the world. We want our authors to change the world through their books. If you have written or are writing a non-academic book on one of the above topics and would like to be considered for publication, contact us at:

http://the7gracesofmarketing.com/contact

Kindly do NOT send your book or full proposal. Send only your topic, title and a one paragraph (250 words max) description of your book.

SPIRIT AUTHORS BOOK PROMOTIONS

Founded upon the 7 Graces in everything we do, Spirit Authors Book Promotions offer full-service Amazon bestseller launches, product launches, affiliate and partner management, branding, Twitter account management, and online platform building.

All authors of new-paradigm, holistic and self-help books are welcome, from first-time self-published authors to established authors from major publishing houses. If you are writing a book or getting ready to publish sometime within the next year, contact us 6-8 months in advance of your publication date to see how we can help you.

We also help social entrepreneurs with their branding, marketing strategies, social media and collaborations. We specialise in creating and motivating strong partnerships to support your cause. If you have a new paradigm project serving humanity and planet, contact us and let us help you get the word out.

*'I was truly blessed when I found Lynn Serafinn...**my book reached #1** in US and Canada due to Lynn leading the way.'*
~ **ALLISON MASLAN**, author of #1 bestseller: *Blast Off! The Surefire Success Plan to Launch Your Dreams into Reality*
Morgan James Publishers

*'**Lynn literally puts you on the map of bestselling authors.** My publisher, Hay House, was impressed.... **I recommend Lynn to anyone who is serious about becoming a #1 bestseller.**'*
~ **ROY MARTINA, MD**, author of #1 bestseller: *Emotional Balance: The Path to Inner Peace and Harmony*
Hay House Publishers

Visit http://spiritauthorscoach.com
There, you will also find a PDF describing our services.

Connect on Social Media

Twitter
@LynnSerafinn
@7GracesMarketng (that's not a typo)
@SpiritAuthors
@GardenOfTheSoul

Facebook
LynnSerafinn
7GracesOfMarketing
SpiritAuthors
GardenOfTheSoul

LinkedIn
Lynn Serafinn

YouTube
gardenofthesoul

Google+
http://bit.ly/LynnGoogle

Contact Lynn

Contact Lynn Serafinn about speaking engagements, book promotions, bestseller launches, media appearances or just to say hello at http://the7gracesofmarketing.com/contact.

Lightning Source UK Ltd.
Milton Keynes UK
UKOW051900290313

208421UK00004B/335/P